Psychotherapy as a Personal Relationship

Psychotherapy as a Personal Relationship

VALERIAN J. DERLEGA
Old Dominion University

SUSAN S. HENDRICK
Texas Tech University

BARBARA A. WINSTEAD
Old Dominion University

JOHN H. BERG
University of Mississippi

THE GUILFORD PRESS
New York   London

© 1991 The Guilford Press
A Division of Guilford Publications, Inc.
72 Spring Street, New York NY 10012

Printed in the United States of America

This book is printed on acid-free paper.

Last digit is print number: 9 8 7 6 5 4 3 2 1

Library of Congress Cataloging-in-Publication Data

Psychotherapy relationship as a personal relationship / Valerian J.
    Derlega . . . [et al.].
        p.   cm.
    Includes bibliographical references and index.
    ISBN 0-89862-554-8
    1. Psychotherapy.   2. Interpersonal relations.   3. Psychotherapist
and patient.   I. Derlega, Valerian J.
RC480.5.P76   1991
616.89′14—dc20   90-3997
                                                                    CIP

Acknowledgments

We first wish to acknowledge those who generously granted permission to use material relevant to this volume. These include the American Psychological Association, the Society for the Psychological Study of Social Issues, Sage Publications, and the *Journal of Social Behavior and Personality*.

We also wish to thank Guilford Publications and our editor, Sharon Panulla. Her encouragement, goodwill, and patience allowed the book to come to fruition. We appreciate the support of the Departments of Psychology at Old Dominion University, Texas Tech University, and the University of Mississippi.

Val Derlega and Barbara Winstead wish to thank the faculty and staff at the Department of Psychiatry and Behavioral Sciences at the University of Auckland Medical School, Auckland, New Zealand, who provided us with an academic home in 1988: *kia ora*. We also thank our children, John, Ann, and Christopher, for providing distractions. Thanks are also extended to Stephen Margulis, who commented on Chapters 3 and 7.

Thanks are also extended to the therapy and counseling clients who taught us about personal relationships in psychotherapy.

Preface

Like two companionable but unacquainted toddlers engaged in parallel play, the fields of personal relationships and psychotherapy have coexisted comfortably in recent years. The former is the new kid on the block; the intense study of intimate relationships by social scientists is a phenomenon largely of the past decade or two. Psychotherapy, on the other hand, has been inventing and reinventing itself in myriad ways for nearly a century. However, the two have stayed relatively separate until the present volume.

What do the perspectives of social psychology, clinical psychology, and counseling psychology (areas represented by the authors of this volume) have in common? Although a number of answers might be considered correct, one basic theme for all three areas of psychology has been "human interaction," persons interacting with other persons—in dyads, in families, in groups—and the resulting successes and failures, joy and pain.

Research on personal relationships has essentially exploded within recent years. It developed largely out of (1) social psychology research on interpersonal attraction, relationship development, and self-disclosure; (2) sociological work on courtship and marriage, sexuality, and relationship satisfaction; and (3) communication research on interpersonal communication (including nonverbal behavior). The field has now broadened to include additional areas of psychology (e.g., counseling, clinical, developmental) and has resulted in the publication of a specialized journal, the *Journal of Social and Personal Relationships*, and various books.

Although relationship researchers come from diverse backgrounds and may use diverse methodological approaches, including standard laboratory research, survey studies, case studies, assessment of marital interaction through videotapes, and analysis of written personal accounts, the binding force is a consummate interest in relationships that are based on familial ties, friendships, or romantic/erotic attachments. For the most part, personal relationships research has remained within the boundaries of family, friendship, and romance. However, previous collaboration among various subsets of the four current authors and ensuing group discussions made the application of theory and research on personal relationships to psychotherapy seem not only natural but inevitable. Thus, it is out of common research interests (all four authors do research in personal relationships) and therapy experience (two authors are also therapists), as well as a shared vision of the applicability of relationships research to therapy, that this book has emerged.

The study of personal relationships encompasses topics such as relationship development, attraction, love, intimacy, jealousy, self-disclosure, conflict, satisfaction, trust, sexuality, social support, and friendship. Some of these topics—for example, attraction, relationship development, self-disclosure, social support—are directly relevant to psychotherapy. In an extensive review of the psychotherapy process and outcome literature, Orlinsky and Howard (1986) included the "therapeutic bond," a major facet of the therapist–client relationship, as one of the five core elements of therapy process. In concluding a lengthy discussion of the therapeutic bond, Orlinsky and Howard noted that "the quality of the therapeutic bond is an extremely important factor in patient outcome" (p. 357). This therapeutic bond and the total therapist–client relationship of which it is a part are important enough to require continuing scrutiny from practicing clinicians.

Although clinicians bring differing worldviews and necessarily differing relationship orientations to the therapy process, all are, to a greater or lesser extent, "in relationship" with their clients. One may choose to reveal oneself fully and authentically in therapy, to be more reserved in sharing personal aspects, or to function primarily as a neutral mirror to the client. But whatever the specific level of involvement, some kind of relationship is being created, moment by moment, therapy hour by therapy hour. And it is to the illumination of this relationship that the current volume is dedicated.

This application of the personal relationships literature to the therapy relationship has been designed to speak to practicing psychotherapists—psychologists, clinical social workers, marriage and family therapists, counselors—and to scholars involved in the areas of relationships and/or psychotherapy. The approach is scholarly, but there are frequent clinical examples and a consistent awareness of the "real world" of therapist and client. Although the book has been crafted for use by professionals and interested scholars, it could also serve as a central or secondary text for graduate courses and seminars in psychotherapy theory and process, interpersonal attraction, interpersonal communication, and the like. It would also be useful in practicum training for clinical and counseling students.

Although the major responsibility for particular chapters resides with each author (V. J. D., Chapters 3 and 7; S. S. H., Chapters 4 and 8; B. A. W., Chapters 1 and 2; and J. H. B., Chapters 5 and 6), the volume is truly a collaborative effort. Extensive exchange of information, commentary, and revision have integrated the words, as well as the ideas, of the authors. The authors' goal was to illuminate the elusive therapist–client relationship with the concepts and research of personal relationships. We hope that we have succeeded.

Contents

CHAPTER 1

Overview of Theory and Research on Therapy as a Personal Relationship

"**P**sychotherapy is first and foremost a species of human interaction" (C. Hendrick, 1983, p. 67). The question remains, *Which* species is it? What follows is an attempt to answer that question. As two social psychologists (J. H. B. and V. J. D.), a counseling psychologist (S. S. H.), and a clinical psychologist (B. A. W.), we have watched with pleasure and have occasionally contributed to the emergence of a dialogue and, eventually, an interface between social and clinical/counseling psychology (Berg, 1987; Derlega, Margulis, & Winstead, 1987; S. Hendrick, 1983, 1987; Winstead, Derlega, Lewis, & Margulis, 1988). The history and significance of the interface has been well presented by others (Leary & Miller, 1986; Maddux, Stoltenberg, Rosenwein, & Leary, 1987). We begin here with the assumption that the value of an active dialogue between clinicians and social psychologists is understood and appreciated.

Our purpose in this book is to explore some of the ways in which information from social psychology and the emerging field of personal relationships is applicable to psychotherapy and vice versa, that is, how social psychological theory and research on interpersonal relationships can contribute to a greater understanding of the therapy relationship and how clinical theory and research concerning the therapy relationship can contribute to a greater understanding of other interpersonal relationships. The book is made possible in part by the development from several disciplines (including communications,

1

family studies, sociology, and social psychology) of an area of endeavor devoted to studying real relationships, instead of encounters between strangers in an experimental setting (Duck & Gilmour, 1981; Duck & Sants, 1983; Kelley et al., 1983). Most of this work has been on close personal relationships. As research and theory establish what constitutes a definition of a personal relationship (Clark & Reis, 1988), attention must also be paid to other sorts or species of relationships and how different species of relationship are similar to and different from one another.

The therapy relationship is an intriguing relationship because it is both personal (even intimate) and professional. Although personal relationships between adults are generally symmetrical, the therapy relationship is asymmetrical. In a symmetrical relationship, each partner is similar in terms of power in the relationship and resources that she or he can provide to the relationship. Thus, each is expected to participate in the relationship in similar ways, for example, by offering similar amounts and levels of intimacy of self-disclosure or amounts of social support. The relationship most likely to contain this equality and reciprocity (and a relationship to which psychotherapy has been compared; see Schofield, 1964) is a close friendship. Romantic relationships are also generally symmetrical, although in heterosexual relationships sex roles may create an imbalance of power and make the sorts of resources that each partner provides very dissimilar. In asymmetrical relationships there is a clear difference in power and in resources provided by each partner in the relationship. Parent–child, teacher–student, and employer–employee relationships are asymmetrical. Therapy relationships are also asymmetrical. The therapist's professional training and expertise give him or her greater power and resources. The client gives a fee to the therapist for the services that she or he provides. The asymmetry of the therapy relationship is in keeping with its professional quality, but the fact that the client's most intimate thoughts and feelings are shared with the therapist and the fact that therapists frequently develop strong feelings of caring and concern for their clients suggest a personal quality to the therapy relationship as well. A goal of this book is to explore how the professional and personal are integrated into the therapy relationship.

There already exists a considerable literature in clinical and counseling psychology on the therapy relationship. This literature does not generally address concepts from the social psychological literature on relationships, for instance, interpersonal attraction, social exchange, role theory (for an exception, see Strong & Claiborn, 1982). Furthermore, this literature has not generally been mined by social psychologists investigating relationships. Our intention is to draw on both the social and clinical psychology literatures in an effort to further our understanding of the therapy relationship as a type of interpersonal relationship and thereby to advance understanding of both therapy and interpersonal relationships in general.

This chapter will provide a brief review of the literature on the therapy relationship, identifying themes that clinicians have used in grappling with this topic, and relevant material from the personal relationships literature. An overview of the remaining chapters will also be presented.

Defining Close Relationship and Therapy Relationship

Berscheid and Peplau (1983) note:

> When the myriad conceptions and usages of the term *relationship* are collected and carefully compared, it becomes apparent that the term essentially refers to the fact that two people are in a relationship with one another if they have impact on each other, if they are "interdependent" in the sense that a change in one person causes a change in the other and vice versa. (p. 12)

Close relationships are those in which individuals have a strong impact on each other and influence each other frequently and in diverse ways and that tend to endure over some period of time. This definition indicates that relationships do not exist as states but as ongoing, everchanging interactions between individuals (Duck & Sants, 1983). In addition to viewing relationships as involving the actions and reactions of two people that occur over time, this perspective (Kelley et al., 1983) also views relationships as being influenced by the "environment" or context in which they exist and as having emergent properties arising from the unique nature of the interaction between the relationship partners. Thus, the *relationship* influences the partners in addition to the partners influencing the relationship.

The therapy relationship is certainly a close relationship. Therapist and client are interdependent, with one person's behavior affecting the behavior of the other. The impact of the therapist on the client is generally stronger and more extensive than the impact of the client on the therapist. Nevertheless, the client's behaviors will influence the therapist's behavior in sessions with that client and sometimes will influence the therapist's behavior outside of therapy as well. The impact of the exchange in a therapy session may be greater, especially for the client, than the impact of interpersonal exchanges of comparable length in other settings.

Although the therapy relationship is, by our definition, a close relationship, its professional quality also makes it different from most close personal relationships. It takes place only at certain times (e.g., weekly 50-minute sessions) and in certain places (e.g., the therapist's office). Despite its emotional content and, in many cases, its apparent lack of structure, it is a task-oriented relationship. The underlying purpose is always to improve the client's well-being. Also, the therapy relationship is meant to end when it has been successful, not from dissatisfaction or disinterest. These restrictions of time, place, purpose, and length make the therapy relationship markedly different from most close personal relationships.

The complexity and importance of the therapy relationship in the psychotherapy process led Greenson (1967) to conceptualize the therapy relationship as made up of three components: the working alliance, the transference relationship, and the real relationship. Using this framework, Gelso and Carter (1985) examined the therapy relationship and how it fares in three broadly defined therapies: those based on psychoanalytic, humanistic, and behavioral principles. The working or therapeutic alliance, on which there is much psychoanalytic writing and recently some research, is the implicit, occasionally explicit, bond between therapist and client that allows them to work together on the client's problems. Psychoanalysts often refer to the healthy part of the client's ego as that which forms a partnership with the therapist to cure the unhealthy part of the ego. Although the concept of working alliance comes from the psychoanalytic tradition (Greenson, 1967; Zetzel, 1956), many clinicians (Bordin, 1979; Gelso & Carter, 1985) argue that a bond or agreement between therapist and client is a component of any therapy relationship.

Transference is also a term from psychoanalysis. Transference is the tendency for the client to establish with the therapist a relationship that reflects relationships the client has experienced with significant others. The techniques of psychoanalytic psychotherapy, discussed later in this chapter, encourage the development of transference; but even when it is not encouraged, it is a part of the therapy relationship. Gelso and Carter (1985) refer to this component of the therapy relationship as the "unreal" relationship in that it "entails a misperception or misinterpretation of the therapist, whether positive or negative" (p. 170). While transference comprises the client's errors in perception, countertransference comprises the errors of the therapist. Countertransference can also occur in any therapy, not just psychoanalysis. Finally, there is between therapist and client a real relationship, based on accurate perceptions and a willingness to be open and genuine with one another. Whereas working alliance and transference–countertransference are concepts associated with psychoanalysis, the concept of the real relationship is associated with humanistic psychotherapy.

Working alliance, transference–countertransference, and real relationship are useful concepts for examining the therapy relationship. They can also be used to examine nontherapy personal relationships. We tend to think of close personal relationships as real relationships in which relationship partners strive to understand one another and to be open and authentic in their dealings with one another. Transference, however, is not unique to psychotherapy; it plays a role in *every* relationship. As a person enters a relationship, her or his expectations, hopes, and fears about the relationship (i.e., her or his internal representations of the relationship) are based on experiences in previous relationships, especially previous important ones. A person's inputs into the relationship and efforts to create a relationship are based on these internal representations.

Some of a person's expectations or efforts to mold a relationship are, given the nature of the relationship partner, unrealistic or irrational. In an ordinary relationship these irrational components are corrected by the input from the partner. For example, when John meets Mary, his goal is to be catered to and pampered just as he was by his mother (on her good days). Mary is responsive but not indulgent; in fact, she wants someone who will look after her. John must change his expectations about this particular relationship or look for another one; otherwise, he will experience frequent feelings of disappointment in his relationship with Mary. In real life one person's transference bumps up against another person's transference, and the individuals will adapt to one another's needs and capabilities, forgo the relationship, or have a relationship marked by constant discord.

It is also possible to speak of a working alliance, or its absence, in personal relationships. For example, friends may have an implicit agreement on the purpose of their friendship. It may be to provide companionship—someone to go places with or to talk to when it is convenient for both partners—but not favors or help in a crisis. Just as in therapy, problems arise when this working alliance is missing. For example, a woman asks her friend to keep her children for a weekend while she visits her ill mother; her friend says she is too busy. The woman is angry and disappointed; clearly, an agreement on the goals of the friendship was absent in this relationship.

Thus, components of close personal relationships apply to the therapy relationship, and concepts useful in examining the therapy relationship can be applied to personal relationships. Next, we will examine now therapists with different theoretical orientations view the therapy relationship.

Therapists' Views of the Therapy Relationship

Psychotherapists of every orientation acknowledge the importance, in some cases the centrality, of the relationship between therapist and client. In both theoretical writing and research, attention has been paid to this relationship. Schools of therapy differ, however, in the emphasis they place on the relationship. Behavioral and cognitive approaches focus on techniques that produce behavior change. The relationship between client and therapist is ancillary and is discussed primarily in terms of how it might be used to improve the chances that the client will follow the prescribed course of therapy and, thus, benefit from it. At the other extreme are humanistic approaches, in which the relationship *is* the therapy. The therapist creates the relationship through authenticity, empathy, and unconditional positive regard; such a relationship allows the client to improve by enhancing unconditional positive self-regard and self-acceptance. The therapy relationship is also central to psychoanalytic therapy. A neutral therapist provides the opportunity for the client to create a relationship of her or his own unconscious design through transference. The examination and explication of that relationship, that is, interpretation of the transference, is at the core of the psychoanalytic approach. The client–therapist relationship is also an element in therapies based on systems theory, but this approach embraces all of the client's important relationships both in the therapy, where other persons are often present (e.g., marital and family therapy), and outside it. Therefore, the client–therapist relationship is seen as only one thread in a rather large web of relationships.

Despite the differing roles played by the client–therapist relationship in the various schools of psychotherapy, many (e.g., Gelso & Carter, 1985; Lambert, Shapiro, & Bergin, 1986; Orlinsky & Howard, 1986; Strupp, 1973) have argued that it is the relationship itself that is the common element among different therapies. Research on factors predicting positive outcomes from therapy, regardless of approach or technique, and research on the process of psychotherapy include many studies relevant to understanding the client–therapist relationship.

The following paragraphs review literature on the therapy relationship from four major schools of psychotherapy: psychoanalytic, humanistic and client-centered, behavioral and cognitive–behavioral, and systems. Table 1.1 summarizes these approaches to psychotherapy and the characteristics of the therapy relationship inherent in each.

Psychoanalytic Therapy

Freud wrote extensively about the therapy relationship. In fact, one could argue that psychoanalysis is essentially an analysis of the relationship between therapist and client. The concept of transference, the tendency of a client faced with a neutral stimulus (the therapist) to establish a relationship with the therapist that mimics relationships the client previously experienced with important others, is central to psychoanalytic psychotherapy. The interpretation of the transference is the technique that distinguishes psychoanalytic psychotherapy from other psychological therapies. As the transference unfolds in therapy, the therapist, rather than enacting this relationship with the client, focuses attention on it and draws parallels between what is happening in therapy, what happens in the client's current relationships, and what happened in her or his past relationships. The analysis of the relationship between therapist and client is the substance of psychoanalytic psychotherapy.

In psychoanalytic therapy the neutrality of the therapist, her or his refusal to either reject or gratify the client's expectations and needs, allows the transference to flourish unimpeded. The therapist can then interpret the client's behavior in the relationship, giving the client the chance to recognize and understand what her or his expectations, needs, fears, and inputs typically are in relationships.

TABLE 1.1. Characteristics of the Therapy Relationship in Four Therapy Modalities

Therapy modality	Component of relationship emphasized	Therapeutic techniques	Therapist stance toward client	Therapist "role"
Psychoanalytic	Transference–countertransference	Interpretation of transference	Neutral	Parent
Humanistic	Real relationship	Unconditional positive regard	Authentic	Friend
Behavioral	Working relationship	Homework, role-playing, changing maladaptive cognitions	Directive	Teacher
Systems	Joining the family	Advice, assignments, paradox	Active (often through indirect means)	Coach

Psychoanalytic therapists acknowledge that therapists, like all human beings, also experience transference; the therapist's transference in the relationship is called countertransference. Through this phenomenon the therapist's internal representation of a relationship, based on her or his relationship experiences, influences what happens in the therapy relationship. In general, psychoanalytic therapists are exhorted to beware of countertransference since it can cause them to behave in ways that gratify their own needs or serve defensive purposes and that do not fulfill therapeutic objectives (Gorkin, 1987; Reich, 1960). Another source of countertransference, however, can be the client's behavior. In trying to create relationships similar to those she or he has experienced in the past, the client will act in such a way as to evoke the desired (familiar) responses from the therapist. For example, a client who has experienced a bullying, controlling parent may behave in such a submissive, apathetic way that the therapist feels inclined to prod and push, much like the parent. In this context, countertransference thoughts, feelings, and behaviors are an important source of information to the therapist about the client and, when understood, can also be of benefit to the client (Gorkin, 1987).

Two of the messages of the psychoanalytic view of relationships are that they are based not solely on behaviors exchanged between two people but, rather, on each person's often unconscious expectation of and goals for relationships and that expectations and goals are the product of a personal history of significant relationships. Shaver, Hazan, and Bradshaw (1988; Hazan & Shaver, 1987) have developed a model of adult love relationships based on this assumption that early relationship experiences influence adult relationships. Their work is more specifically an application of Bowlby's (1969) theory of attachment and Ainsworth's (1982) work on patterns of attachment. Bowlby and Ainsworth had observed and analyzed mother–infant attachment, but they assumed as do all psychoanalytic theorists, that mental models or representations of the mother and the self and the relationship between the two develop in early life and have a profound effect on a person's relationships later in life. Ainsworth, Blehar, Waters, and Wall (1978) identified three types of attachment: secure (66% of infants observed), anxious/ambivalent (19%), and avoidant (21%). Using descriptions of these three types, modified for adult relationships, Hazan and Shaver (1987) found in two studies that adults and college students classified themselves into these three categories in percentages similar to those found by Ainsworth et al. (1978): secure (56%), anxious/ambivalent (19-20%), avoidant (23-25%). They also found that secure subjects in both studies were more likely than others to describe their relationship as friendly and trusting and (in the older sample only) to have long relationships. Anxious/ambivalent subjects reported desire for reciprocity and union, sexual attraction and love at first sight, but also emotional extremes, jealousy, and fear of closeness in their relationships. Avoidant subjects reported fear of closeness, emotional extremes, and jealousy. Subjects were also asked questions about their parents. Discriminant function analyses yielded different results for the adult and student samples, partly because avoidant students gave far more favorable ratings to parents (perhaps, the authors suggest, defensively) than did the older adult subjects. Nevertheless, having respectful, accepting mothers characterized secure subjects in both samples, and in general mothers and fathers were viewed more positively by secure subjects in both samples than by subjects in either of the other categories. Hazan and Shaver (1987) also found that the three groups had different mental models, or beliefs, about relationships.

This research is an important demonstration of the idea that individuals bring into a relationship their own needs and expectations and that these may be formed in part by significant relationships in early life. In ordinary relationships the individual's initial beliefs and wishes may change; the purpose of psychoanalytic therapy is to allow those beliefs and wishes to show themselves fully so that they can be examined and understood.

The therapy relationship also has another role in psychoanalytic psychotherapy. Freud (1937) wrote about the "analytic pact" between therapist and client, the collaborative and realistic part of the relationship (as opposed to the irrational transference) that allowed therapist and client to work together toward alleviating the client's problem. This aspect of the relationship has been refined and clarified by others (Bordin, 1979; Greenson, 1967; Zetzel, 1956) and is referred to as the therapeutic alliance or working alliance. The healthy part of the client (the client's observing ego) agrees to join the therapist (the therapist's analyzing ego) to work together on the unhealthy part of the client, which is being expressed through the transference. In psychoanalytic therapy the therapeutic alliance is the view of the therapist–client relationship that is most similar to that of other therapy orientations. In fact, several clinicians (Bordin, 1979; Gelso & Carter, 1985; Strupp, 1973) have argued that the therapeutic or working alliance is a concept that applies to any type of therapy, not just psychoanalytically oriented ones.

Considering the three components of the therapy relationship proposed by Gelso and Carter (1985), it is clear that in psychoanalytic psychotherapy the working alliance and transference–countertransference play critical roles. The psychoanalytic perspective has much less to say about the real relationship aspect of the therapy relationship. Modifications of traditional psychoanalytic technique, however, have been proposed for working with more disturbed clients. These modifications generally involve being less neutral or abstinent and more "real" (Horwitz, 1974; Kernberg, 1984).

Although most research on psychoanalytic therapy is in the form of case studies, at least one research study has examined changes in the therapy relationship as a predictor of outcome in short-term psychotherapy. Lansford (1986) coded transcripts of six therapies for weakenings and repairs in the therapy relationship during 12 sessions of psychotherapy. Weakenings were defined as negative responses to therapy, such as fear that the therapist would be critical, difficulty coming to therapy or talking in therapy, and difficulty terminating. Repairs were defined as activity in therapy that addressed and resolved the problems between client and therapist. Lansford found that the initial quality of the working alliance and the patient's ability to work on repairing the therapy relationship predicted outcome, as rated by client, therapist, and outside rater. Clients also benefited from discussion of the focus of therapy during repair sequences. When similarities between problems in the therapy relationship and problems outside therapy were discussed, outcome was better. Client response to interventions contributed more to outcome than did quality of therapist's intervention. The sample was small, and Lansford stressed the preliminary nature of her findings, but the results suggest that the client's ability to discuss and resolve problems in the therapy relationship contributes to overall therapy outcome in psychoanalytic psychotherapy (see Orlinsky & Howard, 1986).

Humanistic/Existential Psychotherapy

The humanistic/existential psychotherapies promote insight as a goal of psychotherapy and are sometimes grouped with psychoanalytic therapies as insight-oriented psychotherapies (London, 1986). The role of the therapy relationship in humanistic/existential therapies, however, differs from that in psychoanalytic therapy. Whereas psychoanalytic therapy focuses on *analyzing* the therapy relationship in order to gain insight, humanistic/existential therapy views the therapy relationship itself as facilitating self-exploration and, thereby, insight. The humanistic therapist is authentic, not neutral; and the therapy relationship is not viewed as a medium for transference. The therapist's role is to be accepting and responsive, but not to guide or interpret. There is not necessarily any therapeutic advantage in examining the client–therapist relationship unless it specifically facilitates the client's self-discovery process at a particular time.

Yalom (1980), writing about existential psychotherapy, states that the maxim "'It is the relationship that heals,' is the single most important lesson the psychotherapist must learn" (p. 401). He argues that the therapy relationship is useful for two reasons. One, it provides an opportunity to examine and understand other relationships, present and past, in the client's life; this view is similar to that advanced by psychodynamic psychotherapists. Second, Yalom (1980) writes, "There is enormous potential benefit in the patient's developing a real (as opposed to a transferential) relationship to the therapist" (p. 405). In order for this real relationship to be healing, the therapist must have certain qualities, such as empathy and authenticity. The therapist helps the client not by instruction, advice, or suggestion nor by in any way manipulating or imposing on but by caring deeply about and being with the client, by sharing the client's experience, and by imagining with the client what she or he might become.

Rogers, in his explication of client-centered or nondirective therapy, gives a clear account of the necessary conditions for therapy from his point of view (Rogers, 1951, 1957). The therapist must be authentic and have unconditional positive regard for and empathic understanding of the client. If the therapist provides these ingredients, the client will be free in the therapy relationship to examine her or his experience, thoughts, feelings, and impulses honestly and without distortions.

Rogers assumes that clients experience dissatisfaction with themselves because they are responding to conditions of worth, that is, the *conditional* positive regard expressed by important others. If, for example, expressions of anger are unacceptable to one's parents, then one's own feelings of anger may be distorted and may become self-critical feelings or feelings of moral indignation. Fear of experiencing one's true feelings leads to distortions that lead in turn to incongruence between one's *actual* experiences and what one is conscious of experiencing (incongruence, in Rogers's terms, between the organism and the self). In a relationship with a therapist (or presumably anyone) who *knows* the client (empathic understanding) yet accepts everything the client experiences (unconditional positive regard), the client is able to disregard the "conditions" that have been set on his or her feelings of worth and begins to acquire congruence between actual experience and conscious experience (in other words, insight). Rogers is describing not just a therapy relationship but a relationship that, if it exists between any two people, will promote insight and self-actualization. Rogers downplayed the role of the therapist as an expert or adviser. In fact, a client-centered therapist would *not* ask leading questions, give advice, or make interpretations.

For humanistic therapists it is the real relationship that counts; relatively little attention is given to either the working alliance or transference–countertransference (Gelso & Carter, 1985). If the therapist is genuine and congruent, transference, that is, misperceptions on the part of the client, should disappear over time, not from analysis but from the opportunity the client has to see who the therapist really is. The working alliance is viewed from the humanistic perspective as arising in part from the client's inherent actualizing tendency, or movement toward growth.

Early research on Rogers's necessary and sufficient conditions for effective psychotherapy, that is, genuineness, empathy, and unconditional positive regard, concluded that therapists who have these qualities are effective for nearly any client (Truax & Mitchell, 1971). More recent research and literature reviews, however, claim that these conditions are neither necessary nor sufficient but are facilitative (Gelso & Carter, 1985). Research using the Relationship Inventory, a scale designed to measure level of regard, empathy, unconditionality, and congruence, confirms that clients who perceive their therapists as having these characteristics do have more positive therapy outcomes (Barrett-Lennard, 1986; Gurman, 1977). Therapists' ratings of the degree to which they possess these characteristics are not as strongly related to outcome (Barrett-Lennard, 1986).

The Relationship Inventory (Barrett-Lennard, 1986), although based on a theory of therapy, is well suited for studies of any type of relationship. This is in keeping with Rogers's view that any relationship with the proper conditions is therapeutic. The items assess (1) the subject's perceptions of the other's behavior and feelings toward self and (2) the self's behavior and feelings toward the other. They measure understanding, maintaining regard despite revelations, being genuine, and so forth. Their content is not specific to the therapy relationship. Researchers have found, for example, that marital couples in distress report lower levels of positive relationship characteristics than couples not in distress (B. Thornton, cited in Barrett-Lennard, 1986). Rogers's theory and Barrett-Lennard's operationalization of it offer a model of the essential ingredients of good personal relationships, not just of therapy relationships.

Although the relationship characteristics (empathy, level of regard, unconditionality, and congruence) may be present or not present in either partner in a relationship, in client-centered therapy, as in any other therapy, there is asymmetry. It is the therapist's responsibility to be authentic and to have empathy and unconditional positive regard. The goal of therapy is for the client to obtain these qualities, but she or he is not assumed to have them initially. Thus, whereas the quality of a marriage or a friendship may be predicted by the presence of these characteristics in either or both partners, in therapy the prediction of outcomes is based on ratings of these characteristics in the therapist.

Both psychoanalytic and humanistic therapies stress client self-disclosure and self-exploration and place the burden on the therapist for providing the proper setting for these to occur. Referring to both of these modalities, London (1986) captures the personal but asymmetrical quality of insight-oriented therapy: "As personal as this relationship may be in some ways, it is not sociable—it may look continuous with social states in which people engage each other, but Insight therapy makes clients engage themselves alone" (p. 54).

Behavioral and Cognitive-Behavioral Therapy

Unlike psychoanalytic and humanistic therapies, the emphasis in behavioral and cognitive–behavioral therapies is on interventions, not on the therapy relationship. In behavior therapy the strategy is to define the behavior to be changed and apply an intervention that has been designed according to principles of behavior therapy to change it. The strength of the therapy resides largely in the intervention itself. Thus, for example, with participant modeling, it is the opportunity to observe and then imitate a model coping with an anxiety-producing situation that reduces the client's stress and improves her or his performance in the stressful situation. In behavioral therapy with a token economy, it is receiving a reward contingent on performing desired behaviors that produces behavior change.

The therapist's responsibility is to know how to assess a behavioral problem, to choose or design an appropriate intervention, and then to apply that intervention and assess behavior change. Behavior therapists are aware, however, that client expectations of success predict therapeutic outcomes. Thus, the therapist is advised to present herself or himself as an expert in assessing the problem and applying the appropriate procedures and to convince the client that this procedure has been shown to work in other cases similar to the client's (Goldfried & Davison, 1976). They also acknowledge, and research (Morris & Suckerman, 1974) has demonstrated, that "warm" therapists achieve better results than "cold" therapists using the same techniques. Some behavior therapists (e.g., Goldfried & Davison, 1976; G. Wilson & Evans, 1977) have been explicit about the importance of therapists being warm and caring and a positive social reinforcer, but there is less emphasis on the therapy relationship in this approach than in any of the others. In general, the behaviorist's view of her or his relationship with a client is similar to the physician's: it is important to have a good bedside manner, that is, to be self-confident, concerned, and reassuring, but also to select and apply the best treatment for the client.

Traditional behavioral approaches, such as systematic desensitization, role-playing, and homework assignments, tend to be action-oriented. Cognitive and cognitive–behavioral therapies, like the insight therapies, are talk therapies (although homework assignments and record keeping are often used). But like other behavioral approaches, there is an emphasis on teaching rather than open-ended self-exploration. The assumption is that client problems stem from how clients think about themselves and others. Some examples of cognitions that cause problems for clients are (1) thinking in terms of "shoulds," "oughts," and "musts" (Ellis, 1984); (2) blaming events in one's life on personal failures; (3) selective attention to negative information about oneself or others and ignoring positive information; and (4) "catastrophizing." Cognitive–behavioral therapists help clients identify and test dysfunctional beliefs. Therapists have clients examine evidence that disconfirms their irrational beliefs. They may also have clients introduce positive information and/or statements into their thoughts, sometimes by having them repeat certain phrases to themselves on a regular basis. As with traditional behavioral techniques, being skilled in therapeutic procedures (e.g., being adept at identifying irrational beliefs and at getting clients to question those beliefs and develop more constructive ways of thinking) is the key to effective therapy.

While using these techniques, a therapist might in fact do something that looks much like what a psychoanalytic therapist would do while interpreting the transference. From the cognitive–behavioral therapist's point of view, the relationship between client and therapist is a sample of behavior. The therapist may point out ways in which the client's behavior in her or his relationship with the therapist is maladaptive. If, for example, the client appears nervous during a session, a cognitive therapist may ask what thoughts she or he has about coming to therapy, thereby discovering, say, that the client is afraid of being a poor patient. Further exploration may reveal that the client is engaging in all-or-none thinking: "If I don't say all the right things, then I'm not a good patient." The therapist can then have the client consider whether or not this is a rational belief, point out how this maladaptive thinking has contributed to the client's feeling nervous and uncomfortable, and explore whether or not this occurs (as it probably does) in other relationships.

The difference between analytic therapy and behavioral or cogni-tive–behavioral therapy is that whereas the analytic therapist views the client's behavior toward and thoughts and feelings about the therapist as a continual expression of the client's basic personality structure and, therefore, a central problem, the behavior therapist views the relationship as a sample of behavior that may or may not be relevant to the client's main problems. The analytic therapist focuses on helping the client achieve insight by interpreting the transference. The cogni-tive–behavioral therapist focuses on the client–therapist relationship only if it is seen as related to the client's presenting problem. When focusing on the relationship, the cognitive–behavioral therapist would point out ways in which the client's behavior and/or thoughts are maladaptive, have the client question her or his assumptions about the relationship, and suggest behaviors or ways of thinking.

As with a teacher or doctor, the therapist who is liked, respected, and trusted will be more likely to have clients who comply with instructions and participate in interventions. The emphasis, however, is on having the client use the prescribed techniques. It is the follow-ing of procedures, for example, practicing systematic desensitization or adopting more rational beliefs, that is believed to lead to results rather than the client's perceptions of or feelings about the therapist or her or his insights into those perceptions or feelings. Contrast this with psychoanalytic therapy, where no therapy would take place with-out a relationship, without the client's expression of thoughts and feelings about the therapist. Also compare it with humanistic therapy, where providing a good relationship is considered to be therapeutic *in and of itself*. Although the behavioral and cognitive therapies place the least emphasis on the therapy relationship, it is probably the working alliance and the real relationship that are the most important therapy relationship components from this perspective. The working alliance, for example, includes agreement on goals, an important element in many behavior therapies. Furthermore, cognitive or behavioral thera-pists are generally uninterested in transference–countertransference issues and tend to view their behaviors and those of their clients in the relationship as genuine.

Research on clients' perceptions of what contributed to their improvement during therapy demonstrates that clients have different experiences in behavioral and insight-oriented therapies. Cross, Shee-han, and Khan (1982) found that both groups of clients rated very highly "the therapist helping you to understand your problems," but clients in behavioral therapy gave higher ratings to variables concerning the treatment itself (e.g., practicing behaviors in the session) whereas clients in insight-oriented therapy gave higher ratings to variables concerning the interaction between client and therapist. Thus, the distinction between therapeutic techniques and the role of the relationship in the two styles of therapy was confirmed in this particular study.

Systems Theory Family system

Systems theory regards the individual as a unit in a complex but structured collection of interrelated units. From this view, generally adopted by family therapists, the individual cannot be understood outside of the context of the system in which she or he functions. It is not that family therapists treat disturbed families whereas other therapists treat disturbed individuals from basically healthy families; rather, family therapists treat individuals by treating the whole family. These therapists believe that it is difficult, if not impossible, to understand or treat an individual outside of the context of her or his family. A family may include parents and children, but family therapists recognize that any set of individuals is only a subset of the larger extended family and that psychological problems are passed down from one generation to the next (Bowen, 1978). Therapy with three or even four generations is preferable, and in some cases necessary, according to some family therapists (e.g., Whitaker, 1982).

The family therapist is in relationship not with just one person but with a system of persons. In establishing a relationship with a family, the therapist speaks of "joining" the family or being inducted into the family, indicating that becoming a member of this set of interrelated persons is essential to the therapeutic process.

It is assumed that families in treatment have structures and rules that are dysfunctional and that these create psychological problems for the family members. Such problems eventually emerge as symptoms in at least one of the family members. When there is an individual with a presenting problem, other family members may recognize that she or he has a problem but may believe that they themselves have no problems at all. The family therapist assumes that problems seen in one

individual represent problems in the functioning of the whole system/
family, and therefore the therapist's goal is to restructure and change
the total system.

In order to create change, the therapist must become a part of the
family system. Although techniques for joining the system may differ
among family therapists, there is general agreement that to be effective
the therapist must accomplish this task early in therapy. According to
F. Gottlieb (1986): "The verbal language of joining is validation,
affirmation, confirmation, accommodation, similarity. The body language is mirroring, removing barriers, open arms, palms upward. The
affective language is empathic, often with warmth, agreement, respect,
praise" (p. 265). Bowen (1978) argues that the therapist should present
herself or himself as coaching or supervising the family but should
attempt to remain outside the family's emotional system. He suggests
that therapists deal in reality and facts and adopt the role of expert
professional, preferably without great emotional significance to the
family. Some family therapists use a therapy team, whose members
watch the therapy through a one-way mirror and may interrupt the
therapy session to ask questions or make comments; other therapists
use a cotherapist. These arrangements reduce the intensity of a therapist's emotional involvement with a family and can provide objectivity
so that a therapist does not become overly involved. Clearly, there is a
recognition that a lone therapist, if not careful, may be overwhelmed
by a family and lose her or his perspective.

The family therapist's role is often compared to that of coach,
teacher, conductor, or parent: the therapist gives advice, assignments,
directives. She or he may get distant family members to sit closer
together in the therapy session or to engage in activities together at
home. Like the cognitive–behavioral therapist, the family therapist is
active and directive; unlike the cognitive–behavioral therapist, however, the family therapist often seeks change through strategies whose
purpose may not be, and need not be, clear to the family. Cognitive–
behavioral therapists usually explain how following certain procedures will create change; family therapists may use interventions that
are provocative and paradoxical. For example, a family therapist may
reframe the symptoms of a family member, pointing out to family
members that they all agree that this member has a problem and that
since this is the only thing that they all agree on, the symptom is a
useful source of unity in the family. The therapist's goal is not to
maintain the symptom, but to change the role of the member with the

symptom from scapegoat to creator of unity in the family. Changing the individual's role inevitably changes the family system. The family therapist is trying to change the structure and rules in the family, but she or he often does this indirectly.

The social psychology of relationships has focused on dyadic relationships, for example, friendships, romantic relationships, marriages. Systems theory and family therapy suggest that an understanding of the relationship between two people is always incomplete until one examines the larger system of social relationships in which these two operate.

Clinical Research on the Therapy Relationship

There is a substantial research literature on the role of the therapy relationship; the bulk of this literature is concerned with the therapeutic or working alliance. The terms *therapeutic alliance* and *working alliance* come from the literature on psychodynamic psychotherapy. The idea, however, that client and therapist are collaborators in a process aimed at client improvement and alleviation of symptoms is one that easily applies to any form of therapy (Bordin, 1979; Gelso & Carter, 1985). Research scales measuring the client–therapist working alliance have employed client ratings, therapist ratings, and/or ratings of therapy videotapes or transcripts by trained clinicians who assess clients' and therapists' contributions to therapy and the therapy relationship. These scales have been applied to wide variety of client populations (e.g., college students, drug abusers, bereaved clients, and clients suitable for short-term therapy) and therapy modalities (e.g., psychodynamic, experiential, behaviorally oriented, and Gestalt) (Gomes-Schwartz, 1978; Horvath & Greenberg, 1986; Luborsky, McLellan, Woody, O'Brien, & Auerbach, 1985; Marmar, Horowitz, Weiss, & Marziali, 1986).

Numerous studies have found that positive outcome in therapy can be predicted by patient variables, such as patient participation (from the Vanderbilt Psychotherapy Process Scale, rated from videotapes; Gomes-Schwartz, 1978), patient's perception of therapist helpfulness and collaboration with therapist (from the Penn Helping Alliance Scales, rated from transcripts; Alexander & Luborsky, 1986), and patient's positive contributions to therapy (from the Therapeutic Alliance Rating System, rated by patient, therapist, and external rater; Marmar et al., 1986).

Therapist variables have been less consistent and less powerful but still have been positive predictors of outcome. Alexander and Luborsky (1986) reported little predictive capacity for measures of therapist facilitative behaviors (rated from transcripts) and Gomes-Schwartz (1978) found only a weak relationship between measures of a therapist-offered relationship (i.e., therapist warmth and friendliness and negative therapist attitude) and outcome. On the other hand, Marmar et al. (1986) found that the therapist's positive contribution to therapy (rated by client, therapist, and external rater) was significantly related to outcome for 8 of 18 correlations. In comparison, the client's positive contribution to therapy yielded 10 of 18 significant correlations. These measures of client and therapist variables are made in early sessions (first to fifth) and predict outcome months later, at the end of therapy or some time following termination. Thus, client and therapist perceptions of the therapy relationship established early in the relationship affect outcome. (See Chapter 5, in this volume.)

While it appears that patient behavior, attitudes, and perceptions are more important in predicting outcome than are therapist variables, it is possible that therapist behaviors contribute to what the client does and how she or he experiences the therapy relationship. Suh and O'Malley (1982, cited in Suh, Strupp, & O'Malley, 1986) found that positive *changes* in therapist warmth and exploration from the first to the third session were powerful predictors of positive versus negative therapy outcome. For low prognosis, but not high prognosis cases, these positive changes in therapist behavior were accompanied by positive changes in client participation across the first three sessions.

Whereas client and therapist contributions to therapy, as well as client and therapist perceptions of themselves and of one another, are relevant to the therapy relationship, they focus on participants in the relationship and are not measures of the relationship itself. Some researchers have looked at the therapy relationship more directly. Using ratings of audiotapes of segments of the first three therapy sessions, Sandell (1981, cited in Suh et al., 1986) found that the combination of poor therapeutic relationship and poor collaboration (Patient–Therapist Interaction from the Negative Indicators Scale) had negative correlations with overall improvement for all three sessions. With a sample of 18, however, only the correlation for session three was statistically significant. Horvath and Greenberg (1986) developed the Working Alliance Inventory to measure the components of the alliance described by Bordin (1979). Specifically, the inventory measures (1) Goal, agreement on the goals of the helping process; (2) Task, agreement that the tasks required of client and therapist are reasonable and relevant; and (3) Bond, an experience of mutual trust, liking, understanding, and caring. Both client and therapist filled out the Working Alliance Inventory in the third session. All three components of the working alliance were significantly related to some measure of outcome. Using stepwise regression analyses, Horvath and Greenberg (1986) found that the Task dimension was the most useful in predicting client-reported outcomes.

In general, these studies support the assumption that a positive therapy relationship contributes to positive therapy outcomes. As with research on other relationships, it is difficult to measure the therapy relationship per se, independent of client and therapist perceptions of that relationship. Interestingly, when client and therapist variables are measured separately, client variables appear to have the stronger relationship with outcome variables.

Overview of Chapters

The remaining chapters of this volume examine theories and research in the area of personal relationships and consider how they might be applied to the therapy relationship.

Chapter 2 uses the sociological definition of roles, that is, behavioral expectations shared by individuals within the society, to explore the therapist role and the client role. Roles are helpful in that they structure behavior and increase predictability in interpersonal interactions, but they also limit what is likely to occur in the therapy relationship. The chapter also examines the ways in which gender roles influence therapist, client, and the therapist–client dyad.

Chapter 3 presents the social exchange theories of relationships. These include Thibaut and Kelley's (1959) interdependence theory, which asserts that satisfaction in a relationship is a function of rewards, costs, and comparison level and that commitment depends on the comparison level for alternatives (i.e., other relationships available to an individual), and Rusbult's (1980a) investment model, which adds the concept that investments in the relationship will also influence commitment. Aspects of therapy that contribute to rewards, costs, comparison level, comparison level of alternatives, and investments for both client and therapist are discussed. A theory of relationship that has proven utility for predicting satisfaction and commitment in personal relationships is applied to the therapy relationship.

Chapter 4 reviews the literature on variables that influence attraction and how these may influence the therapy process. It also takes a recent development in personal relationship research, love attitude, and uses this as a framework for examining the relationships that are typical in different modes of therapy. Finally, the chapter considers the issue of sexual attraction in therapy and its implication for therapist and client.

Chapter 5 applies models of relationship development to therapy. Most models assume a gradual increase in closeness, intimacy, and self-disclosure in successful relationships, and the chapter explores how this occurs in therapy. The chapter also explores the possibility that client and therapist impressions or actions in the first few sessions may predict therapy outcome.

Chapter 6 reviews the research on three characteristics of responsiveness: content of response, style of response, and timing of response. The chapter interprets clinical literature on therapist behavior, especially therapist self-disclosing and self-involving statements, in terms of responsiveness and argues that therapist responsiveness in content, style, and timing is critical for the development of a *therapeutic* relationship between therapist and client.

Chapter 7 also examines how and why clients reveal and conceal information. The functions of self-disclosure (expression, self-clarification, social validation, relationship development, and social control) are reviewed. The chapter also discusses client and therapist concerns about boundary regulation and the amount and level of intimacy of information exchanged between client and therapist and between the therapy dyad and others (i.e., confidentiality in therapy).

Chapter 8 applies the literature on social support in personal relationships to the therapy relationship. Sources of support from family and friends are compared to support in therapy. Negative, as well as positive, aspects of support are also considered.

Chapter 9 reiterates major themes in the book. These include the necessary balance in the therapy relationship between personal and professional qualities, the need to examine therapy in the light of the different stages of the therapy relationship, and the impact of the therapy relationship on both the therapist and client. The chapter also describes research strategies to test hypotheses suggested in the preceding chapters.

In every chapter we review research on personal relationships and research on the therapy relationship and therapy outcome, and we give examples of how concepts presented in the chapter may affect the relationship between client and therapist. We hope these chapters speak to the personal relationships researcher, the clinical researcher, and the practicing psychotherapist.

CHAPTER 2

Roles in the
Therapy Relationship

W e often discuss relationships as if they are solely the product of individuals' perceptions (e.g., attraction to another, experience of rewards or costs) and actions (e.g., self-disclosures, social support) and as if these perceptions and actions are affected only by differences among the individuals. Relationships, however, occur with social structures that are composed of roles. Roles are behavioral expectations shared by individuals within the society (Stryker & Statham, 1985). These expectations limit the perceptions and behaviors of individuals both in terms of their own performance within a role and their responses to others in their roles. Some roles, such as gender roles and family roles, may apply to everyone in the society, others to relatively few, such as those in specific occupations. This chapter focuses on how social roles influence the therapy relationship. First, we will examine the roles of the therapist and the client and then discuss how gender roles may influence the therapy relationship.

Therapist's Role

In Chapter 1 we acknowledged that we were using the word *therapist* to include a variety of professionals whose work includes forming a therapy relationship with a client. Although the specific roles of therapists representing different specialities or orientations will differ, there are core characteristics. The therapist is a professional who has received special training in providing the services that she or he delivers: the therapist has knowledge and expertise. The therapist's responsibility is to apply his or her skills in ameliorating or preventing the client's psychological and/or behavioral problems (American Psychological Association, 1987). In general, then, the therapist's role is one of an expert in treating psychological/behavioral problems.

The attitudes and behaviors that are central to the role of the psychotherapist have been described by clinicians. Basch (1980) writes, "In encounters with patients we do not have the armamentarium of laboratory tests or X rays or an assortment of 'scopes' to let us know what is going on. Our only instrument is our personality" (p. 5). In describing the personal qualities needed by a therapist, Strupp and Binder (1984) write, "The therapist's attitude should consistently reflect interest, respect, a desire not to hurt (even when provoked), a suspension of criticism and moral judgment, and a genuine commitment to help (within the limits set by the therapeutic role and by being human)"; for Strupp and Binder, doing therapy "calls for receptive and quiet listening, attempting to understand, and simply being there" (p. 41).

For Dinkmeyer, Pew, and Dinkmeyer, Jr. (1979), "the relationship that Adlerian counselors seek to establish is a relationship between equals, a collaborative effort in which counselor and counselee are active partners working toward mutual agreed-upon goals" (p. 58). The following conditions, they write, are essential for good counseling: "1. Empathy. 2. Caring and concern. 3. Genuineness and openness. 4. Positive regard and respect. 5. Understanding and clarification of the meaning and purpose of the individual's behavior. 6. Action-oriented techniques [such as confrontation and encouragement]" (p. 74).

These characteristics are echoed by Beck, Rush, Shaw, and Emery (1979), who write, "The general characteristics of the therapist which facilitate the application of cognitive therapy (as well as other kinds of psychotherapies), include warmth, accurate empathy, and genuineness" (p. 45). Furthermore, "The relationship involves both the patient and the therapist and is based on trust, rapport, and collaboration. Cognitive and behavior therapies probably require the same subtle therapeutic atmosphere that has been described explicitly in the context of psychodynamic therapy" (p. 50). Cognitive therapists also use specific techniques to help patients identify, observe, and evaluate their thoughts and then test the validity of their assumptions about themselves and the world. All of these writers emphasize the therapist's personal qualities and interpersonal skills.

Texts on behavior therapy generally have less to say about therapist characteristics or the client–therapist relationship. Wolpe (1982)
writes, "1. The emotional climate is at all times a blend of objectivity
and permissiveness. 2. The patient must be assured that his [or her]
unpleasant reactions are reversible. If they have been learned, they can
be unlearned" (p. 62). The focus is on techniques which the clinician
uses to help the client unlearn maladaptive habits. G. Wilson and
O'Leary (1980) write, "Behavior therapists are professionals well-
versed in the scientific foundations of behavior therapy *and* are pos-
sessed of the clinical and/or interpersonal skills required to design and
implement effective behavior change methods" (p. 29, emphasis in the
original). But there is no discussion of the interpersonal skills that are
required.

Malan (1979), a psychodynamic therapist, stresses the personal
aspect of the therapy relationship balanced with the professional. He
writes that a clinician needs "to *use his knowledge of his* [or her] *own
feelings* . . . to know not only *theoretically* but *intuitively* what [is]
needed . . . [and when] not to obtrude one's own personal feelings into
what one says to the patient" (p. 25, emphasis in the original).

There are other professionals who are also service providers, and it
is informative to compare the therapist's role to theirs. Physicians
(excluding most psychiatrists, who function as therapists), dentists,
accountants, and lawyers, for example, treat or advise patients/clients.
Professional relationships are established in these cases, but they differ
in important ways from the professional relationship that is also a
therapy relationship. Interactions with physicians, dentists, accountants, or lawyers occur on an as-needed basis, and the helping aspects
of the relationship itself may be acknowledged but are never believed
to be the main ingredient of the intervention. (An exception to this
latter point would be cases in which physicians see individuals who
have primarily psychological, not physical, problems. Rather than
referring them to a psychotherapist or upon the patient's refusal to see
a psychotherapist, the physician may "treat" the patient with encouragement and reassurance.) Even among providers of psychological
services, the therapy relationship is sometimes seen as playing a minor
part in therapy (see Chapter 1): some behavioral or biofeedback interventions, for example, emphasize the technical, rather than the relational, aspects of the therapeutic process. Most therapy relationships,
however, involve regular, ongoing interactions that may be time-
limited but usually do not vary as a direct result of the client's current

state, until client and therapist agree that sufficient improvement has occurred.

Furthermore, with medical or legal problems there is a tendency, even an expectation, that the case will be "turned over" to the professional. In other words, the physician or lawyer will determine what the problem and its solution are and proceed from there with the assumption that the patient/client will willingly follow her or his prescriptions and advice. In psychological therapy, the therapist may or may not give advice and there is generally an emphasis on the client's participation in and responsibility for her or his "cure" and an understanding that the client and therapist *together* will find the path to improvement. The asymmetry in the professional–client relationship is much clearer in medical and legal situations: an individual has a problem, she or he goes to an expert, and the expert does her or his best to solve the problem. An individual with a psychological or behavioral problem may go to a therapist with similar expectations, that is, that the therapist will assess the problem and provide a cure or solution. Certain behavioral techniques (systematic desensitization as a cure for a phobia or biofeedback as a cure for headaches or other ailments) may confirm the expectation. In most cases, however, the client is likely to discover that the therapist is unwilling to assume the role of one who provides cures or solutions. Therapists generally view their role as working with clients to help *them* define and find ways to ameliorate their problems themselves.

In general, when therapists write about the functions and characteristics of the therapist, they focus on the therapist's personal qualities and the need to establish a good working relationship with the client along with the therapist's mastery of theory and technique. It is not enough to "know your stuff," as it might be for a physician or lawyer. A therapist must have the qualities of a good friend (listening, being empathic) as well as a good professional. The balance between the personal and interpersonal aspects of the therapist role and its professional aspects makes it unique. Framo (1982), writing about marital therapy, remarks on this delicate balance: "In an attempt to decrease the distance between us, I will at times make social comments and even relate something personal about myself when relevant. . . . It should be remembered, however, that the therapy situation is a professional rather than a social situation" (p. 136).

The props on the stage where these professional roles are played are indicators of the nature of the roles. Professional service providers, including therapists, display their professional degrees, certificates, and licenses on the walls of their offices. (State law may, in fact, require that a professional license be displayed.) Other props are also used; physicians generally wear white coats and carry special equipment (e.g., stethoscopes), and they move from room to room attending to patients who are seen briefly, with a clear focus on the patient's medical problem. The patients themselves usually collude in the dissociation of person from physical symptom as a defense against the potentially embarrassing or upsetting acts of looking and touching that characterize the behavior of a physician who must make a diagnosis. In a lawyer's or accountant's office the professional generally sits behind a desk when interacting with a client. The desk serves not only as a physical barrier between professional and client but also as a way of signifying that the professional is *at work*. The lawyer may refer during the meeting to books or legal codes as a way of substantiating points; but these behaviors also validate her or his role as a guide through the legal system. The therapist, however, usually sits facing the client in an office that is designed to be comfortable and pleasant. There may be a desk in the office (a signal that this is where the therapist *works*), but the therapist rarely sits behind it when interacting with a client. The therapist often has books on shelves in the office—and may even recommend one to a client—but would rarely "look something up" during a session. Whereas the props of the physician and lawyer distance them from the patient/client, the therapist has few props and tends to behave in a manner that decreases the distance between therapist and client. A common caricature of the psychotherapist is of a bespectacled male with a beard, perhaps smoking a pipe. It is an empirical question whether therapists are more likely than other professionals to wear glasses or beards or smoke pipes, but in our culture these characteristics connote a person of authority and wisdom.

Two anecdotes will illustrate the importance of props and the balance that therapists attempt to create between the professional and the personal aspects of their role. Therapists usually have a chair in the office that is *theirs*, and upon first meeting with a client in the office they may indicate where the client is to sit. The chairs in the office may be all of the same type, but often the therapist's chair is different—larger or more elaborate in some way. In one case the therapist's chair was so large that a group of psychologists meeting in his office commented among themselves; the image of the therapist "enthroned" contradicted their ideal of a more symmetrical and egalitarian relationship between therapist and client.

Although therapists do not wear uniforms or white coats, they do generally dress in a professional style. The code of dress, however, surely varies more than it does for lawyers. Nevertheless, a group of graduate students who had begun to wear the same casual clothes to their practicum settings that they were wearing to class were instructed to dress more formally in the clinical setting and were reminded that they were professionals in training. No one believed that style of dress correlated with therapeutic skill, but dress is role related and the students were reminded that a professional "ought to dress for the part."

Client's Role

For every role there is a counter-role. Indicative of the two views of the role of the recipient of therapy, there are two labels used to refer to this person: *client* and *patient*. The use of the label *patient* is the older and more traditional. The definition in *Webster's Seventh New Collegiate Dictionary* (1963) of patient is simply "a person receiving care or treatment," but its use in the medical setting has given the word the connotation of a person with a physical illness. Carl Rogers adopted the term *client* and incorporated it into the name for a style of therapy: client-centered therapy. As Rogers saw it, *client* means "one who comes actively and voluntarily to gain help on a problem, but without any notion of surrendering his [or her] own responsibility for the situation," and "it avoids the connotation that he [or she] is sick" (Rogers, 1951, p. 7).

Counselors generally use the term *client*, as do psychotherapists with a behavioral orientation (e.g., Goldfried & Davison, 1976; G. Wilson & O'Leary, 1980). Psychodynamic, cognitive (unless they are especially behavioral), and family therapists typically use the term *patient*. The use of these terms may indicate little more than the degree of influence of psychiatrists, who have received medical training that instills a doctor–patient frame of reference. Psychiatrists have been prominent figures in psychodynamic, cognitive, and family therapies but are relatively uninvolved in client-centered and behavioral therapies. On the other hand, choosing to refer to the recipient of therapy as a client may reflect important assumptions about the roles played by therapist and client, de-emphasizing the therapist's curative or doctoring role and emphasizing the psychological (rather than medical/physical) nature of the client's problem and the client's responsibility for seeking therapy and using the aid she or he obtains from it.

Another issue vis-à-vis the client's role is the individual's relative unfamiliarity with it. The therapist has had years of course work and supervised practical experience that provide socialization for the therapist role. The client, upon entering therapy for the first time, may have only fictional accounts (e.g., from novels, movies, or television) or the stories of friends to serve as guides to the proper attitude and behavior of a client. Some clinicians have advocated role induction, a process in which clients are informed prior to beginning therapy by means of pretherapy interview, videotape, or written material, about behaviors expected of clients and therapists, about potential problems in therapy, such as resistance, and about what they can expect in terms of positive outcomes. In a review of the research literature on the results of this pretherapy training, Orlinsky and Howard (1986) report that of 34 studies, 24 found positive results in terms of process (e.g., individual self-disclosure, ratings of the client–therapist relationship, attendance record for sessions) and/or outcome for clients who had some form of role preparation. No study found negative effects. Some studies have found that clients who are likely to have inappropriate role expectations (e.g., clients from low socioeconomic groups) are particularly likely to benefit from this training. One criticism of the research is that most role inductions manipulate expectations for therapy outcome as well as inform the client about appropriate role behaviors (Kaul & Bednar, 1986). Inducing positive expectations definitely improves outcomes; it is not clear whether efforts to familiarize clients with client and therapist roles *without* enhancing their expectations would be equally beneficial.

Despite the positive findings on role induction, it does not appear to be widely used. Most clients learn their roles through altercasting, a process in which the therapist elicits the appropriate behaviors from the client. Therapists may be relatively direct in letting clients know what they are expected to do—by, for example, spending a few minutes in the first session describing their approach to therapy. It is likely, however, that these descriptions are brief and general, with few examples or specific instructions to clients. Other therapists may say nothing at all about the process of therapy, expecting either that the client has some ideas about this already or that they will learn "by doing."

Most therapists would begin an initial session by asking the client what brought her or him into therapy. At the beginning of subsequent sessions, however, the therapist may say nothing. If the client expresses uncertainty about what to say, the therapist will prompt the patient to behave in whatever manner is appropriate for the therapy being conducted. Dynamic and humanistic therapists would probably wait in silence longer than would be comfortable in a social encounter in order to give the client a chance to begin, thereby indicating to the client that he or she is expected to begin. To relieve a period of awkward silence, such a therapist might say, "We could start with whatever you have on your mind right now," or "Well, what today?" After a while the well-socialized client will sit down and begin to talk without prompting. When silence occurs at the beginning of a session with such a client, the therapist may inquire about what makes it difficult to begin. (On occasion, sitting in silence with a client can be the most therapeutic response, and experienced therapists advise against interrupting silences.) A cognitive or behavioral therapist generally takes a more directive approach, beginning a session by asking about progress on issues discussed during the last session or asking about homework assignments. Again, in time clients may themselves report on these things without being asked.

Throughout the session the therapist's questions and comments and even nonverbal behaviors (e.g., nods, smiles, frowns, looks of boredom) indicate to the client what is appropriate and inappropriate material for therapy. These therapist responses may be intentional or unintentional, but they do reflect the therapist's conscious and unconscious assumptions about what clients in therapy should do. Over the course of therapy a client in dynamic therapy will almost certainly talk more about family history and dreams than will a client in behavioral therapy. Sometimes a therapist's expectations will be directly expressed (e.g., "I often find that a client's dreams are very meaningful and useful material in therapy"); other times it is simply the therapist's enthusiasm and interest in the presentation of a dream that informs the client about her or his role.

Some aspects of the therapy relationship are distinctly different from other social relationships and are more in line with business relationships. For example, while a small amount of small talk may serve as a warm-up, prolonged social chitchat, highly appropriate in social or friendly relationships, is directly or indirectly discouraged in therapy relationships. It is regarded as a waste of valuable time, much

as it would be in a business meeting. Furthermore, small talk in therapy would probably be difficult to maintain even if it occurred. Although the therapist generally knows a great deal about the client, the client knows very little about the therapist, and many forms of therapy (especially psychodynamic) advise against disclosure of personal information by the therapist. Thus, after "How are you?" (when during an ordinary social encounter one might go on to inquire, "How's work?" or "How are your children?") the client is unable to continue with such inquiries because the therapy session *is* the therapist's work and the client may not know if the therapist has children. Certainly therapists will avoid ritualized social questions, which generally encourage rather superficial responses, because their task is to get the client to disclose personal problems in depth. (Goffman, 1971, points out the awkwardness, for example, of saying "How are you?" as a greeting to someone who is gravely ill.)

Some therapists are comfortable with abbreviated social amenities at the beginning or end of sessions (e.g., the exchange of remarks about the weather, the offer of a cup of coffee, farewells). Others dispense with these altogether. Traditionally, psychoanalytically oriented therapists have viewed the therapist's role as one of neutrality and anonymity and have condemned even casual social remarks. They argue that these interfere with neutrality and, therefore, the development of the transference and that they inappropriately gratify the client's need for a social relationship (which the therapy relationship is *not*). For example, nearly all respondents to a survey sent to members of the British Psycho-analytical Society reported "avoidance of social ('fringe') contact during analytical sessions" and "limitation of small talk" (Glover, 1955).

Reflecting a more moderate, and perhaps more humane, view of the client–therapist relationship in dynamic therapy, DeWald (1969), Stone (1961), and others have acknowledged that an unresponsive therapist may easily be experienced by the client as hostile and insulting rather than neutral. DeWald (1969) recommends responding in a friendly way at the beginning of therapy but drawing the client's attention to these activities as therapy progresses and encouraging the client to explore their meaning. Such an approach generally leads to their being seen as merely social rituals or to the revelation of the personal meanings they hold for the client and, ultimately, to their being dispensed with. Goffman (1971) refers to ritualized greetings and leave-takings as supportive interchanges. He makes the point that in

Superficial chatter
social chatter
can be distressing

business interactions "supportive rituals *can* (although they need not) be performed in passing" (p. 71). The fact that supportive rituals are unnecessary in the therapy relationship highlights its professional, rather than its personal, qualities.

When client and therapist find themselves in situations that require informal social talk (e.g., riding the same elevator to the therapist's office or attending a social function) they may find that they feel uncomfortable and at a loss for words, despite the fact that inside the therapist's office words flow easily. (Two-thirds of the psychoanalysts responding to the aforementioned survey reported that they took special measures to avoid encountering clients outside of sessions [Glover, 1955].) As mentioned earlier, the asymmetry of the therapy relationship will make it difficult for the client to reciprocate in the manner expected in ordinary social relations. Furthermore, the superficiality of most social talk belies the intimate nature of therapy talk. In this way the therapy relationship is unlike other professional relationships, where the partners are generally at ease in casual conversation although they may avoid it when there is business to do.

There is at least one other context in which the superficiality of social chatter is distressing. When individuals are just entering an intimate relationship or when they are in the midst of serious discussions (e.g., deciding whether or not to continue the relationship), knowing that they have more important things to talk about may cause them to feel that social talk is inappropriate. In these relationships reciprocity is not the issue. The intensity of the personal relationship during periods of relationship development or uncertainty is similar to the intensity often experienced in therapy relationships. Thus, two factors—lack of reciprocity or symmetry and expectation of a high level of intimacy—inhibit social talk between client and therapist. The former factor distinguishes therapy relationships from personal relationships, the latter from other professional relationships.

This aspect of the nature of the therapy relationship—being neither entirely personal nor entirely business—is reflected in ethical principles regulating providers of psychological services. The "Ethical Principles of Psychologists," adopted and published by the American Psychological Association (1981), include the following:

> Psychologists make every effort to avoid dual relationships that could impair their professional judgment or increases the risk of exploitation. Examples of such dual relationships include, but are

not limited to, . . . treatment of employees, students, supervisees, close friends, or relatives. Sexual intimacies with clients are unethical. (p. 636)

In addition to not accepting into treatment individuals with whom the therapist has a prior relationship, this statement warns therapists against establishing other relationships with clients while they are in therapy. Establishing personal or business relationships with clients even following termination of therapy is questionable. The therapist is in possession of personal information about the client that the client does not have about the therapist. The therapist retains this power of information after therapy, and thus a relationship with a former client is unlikely to be a fully symmetrical one. A female client propositioned by her former therapist 2 years following termination of therapy stated, "It's taking unfair, personal advantage of knowledge that he gained in a relationship of professional trust and confidence" (Finney, 1975, p. 595).

Bayles (1981) discusses three models of the therapy relationship that professionals *might* use and has evaluated them in terms of their appropriateness. He states that a model that presents the therapy relationship as a friendship in which both partners are equal and free to engage in personal exchanges is not appropriate because the therapy relationship is not symmetrical. Only the client is intended to receive help; and power is unequally distributed, since therapists do in fact have more status in the relationship. Bayles argues that a model that portrays either the client or therapist as fully in control is also inappropriate because it fails to acknowledge the client's possible impaired judgment in the former case and the need for truly informed consent of the client in the latter. Bayles concludes that a relationship model in which the therapist's expertise is recognized but the client's right to informed consent and ultimate responsibility for decision making are protected is the most ethical one for the therapy relationship.

Gender Roles

Some roles affect everyone. Being female or male places an individual in a category for which there are societal expectations. Most people readily acknowledge that their relationships with members of the same sex are different from their relationships with members of the opposite sex. Research on personal relationships also indicates that females and males tend to have different experiences and expectations in relationships (Peplau, 1983; Winstead, 1986). How do sex of client, sex of therapist, and sex composition of the dyad (i.e., same sex or not) affect the therapy relationship?

The degree to which male and female clients are perceived and/or treated differently by therapists has received much research attention. The results of this research, however, are equivocal. Broverman, Broverman, Clarkson, Rosenkrantz, and Vogel (1970) in their frequently cited study found that clinicians are more likely to ascribe socially desirable masculine traits to a typical mentally healthy male and socially desirable feminine traits to a typical mentally healthy female. This suggests that clinicians are not free of the gender stereotypes held by most people. A more worrisome finding in this study was that the description of a mentally healthy adult (sex unspecified) did not differ significantly from the description of a mentally healthy male but did differ significantly from the description of a mentally healthy female. Subsequent research indicates that clinicians' gender stereotypes have become less pronounced (Petro & Putnam, 1979).

Research suggests that both female and male clients are likely to be judged as more disturbed when their behavior deviates from culturally prescribed gender norms (Tilby & Kalin, 1980), for example, female adolescents with nontraditional vocational goals (Thomas & Stewart, 1971) and depressed males (Kelly & Kiersky, cited in Zeldow, 1984). Other studies examining similar phenomena, however, have failed to yield significant results (C. Hill, Tanney, Leonard, & Reiss, 1977; Zeldow, 1984). In some studies deviant females have been judged more harshly than deviant males (Coie, Pennington, & Buckley, 1974).

Some diagnostic labels are more likely to be applied to males than to females and vice versa. Clients in clinical vignettes with ambiguous symptomatology were more likely to be diagnosed by clinicians as hysterical when they were represented as female and antisocial when they were represented as male (Warner, 1978, 1979). When clinical psychologists were given a clinical vignette unambiguously matching the DSM-III diagnosis for antisocial personality disorder, they were more likely to accurately diagnose a male (73%) than a female (53%) client (Fernbach, Winstead, & Derlega, 1989). Similarly, Ford and Widiger (1987) found that clinical psychologists were more likely to give the diagnostic labels Histrionic Personality Disorder to female clients and Antisocial Personality Disorder to males, even though a separate group of psychologists was not affected by sex of client when rating specific behaviors as representative of these two diagnostic labels. Diagnoses of female and male clients were not affected by sex of clinician in any of these studies, indicating that sex of client influences the diagnostic judgments of both female and male clinicians. It is reasonable to assume that differences in diagnoses will also yield differences in treatment.

Research examining whether female and male clients are *treated* differently by clinicians has yielded mixed results. Some who have reviewed the research literature have concluded that there is no sound evidence that either sex of therapist or sex of client influences the treatment of clients (Smith, 1980; Stricker, 1977). A recent study (Fernbach et al., 1989) in which clinical psychologists were asked to diagnose and give treatment recommendations for written cases that varied only in terms of client's sex found that when diagnosis was held constant (data analyses included treatment recommendations only from subjects who gave the cases the correct diagnosis), clinicians recommended nondirective therapy more often for female clients, legal constraints more often for males when the diagnosis was antisocial personality disorder, and medical workup by a physician more often for females when the diagnosis was somatization disorder. Fifteen other treatment variables yielded no significant differences. When diagnosis was not held constant, there were two additional sex-of-client differences: individual therapy and insight-oriented therapy were recommended more often for female than for male clients, suggesting that sex differences in diagnosis may also create sex differences in treatment.

Well-controlled studies in which clinical information and sex of client are determined by the experimenter are, of course, analogue studies. The processes in real life that may influence whether or how female and male clients are treated differently in therapy are numerous and have not been carefully studied (Marecek & Johnson, 1980). At least one study of therapy relationships revealed that the manner in which sex of therapist and sex of client influence therapeutic outcome is complex. Orlinksy and Howard (1980) found that for female clients diagnosis, marital status, and age of the client interacted with sex and years of experience of the clinician in predicting outcome. Female therapists were more successful than male therapists with female clients with anxiety reaction and schizophrenia but there were no sex-of-therapist differences for depression and personality disorder. Female therapists were more successful than male therapists with young single and family women whereas male therapists were more successful with single mothers. Experienced male therapists were considerably more successful with these female patients than less experienced male therapists whereas experience made little difference for female therapists. This study suggests that the answer to how sex of therapist and sex of client influence the therapy relationship is a complicated one.

Furthermore, it is likely that the composition of the dyad in the therapy relationship (female therapist–female client, female therapist–male client, male therapist–female client, male therapist–male client) may be more important variable than sex of therapist or sex of client alone. If we look at the literature on same-sex *personal* relationships, we find that female friends talk more than male friends about personal topics (Aries & Johnson, 1983; F. Johnson & Aries, 1983), that they experience more attachment, trust, and intimacy in same-sex friends than do males (Powers & Bultena, 1976; Sharabany, Gershoni, & Hofman, 1981), and that they are more willing than males to express feelings about their friend or the relationship to their friend (Hays, 1984; Rands & Levinger, 1979). If these results generalize to same-sex therapy relationships, we would expect to find more self-disclosure, more commitment and trust, and more discussion of transference (in psychodynamic therapy) in female therapist–female client pairs than in male therapist–male client pairs. To date there is no research that directly addresses these hypotheses; but using research on personal relationships to generate hypotheses concerning sex roles in the therapy relationship may be a useful strategy.

Most clients (60% or more) are women, especially in outpatient therapy, and most therapists are men. Feminists have argued that the therapy relationship between a male therapist and a female client is likely to mirror traditional male–female relationships in which the male is powerful, knowledgeable, and protective and the female is weak, helpless, and dependent. In at least one arena, sexual attraction and sexual behavior, this dyad *is* more vulnerable. Holroyd and Brodsky (1977) found that 5.5% of male therapists and 0.6% of female therapists reported having engaged in sexual relations with clients; Pope, Keith-Spiegel, and Tabachnick (1986) found that 9.5% of male therapists and 2.5% of females reported engaging in sexual intimacies with clients. Data on therapists' sexual attraction to clients confirms that males (95%) are more likely than females (66%) to experience sexual feelings about their clients, although most therapists (73% of males, 60% of females) believed that sexual attraction had been beneficial to the therapy process in at least some instances (Pope et al., 1986), presumably in terms of the therapist understanding the patient and/or self-understanding by the therapist. Most of these behaviors or feelings involve heterosexual dyads. (For additional discussion see Chapter 4.)

The fact that female therapists in female–male dyads are less likely than their male counterparts to engage in sexual behavior with clients or to experience sexual attraction toward clients may also reflect sex role norms. A female therapist, who expects a man to be a protector and provider, may find that a man coming to her to seek help and advice for psychological problems is far from her ideal. That sexual attraction in the therapy relationship is governed to some extent by sex role stereotypes is supported by Pope et al.'s (1986) finding that male therapists mentioned "physical attractiveness" as a characteristic of clients to whom they were sexually attracted more often than female therapists did and female therapists mentioned "successful" more often than male therapists. These findings correspond to differences between ratings by men and women of characteristics that are desirable in a mate (Buss & Barnes, 1986).

As with same-sex therapist–client relationships, we might generate testable hypotheses about processes within the cross-sex therapy relationship from information about other male–female relationships. Although most heterosexual couples see their relationship as egalitarian, when a relationship is not it is much more often the man rather than the woman who is seen as dominant (Peplau & Gordon, 1985). Not surprisingly, marital satisfaction is found to be higher in egalitarian and male-dominant marriages than in female-dominant marriages (Peplau, 1983). Other research suggests that a wife who perceives her husband as he perceives himself and who conforms to his expectations contributes to marital satisfaction whereas a husband's ability or willingness to do these things does not affect satisfaction (Laws, 1971). B. Gottlieb (in press) found that wives report changing their coping strategies to suit their husbands' coping needs. Usually this meant being less emotionally expressive about the stressor (i.e., a child's chronic illness) because the husband was disturbed by the wife's affect. This last finding also supports other research that suggests that women and men tend to have different coping styles; men are more likely than women to use problem-focused or direct action strategies (e.g., looking for another job when the current one is a source of stress) whereas women are more likely to use emotion-focused strategies such as talking with friends about stress created by one's job (S. Miller & Kirsch, 1987). Sex differences in preference or use of coping strategies, if they exist among therapists, may also influence the therapy relationship, since a common goal in therapy is helping the client learn how to cope with stress. Differences also exist in how men and women cope with conflict in a heterosexual relationship (which may reflect to some degree differences in power). Men are more likely than women to report using bargaining or logical argument whereas women are more likely to report using withdrawal or pouting (Falbo & Peplau, 1980). Other data indicate that women are more likely to cry and sulk but want to confront conflict and discuss problems and feelings. Men, however, show anger and call for a logical approach to the problem but also want to delay discussion and avoid the conflict and its emotional displays (Kelley et al., 1978).

The results of these studies suggest that if the male therapist–female client relationship reflects sex roles as they are expressed in a personal heterosexual relationship, then certain hypotheses about the course of therapy can be proposed. Satisfaction with therapy should occur when the client–therapist relationship is perceived as egalitarian or therapist-dominant but not if the therapist is perceived as weak or not in control. There may be a tendency for female clients to accommodate themselves to male therapists' expectations for them. This may even be seen as therapeutic progress by both client and therapist. Female compliance with male-established norms in a traditional male-dominant relationship is precisely the scenario that feminists have predicted and criticized. Research on sex differences in diagnosis, treatment recommendations, or therapy outcome does not address this problem. Research modeled on some of the work done on marriages or dating relationships may be fruitful in determining whether this concern is well founded or not. Finally, male therapists may directly or indirectly suggest problem-solving or logical approaches to coping and may consciously or unconsciously limit the emotional expressivity of their female clients.

What about female therapists with male clients? This dyad poses a dilemma because whereas the tilt in power differences in the therapy relationship is toward the therapist, the tilt in traditional heterosexual relationships is toward the male. A female therapist may find that an egalitarian relationship with a male client is satisfactory but that an attempt on her part to assert her authority will lead to client dissatisfaction. Likewise, there may be a conflict between the male client's expectation that a woman will accept his point of view and the fact that his therapist has expert knowledge regarding his problem and its potential solution. Finally, the female therapist may encourage the expression of feelings and discussion of conflicts within the therapy relationship, behaviors that fit her sex role as well as some models of good psychotherapy, only to find that her male clients are intolerant of and disturbed by this approach.

We have focused on the sex of the client and sex of the therapist in terms of their impact on the therapy relationship. But, congruent with the discussion of Chapter 4 on the role of similarity in interpersonal attraction, the degree to which clients and therapists conform to socially defined gender roles (gender role identity) may be a more important variable than sex per se. The assumption is that the behaviors, feelings, and attitudes of some clients and therapists would be influenced by gender role stereotypes more than would others and that the hypotheses suggested earlier would more likely be confirmed for such individuals.

Conclusions

We have identified ways in which social roles direct, enable, and limit the behaviors of therapist and client and the ways in which gender roles serve as yet another source of influence. For the therapist, learning one's professional role generally begins in graduate school and includes learning specific techniques (e.g., how to administer a mental status exam or a psychological test), ways to deal with probable events (e.g., what to do when a client neglects to pay for services), and the standards for acceptable behavior (e.g., avoiding dual relationships). Learning occurs in courses, in supervision, and from simply being around and modeling oneself after other clinicians. Novice therapists are often anxious about meeting with clients; they wonder if they will know what to say or do in this or that situation. Knowing and practicing the therapist role reduces this anxiety. Presumably, behaviors corresponding to the role—such as instilling confidence in the client about one's expertise (directly by establishing client expectations about therapy outcome or indirectly through therapist's manner, dress, displayed degrees, and office decor), listening attentively, and maintaining a professional, as opposed to a personal, relationship—build confidence and expertise.

Clients, having had less training, are less well prepared for their role. Studies reviewed in Chapter 5 suggest that over time clients develop expectations and perceptions of therapy that are similar to those held by their therapists and that, if they do not, they are likely to leave therapy (Carr, 1970; Hunt, Carr, Dagadakis, & Walker, 1985). Role induction (i.e., formal preparation of clients for their role) has been recommended as a method to decrease the incidence of premature terminations and as a way to provide those clients least likely to be knowledgeable about the client role with important information about how to take advantage of therapy. Research results, as reviewed earlier, indicate that role induction is often useful. Still, for the majority of clients learning the role will require on-the-job training.

Gender roles are learned so early and so thoroughly that we are often unaware of the ways in which they affect our relationships. Research on personal relationships suggests that the sex composition of the client–therapist dyad will influence important aspects of therapy such as amount of self-disclosure, commitment, and willingness to discuss relationship issues. Furthermore, because of power differences between women and men in our society, the therapy relationship in cross-sex dyads may reflect these differences. An interesting question is, To what degree does assuming the role of therapist override one's gender role? It is unlikely that female and male therapists will, even after identical training, behave in exactly the same fashion or that female and male clients will be treated in a manner completely free of sex bias.

CHAPTER 3

A Social Exchange Analysis of Satisfaction and Commitment in the Therapy Relationship

Human relationships can be considered as a series of social interactions that to some degree satisfy or frustrate the needs of individuals. The consequences of interaction can be described in terms of the rewards that persons receive and the costs that they incur; relationships are expected to be satisfying to the degree that rewards exceed costs.

The last three decades have seen considerable interest in studying the reward–cost aspects of social relationships and the pattern of interdependence that emerges between individuals. Well-known analyses have been provided by Kelley and Thibaut's theory of social interdependence (Kelley, 1979; Kelley & Thibaut, 1978; Thibaut & Kelley, 1959), Homans's (1961) exchange theory, Altman and Taylor's (1973) social penetration theory, Levinger's incremental exchange theory (Levinger, 1980; Levinger & Snoek, 1972), and Rusbult's investment model (Rusbult, 1980a, 1980b, 1983; Rusbult, Zembrodt, & Gunn, 1982). All these theories emphasize how the behaviors of interactants have consequences for both individuals involved in the relationship in the form of rewards and costs. But these theories also emphasize how satisfaction with and commitment to a relationship depend on how we compare current outcomes with outcomes obtained in previous relationships, with potential outcomes that are currently available in other relationships, and with the investment made to keep the relationship going. Ideas such as these are found across the various so-called exchange theories and will be considered here.

The present chapter is based on the assumption that the exchange of rewards and costs will affect the kind of personal relationship that develops between a client and therapist. For the client rewards, costs, investments, and comparisons with other relationships may be important determinants of degree of participation in the therapy relationship and/or of the decision to continue or terminate therapy. Knowing how these factors influence relationships suggests interventions that can increase client satisfaction and commitment to therapy.

A social exchange analysis can also illuminate the therapist's experience. The therapist, however, has a professional as well as a personal role in the therapy relationship. This professional role places constraints on her or his behavior in the relationship. Whereas a client may leave the therapy relationship if costs exceed rewards, the therapist typically would not. The therapist may calculate outcomes in the therapy relationship in a more global fashion, that is, in terms of outcomes or relationships with clients in general rather than with any particular client. On the other hand, all therapists know that some clients are more rewarding than others. As a participant in an unsatisfactory relationship, the therapist will feel pressure to change her or his own behavior or that of the client to make the relationship more rewarding or, if this is impossible, to avoid the relationship. The therapist's professionalism should prevent him or her from acting in a way that would be harmful to the client, but therapists do on occasion let their own needs in the relationship obscure the client's needs. A social exchange analysis can be useful in predicting when a therapy relationship is likely to be dissatisfying to a therapist and can thereby allow the therapist to anticipate and avoid untherapeutic behavior.

Reward-Cost Dynamics in Social Interaction

According to Thibaut and Kelley (1959), "When the interactions of a number of persons are observed it usually becomes quite apparent that interaction is a highly selective matter . . . with respect to who interacts with whom" (p. 12). It is more satisfying to have a relationship with some people than with others. Social exchange theory assumes that individuals are motivated to maximize rewards or benefits while minimizing costs. Thus the "goodness" of outcomes in a relationship depends on the rewards outweighing the costs incurred for each participant. According to this theory, selection of a relationship partner will be based on goodness of outcomes. A person should approach another with whom net rewards are anticipated and stay in the relationship as long as net rewards continue. (Modifying variables, such as comparison level, equity, and transformations of rewards, are discussed later in this chapter.)

A number of factors determine how a client and therapist meet one another for the first time. According to social exchange theory, the ideal beginning would be one in which the client approaches a therapist who has been highly recommended as someone who can help her or him quickly and easily (i.e., provide rewards at low cost). On the basis of contact with the referral source or initial phone conversation with the prospective client, the therapist (in the ideal beginning) anticipates a highly motivated client without serious pathology (assuming that these characteristics are associated with rewards for most therapists).

Whatever the initial expectations for therapy, satisfaction with the relationship will depend on the outcomes that are experienced. Positive outcomes experienced in the initial interactions will lead to the expectation that positive outcomes will be experienced in the future. The experience of benefits and costs early in the therapy sessions can help both the client and therapist forecast how worthwhile it will be to continue in a relationship. By spending time with one another the client and therapist get a sample of what it is like to interact, and they calculate whether or not they should continue in the relationship. For instance, clients may use the therapist's reactions to what is said early in therapy to assess rewards (e.g., "Did the therapist care about what I said?"; "Is she helping me with my problem?") and costs (e.g., "Can I afford the fee?"; "Is it too painful to talk about this?") and to determine whether they should stay in therapy.

Although initial interactions may forecast outcomes, they are not always representative of what will occur in future sessions. For instance, in early sessions the client may be concerned about conveying a good first impression to the therapist and limit the conversation to what may appear to be correct to say when meeting someone for the first time (Thibaut & Kelley, 1959). Positive self-presentation should decrease as therapy progresses. The client's initial pleasure at finding someone who is willing to help with personal problems may not prove as satisfying later in therapy, when the client experiences the costs associated with talking about serious emotional problems. Also, the therapist's initial satisfaction at being selected as the therapist by a particular client (based on a favorable recommendation) may significantly decrease when a client's problems seem intractable later in psychotherapy.

A major consequence of the relative balance of rewards and costs in a relationship is its continuation or termination. There are two points in therapy when a client is likely to terminate prematurely (from the therapist's point of view): at the beginning of therapy and when some gains have been made and more gains will require another set of changes or a higher level of self-awareness (i.e., when the client is at a sort of plateau in therapy). When starting therapy, a client may quickly decide that rewards are less or costs are more than anticipated. Clients who expect a "quick fix" may be disappointed by the therapist's unwillingness to give advice or by the therapist's assumption that therapy will continue for weeks, months, or years. Clients may find talking about their problems embarrassing or anxiety-provoking, especially if the therapist probes too deeply too soon or appears in any way judgmental. A client may feel rewarded by an initial session but less so by a subsequent session or sessions and may decide that she or he has gotten all there is to get out of therapy. This latter example is similar to what may happen during therapy plateaus. An important reward for the client in the therapy relationship is "getting better," not just "feeling good." A pleasant therapy relationship is not enough. When a client has experienced improvement that she or he attributes to therapy and then experiences a series of sessions without demonstrable change in her or his condition, the cost of therapy may appear to exceed rewards and may lead to termination. (For some clients "feeling good" may be enough, perhaps because of the poor quality of other relationships in their lives. These clients may not work hard in therapy or improve very much, but they may continue to come to sessions. Such therapy relationships may be rewarding for clients but frustrating for therapists.)

Although therapists will not necessarily terminate a therapy relationship where costs exceed benefits, as social exchange theory would predict, there are times when this may occur. In a discussion of countertransference reactions to suicidal clients, Maltsberger and Buie (1974) warn clinicians of the temptation to refer such clients elsewhere by rationalizing that the therapy is not working and that some other therapist will be more helpful. They discuss such behavior as a defense against intolerable feelings of hate toward the suicidal patient. But it is also true that relationships with such patients may have high costs, with few rewards; like anyone in such a relationship, the therapist wants to avoid this costly relationship. Acknowledging and accepting one's negative feelings about a suicidal client, as Maltsberger and Buie recommend, may be one way to reduce the costs. Focusing on the global rewards and costs of one's profession rather than on client-specific rewards and costs may be another strategy for avoiding unprofessional behavior in a costly therapy relationship.

Therapists also select clients based on anticipated rewards and costs. One psychologist was contacted by a former client when the psychologist no longer had a clinical practice. The client was depressed and threatening suicide. The psychologist contacted several clinicians before one would accept the client for treatment. Reporting that they currently had enough self-destructive clients, the other therapists felt that they could not afford another; thus, they were containing the costs of doing therapy.

Definition of Rewards and Costs in Psychotherapy

The consequences or "goodness of outcomes" of an interaction have been represented in social exchange theory in terms of rewards and costs. What exactly are the rewards and costs for the client and therapist in psychotherapy?

A useful definition of rewards and costs experienced in social interactions is provided by Thibaut and Kelley (1959):

> By rewards, we refer to the pleasures, satisfactions, and gratifications the person enjoys. The provision of a means whereby a drive is reduced or a need fulfilled constitutes a reward. (p. 12)

> By costs, we refer to any factors that operate to inhibit or deter the performance of a sequence of behavior. The greater the deterrence to performing a given act—the greater the inhibition the individual has to overcome—the greater the cost of the act. Thus cost is high when great physical or mental effort is required, when embarrassment or anxiety accompany the action, or when there are conflicting forces or competing response tendencies of any sort. (pp. 12–13)

Consider the rewards and costs that may be experienced by the client and therapist. Most of the client's rewards, at least early in therapy, may be in the expectations for improvement and in the fact that someone is listening and is apparently concerned about her or him. Over the course of therapy an important reward is experiencing improvement in one's thoughts, feelings, and behavior. One client, who cried in nearly every session and felt anxious and embarrassed in talking about her problems, reported that despite disliking therapy and her therapist she stayed in therapy because she knew she was getting better.

The obvious costs are, of course, the financial expenditure and the time and effort associated with going to therapy. In addition, a cost for clients, at least initially, is in labeling oneself as having a problem: some clients may feel that they are "crazy." Therapists can reduce this concern initially by telling the client that her or his problems are "normal" and treatable. There is also the cost for the client of making oneself vulnerable and presenting negative aspects of self. The implicit requirement that the client make changes may also be a cost; some clients may leave therapy because they are not ready to accept the cost of changing.

Even when clients have been able to make self-disclosures in initial phases of therapy, they may reach a therapeutic impasse. Clients may decide not to share some critical information that makes them feel uncomfortable and upset. They may prefer to avoid the unpleasantness (including fear of rejection or discomfort) represented by talking about new material that enters an area not previously discussed. In ongoing therapy the rewards may be relatively constant and the costs may have been decreasing over the course of therapy (because of increased comfort in dealing with already exposed issues), but the exploration of new issues may expose the client to new costs.

Money is an obvious cost for patients. But the necessity of paying may be either a cost or a reward or a bit of both. Payment indicates that the therapy relationship is a professional relationship, not just a personal relationship, but as a "cost," payment may negate the feeling that the therapist cares ("I pay you; that's the only reason you listen to me."). As a "reward," the payment may represent the client's taking responsibility for her or his problems. It may also make it easier to express negative feelings ("I pay you to listen, so if I'm angry you have to hear me through and not talk back.").

For therapists, rewards include seeing clients improve and experiencing oneself as doing good work. Earning an income is also a reward. Relationships with clients who are interesting and actively involved in therapy may be rewarding, but relationships with other clients may be boring or difficult. Therapists report that the greatest source of stress in their clinical work is clients' threats of suicide (Deutsch, 1984; Rodolfa, Kraft, & Reilley, 1988). Another, more frequent, source of stress is clients' expressing anger toward the therapist (Deutsch, 1984). Clients can also be demanding and call at all hours of the day and night. This represents a cost to the therapist, as does the nonpayment of fees, the fear of a lawsuit from a disgruntled client (Deardorff, Cross, & Hupprich, 1984; Fisher, 1985), and working with a client who does not improve (Deutsch, 1984; Rodolfa et al., 1988).

Research on the Impact of Rewards and Costs

Research on the impact of rewards and costs on satisfaction in psychotherapy is still to be done, but studies of college students living together in dormitories and studies of dating partners suggest some interesting implications. For instance, Berg (1984) studied 48 pairs of previously unacquainted roommates at a university dormitory. Subjects completed questionnaires describing their relationships with roommates 2 weeks after the beginning of classes and approximately 6 months later. Overall, subjects reported receiving more help from their roommates over time. Subjects who planned to continue living together or who were undecided about living together during the next school year reported an increase in receiving help from their roommates from fall to spring, whereas those who did not plan to live together reported decreases in help. In both the fall and spring semesters, rewards received predicted how much subjects liked and were satisfied with their roommates. Research by Hays (1985) on college roommates and by Berg and McQuinn (1986) and Rusbult (1980a, Studies 1 and 2) on dating couples indicates that rewards received predicted partner degree of satisfaction with a relationship.

The finding that rewards (or benefits) received predict the success of a relationship provides support for social exchange theory. However, costs incurred in a relationship should be negatively correlated with a relationship's success, and the value of rewards minus costs should be the best predictor of all of success (Clark & Reis, 1988). Some studies have found that costs are negatively related to satisfaction with a relationship (Rusbult, 1980a, Study 2), but other studies have found that costs are not related to relationship success (Hays, 1985; Rusbult, 1980a, Study 1, 1983). Hays (1985), in a longitudinal study of the relationship between college roommates during their first term at a university, found positive correlations between friendship closeness (based on rating one's roommate on a scale ranging from "acquaintance" to "friend") and ratings of costs. Furthermore, a "benefits-plus-costs" rating (based on the sum of benefits and costs) was positively correlated with friendship closeness, indicating that the experience of rewards *and* costs both increased as the relationship progressed.

Researchers have reported that conflict and ambivalence may increase as a relationship develops (Braiker & Kelley, 1979; Eidelson, 1980). Hays (1985) found that roommates reported greater expenditure of time and more feelings of emotional aggravation as their relationship developed, whether they reported being close or not. Roommates did not report emotional aggravation at early stages of their relationship, but this response sharply increased after 9 weeks of acquaintanceship. The emotional aggravation seemed to accompany increased knowledge and familiarity between the roommates. Typical comments included the following:

> We now every once in a while have tension between us. There are things that do bother me about her which I have never noticed before. (p. 921)

> During this time she and I have had time to learn of each other. I've found faults in her, not that I'm looking for them. (p. 922)

> His personality is coming out. He is inconsiderate, back stabbing, obstinate, irrational, and just a jerk. I don't like him nearly as much. (p. 922)

> I've gotten to know her better and I feel we are closer but I also know her bad points more, which causes her to get on my nerves at times. (p. 922)

Hays's subjects also emphasized the time and energy associated with maintaining relationships:

> Of course a friendship takes effort, but the rewards are worth it. (p. 922)

> I am a little less independent around her, but it doesn't bother me. Being with her does take a lot of time and sometimes I feel guilty when I don't get much else done, but the benefits outweigh this. (p. 922)

These findings suggest, contrary to the traditional position, that costs are positively correlated with relationship development and that "costs are inescapable aspects of personal relationships" (Hays, 1985, p. 922). Inevitably, individuals must be willing to absorb the costs that go along with the development of a degree of personal closeness.

Berg (1984) found that as a relationship develops between room-mates in a university dormitory, individuals are more likely to receive benefits that meet their unique personal needs. If relationship partners feel more responsible for satisfying each other's needs as a relationship develops over time, an increase in benefits will be accompanied by an increase in costs as partners spend more time helping one another (Clark & Reis, 1988).

Given these results, we predict that costs in therapy increase close-ness in the relationship and perhaps client or therapist participation in therapy: the client and therapist tolerate present costs in anticipa-tion of future benefits. Cooper and Axsom (1982) have predicted, on the basis of cognitive dissonance and self-presentation theories, not social exchange theory, that effort expenditure by clients can be an important ingredient of successful therapy. According to cognitive dissonance theory (Festinger, 1957), clients who voluntarily place themselves in a situation where they experience considerable discom-fort (spending money and time, disclosing personal information) may develop a positive opinion of therapy out of an *internal* need to justify their efforts to themselves, thus reducing cognitive dissonance. Accord-ing to self-presentation theory (Tedeschi, Schlenker, & Bonoma, 1971), clients may develop a positive opinion of therapy out of an *external* need to justify their efforts to others. In either case, clients who incur more costs are more likely to feel that the therapy has been worthwhile and helpful. In an empirical study supporting this prediction, Axsom and Cooper (1985) found that overweight women in a weight-loss program who did difficult perceptual and cognitive tasks (tasks that had nothing to do with weight loss) lost more weight after four sessions and showed greater weight loss at a 6-month follow-up than women who did relatively easy tasks. Thus, effort predicted therapy outcome.

From the therapist's point of view, costs in the therapy relation-ship may well predict relationship closeness and satisfaction. A suici-dal client or a client who expresses anger toward the therapist is rated high as a source of stress to therapists (Deutsch, 1984). On the other hand, such clients may also have much to gain from therapy and may represent a challenge and an opportunity for the therapist to do good work; that is, these are the sorts of clients who require effort on the therapist's part. Assuming that Cooper and Axsom's (1982) predictions about the effects of effort expenditure on evaluation of a task are correct for therapists as well as for clients, it follows that therapists who are working hard should feel positive about and committed to the therapy of challenging clients. On the other hand, an unmotivated client may create costs for the therapist that are not offset by rewards or potential rewards.

Types of Rewards and Costs in Research on Relationships

Hays's (1984, 1985) research on the development of friendships among first-term college students suggests interesting hypotheses on possible changes in the types of rewards and costs that persons experience as a relationship develops. We noted earlier Hays's finding that reports of emotional aggravation and time expenditure experienced in friendships increased as the students' relationships developed. This pattern occurred whether subjects' friendships were close or not.

The major benefits of friendship for Hays's subjects were provision of a confidant and emotional support. Nonclose friends infrequently mentioned having a confidant and emotional support as benefits of their friendship; close friends frequently mentioned them. These findings suggest that an opportunity to confide personal knowledge as well as to receive expressions of concern and support are ingredients that people look for in a close relationship (Hays, 1985).

Berg and McQuinn's (1986) longitudinal study of dating couples indicates that some rewards may not appear until a relationship has progressed. The couples in this study had only recently begun to date each other at the beginning of the research. Couples who were still dating after 4 months, compared to those who had broken up in the same 4-month interval, reported receiving benefits that were more likely to meet their particular needs and desires, but this difference in receiving benefits did not appear earlier in the relationship. Berg (1984) also reported, in a study of roommates at the beginning and the end of a school year, that roommates in a close relationship were more likely than roommates who described their relationship as nonclose to be receiving unique rewards that would help them meet their particular needs and desires at the end of the school year than they were at the beginning of the school year. Thus, the exchange of resources became more selective among dating couples and roommates who became closer.

L. Miller and Berg (1984) define a *selective resource* or reward as one that satisfies a specific need or desire of the recipient. It may be that the passage of time is required to acquire the knowledge of the other person's specific needs and desires. Hence, a period of time may have to elapse before selective resources, which are uniquely intended to meet the needs and desires of a relationship partner, are exchanged (Berg & McQuinn, 1986).

As therapy progresses, client satisfaction may be based on the degree to which clients feel that therapists are providing responses based on their unique needs and problems. One therapist found that clients often remarked with surprise and pleasure when the therapist remembered names or details from their personal history. In another case, a client was annoyed and disappointed when a psychoanalytic therapist suggested that as a young boy he had viewed his parents engaging in sexual intercourse (the primal scene). From his own knowledge of psychoanalytic theory the client knew that this was a fairly standard childhood trauma, and he felt that the therapist was using a textbook interpretation rather than responding to his own unique history.

Therapists may also receive selective rewards from clients. Although the therapist does not generally reveal much personal information to clients, clients may nevertheless develop a sense of who the therapist is. Searles (1979) has written about how clients can make therapeutic interventions on behalf of therapists and cites examples from his own clinical work of clients helping him to overcome personal problems.

Expectancies and the Evaluation of Outcomes in the Therapeutic Relationship

Comparison Level

Rewards and costs alone do not determine the client's and therapist's satisfaction with and attraction to the therapy relationship. The value of the relationship is also a function of expectations about what the relationship should be. A useful concept for describing people's expectancies for relationships is what Thibaut and Kelley (1959) named the "comparison level" (CL). The CL represents a standard for evaluating one's degree of satisfaction with a relationship and is based on one's own past and present experiences in relationships as well as on the relationships other people similar to oneself have or are believed to have. The CL represents a level of outcome that is experienced as neutral in value. A relationship is satisfying and attractive to a person to the extent that outcomes are above the CL while a relationship is unsatisfying and unattractive to the extent that outcomes are below the CL.

The location of the CL depends largely on previous personal experiences. According to Thibaut and Kelley (1959), "It may be taken to be some modal or average value of all known outcomes, each outcome weighted by its salience, or strength of instigation, which depends, for example, upon the recency of experiencing the outcomes and the occurrence of stimuli which serve as reminders of the outcome" (p. 21).

The CL, in Thibaut and Kelley's view, is a relatively realistic expectation about outcomes in a relationship. For instance, relationships and interactions with other people that are unattainable are not considered to play a major role in influencing the location of the CL. Also, the outcomes that are salient for individuals are believed to be affected by their beliefs about how much power or control they exercise over their own fate. Persons with high confidence and competence are predicted to focus on the reward aspects of outcomes, because their behavior usually results in their attaining these outcomes. Persons with low confidence are predicted to focus on the cost aspects of outcomes, which allows them to avoid pursuing outcomes that they believe are unattainable. Hence, the confident person, who believes that he or she has a low probability of attaining a favorable outcome, should have a high CL; the less confident person, who believes he or she has a low probability of attaining a favorable outcome, should have a low CL.

Although the location of the CL is considered to be a realistic expectation, it is possible that the comparison level may be affected by ideal or desired social relationships as much as by actual past and present relationship experiences. In therapy, for instance, persons may overestimate the levels of outcomes to be achieved in the therapy relationship, based on exposure to mass media or stories that they have heard. For instance, media presentations of therapy such as television's "Bob Newhart Show," in which the lead character was a clinical psychologist, and the stage play *Equus*, which portrayed a psychiatrist–client relationship, may shape unrealistically high expectations about the relationship between therapist and client and about the outcomes that occur. Therapists in these fictionalized portrayals are shown as more involved with their clients (or perhaps even with one client) than would ordinarily be the case. A therapist may in reality see 20 to 30 clients a week whereas the media show therapists spending large amounts of time with a client and perhaps being preoccupied with that client. The CL set by media therapists may make "real" therapy seem less personal or less intense than it "should be."

According to social exchange theory, satisfaction with a relationship is a function of the discrepancy between the value of outcomes in the relationship and the individual's expectations about what should happen (i.e., his or her CL). Thus, clients who have unrealistically high expectations concerning the quality of therapy may be predicted to have considerable dissatisfaction with the relationship. If expectations become more realistic (so that CL is lowered) as therapy unfolds, satisfaction with therapy may increase.

Some clients may approach therapy with relatively low expectations about the relief that therapy can provide. Individuals may have exhausted other forms of social support such as family and friends and have come to psychotherapy as a last resort for help. If the location of the CL for these individuals is initially low and they perceive that the therapist is interested in their problems and willing to help, they may experience relatively quick gratification with therapy.

There has been little research in personal relationships on the role of expectancies about what one deserves as outcomes. Nevertheless, research in other settings provides empirical support for the concept. For instance, in a study of military personnel in World War II, noncombat soldiers overseas had higher satisfaction with life in the military than noncombat soldiers stationed in the United States. The difference in satisfaction presumably reflected different expectancies for the soldiers overseas versus those in the United States. The noncombat soldiers overseas had as a standard the dangers and rigors of the combat soldier whereas the soldiers in the United States compared their situation to well-off civilians (Stouffer, Suchman, DeVinney, Star, & Williams, 1949).

Comparison Level for Alternatives

Although a person may be relatively satisfied with a relationship, she or he may not continue in it if it is possible to obtain better outcomes in some alternative relationship. According to Thibaut and Kelley (1959) the "comparison level for alternatives" (CLalt) is the standard used by a person to determine whether to leave or remain in a present relationship. The CLalt is the lowest level of outcomes a participant will accept in a current relationship in light of available alternative relationships and refers to the best single alternative available. According to this theory, if outcomes fall below the CLalt, the person will leave the relationship in favor of another relationship.

Research by Rusbult on partners' commitment to ongoing relationships (e.g., a dating relationship) indicates that the CLalt is a good predictor of an individual's willingness to continue in a relationship. Individuals who report having alternatives that are less appealing than the current relationship are likely to remain in the current relationship (Rusbult, 1980a; Rusbult et al., 1982).

The term *dependency* is used by Thibault and Kelley (1959) to refer to the person's likelihood of staying in or leaving a relationship. The more likely a person is to stay in a relationship, based on the belief that other relationships cannot aid in achieving important outcomes, the more dependent the person is on that relationship. Dependency is a function of outcomes minus the CLalt. People will stay in a relationship if outcomes are higher than the CLalt.

An individual can remain dependent on a relationship without feeling satisfied with the relationship. This occurs when a relationship deteriorates (i.e., the individual's outcomes fall at or below his or her CL) and alternative partners are not known or available to the person; or alternative partners may appear to be no better than the current relationship partner in mediating outcomes (i.e., CLalt is less than or equal to CL). Under such conditions, the individual will remain dependent on the current partner.

If a relationship is to develop and be maintained, the jointly experienced outcomes by both partners in the relationship must exceed each person's CLalt. Although the levels of outcomes may be located above CLalt for one person, outcomes may be below CLalt for the other. Again using therapy as an example, it is possible that a client's good outcomes—high rewards and low costs—may be achieved only at high personal costs to the therapist (so that the therapist's outcomes are below her or his CLalt). For instance, a client who pays a very low or no fee (e.g., in a clinic or with 100% insurance reimbursement) and is not charged for missed sessions—coming when it is convenient, missing when it is not, enjoying the support but from the therapist's point of view never working in therapy—may stay in therapy. The frustrated therapist—whose outcomes fall below her or his CLalt— may feel it is worthwhile to terminate the therapy and spend more time with other clients.

The concept of comparison level for alternatives is useful in predicting whether or not clients choose therapy or decide to continue therapy. Clients may have other possible relationships, such as friend-ships, that could provide some emotional support. However, choosing therapy or continuing therapy implies that the individual's best avail-able alternative is below the level of outcomes that can be found in the therapy relationship.

There is a possible paradox represented by having the therapist become highly important with respect to satisfying the client's needs (see Margulis, Derlega, & Winstead, 1984). As persons become more dependent on someone, they may stop looking for or relying on others. For instance, M. Johnson and Leslie (1982) found that as dating couples increased their romantic involvement, their friendship net-works decreased and those friends who remained in the network were seen as less important and were confided in less intimately. For clients, as the strength of the relationship with the therapist increases, the desire to form new relationships or improve existing relationships (with friends, family, etc.) may decrease. However, if the therapy rela-tionship turns unsatisfactory or the therapist becomes unavailable (e.g., the therapist goes on vacation or moves), the client is left alone, perhaps without alternative relationships. For therapists, the relation-ships with clients may deplete emotional reserves and decrease emo-tional involvement with family and friends (Guy & Liaboe, 1986). The paradox for the client as well as the therapist is that as the value of therapy increases in mediating important needs and goals, the quality of one's other relationships may suffer.

On the other hand, if clients are better able to function in other relationships as a result of therapy, the rewards associated with these other relationships may increase and their costs decrease. For instance, a lonely person may acquire social skills in a cognitively oriented behavior therapy that make it easier to initiate friendships outside of therapy (Young, 1982, 1986). The value of outcomes in the best alternative relationship (CLalt) may thus increase, and the client's commitment to therapy may decrease—even if the outcome values earned in therapy remain the same.

It is possible to exaggerate the dependency that the client (and therapist) may have on the therapy relationship for satisfying important socially based needs. The client may be dependent on the therapist for satisfying certain needs that other people may not be able to help with (e.g., providing professional and expert advice on how to solve psychological problems). Although the client and therapist may draw closer as they form an alliance to solve the client's problems, the client must rely on nontherapy relationships to fulfill certain needs that cannot be satisfied in therapy. For instance, individuals may have needs to provide nurturance, support, and protection to others. The client's role makes it difficult to fulfill these needs in therapy; it would be easier and more appropriate to satisfy these needs in other personal relationships, such as those with friends or family members.

3-11-96

Investment in and Dependence on the Therapy Relationship

Commitment to a relationship is affected not only by outcome values of the present relationship and the best possible alternative but also by the size of one's investment in the relationship (Rusbult, 1980a, 1987). Investments represent resources that a person has put into a relationship and that would be lost if the relationship ended. Investment can represent the time, energy, effort, or money put into making the relationship work. Because of these investments, the person who has made them feels dependent on the relationship. A person who has made a considerable investment in forming a relationship may feel trapped because of the high investment, even though current attraction to and satisfaction with the relationship are low.

Support for the prediction that resources invested in a relationship increase dependency is reported by Rusbult (1980a, 1983). She found that the size of the subjects' investment positively predicted subjects' willingness to continue in a personal relationship in a heterosexual dating situation.

Rusbult's concept of investment is applicable to clients' dependency on the therapy relationship. The investment in therapy may be represented by the self-disclosure that has occurred as well as the time and money that have already been spent. Starting again with another therapist or quitting altogether may be unattractive, given all the investment that has been made. On the other hand, it is probably easier for clients to quit fairly early in therapy, when the investment of resources in the relationship is small (and the outcome values might be low at this stage too).

The presence of high investment in the therapy may make clients feel trapped, and they may have difficulty terminating the relationship even it if is not helpful. Occasionally, termination with a therapist must occur prematurely (e.g., client or therapist moves). Because of a high investment in the therapy the client may find the idea of continuing in therapy with someone else unattractive. To help the client accept the situation, the therapist might tell the client: "Yes, you may have to begin again with another therapist, but you have gotten a lot out of therapy already." This approach emphasizes that the investments are counterbalanced by the rewards that have already accumulated in the therapy, and it may make it easier for the client to end the relationship and perhaps begin therapy with another therapist.

An explanatory note is necessary about the conceptual distinction between costs and investments. As Kelley (1983) and Brehm (1985) suggest, past costs become the current investments in a relationship. Costs (as well as rewards) are events that are *now* taking place in a relationship (e.g., the time presently spent driving to the therapy, the fee being paid for current therapy sessions, or the embarrassment experienced now by the client and/or therapist in talking about certain topics). On the other hand, investments refer to contributions that have been made to the relationship *in the past*. Investments would include, for instance, the time previously spent driving to therapy, fees paid in the past, or prior distress in talking about embarrassing topics.

The "goodness" of outcomes of a relationship in terms of *current* high rewards and low costs contributes to satisfaction with a relationship. Depending on prior investments, present "goodness" may not influence commitment to the relationship. A relationship where costs now outweigh rewards is likely to continue if it has a previous history of both rewards and some costs. The costs that were incurred in the past were not high enough at the time to lead to the relationship's being terminated but now become part of one's investment and affect commitment to the relationship.

Interdependence in the Psychotherapeutic Relationship

On the issue of who controls outcomes as two persons interact, Kelley and Thibaut (Kelley, 1979; Kelley & Thibaut, 1978; Thibaut & Kelley, 1959) distinguish three bases of dependence: reflexive control, fate control, and behavioral control. Reflexive control deals with how much each person's outcomes are influenced by that person's own actions, that is, the amount of control by each person over his or her own outcomes. Fate control deals with how much each person's outcomes are influenced by the other person, that is, how much one person controls the other's outcomes. Behavior control deals with how much each person's outcomes are affected by the combination of their behavioral choices.

How much one person is influenced by the other and how much two individuals' outcomes depend on their joint actions create different bases of interdependence. As an illustration, consider how therapist and client feel discussing a topic pertinent to the client's problems during a therapy session. In an extreme example of mutual fate control each person's actions (i.e., choosing to talk about the topic or not) influence the other's outcomes but not their own outcomes. The goodness of the outcomes experienced by the therapist and client for the different interaction possibilities of their discussing or not is represented by the matrix in Figure 3.1. The rows represent the client's choice to talk about the topic or not, and the columns represent the

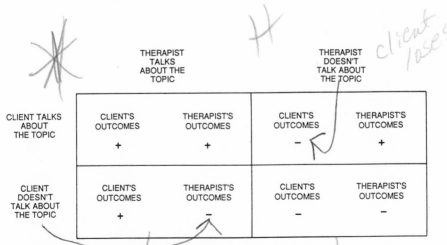

FIGURE 3.1. An extreme example of mutual fate control where each person's outcomes are determined by the other person's behavior.

therapist's choices. The "goodness" of outcomes experienced by the client and therapist is represented by the pairs of signs in the intersection of each row with each column. The first sign indicates the outcomes for the client (or the "row" person), and the second sign shows the outcomes for the therapist (or the "column" person). The signs in the matrix represent the goodness of outcomes or consequences for each person. A plus sign indicates high rewards and low costs; a minus sign indicates low rewards and high costs associated with a particular combination of the client's and the therapist's behaviors.

In this illustration of mutual fate control, the client and therapist can affect the other's outcomes regardless of what the other person does. For instance, the client can, by refusing to discuss the topic, reduce the therapist's outcomes from (+) to (−), perhaps making the therapist feel that she or he is not doing good enough work because, as the therapist sees it, the client is refusing to participate in therapy. Even if the therapist does not discuss the topic, the client's avoidance of it represents failure to the therapist. The therapist can affect the client's outcomes in a similar manner. If the therapist talks about the topic, the client's outcomes are (+). If the therapist doesn't talk about the topic, the client's outcomes are reduced to (−) in this example. It may be that if the therapist fails to take up a topic raised by the client, the client feels that the therapist is uninterested or uncaring. Even if the client has not mentioned the topic in the session, she or he may expect the therapist to know that it is important and not to be ignored. The degree of fate control is affected by the extent of change in another's outcomes that one person causes. (Incidentally, in the situations illustrated in Figure 2.1 there is no basis for predicting whether either the client or therapist will discuss the topic or not, because the individuals' actions don't affect their own outcomes; see Kelley, 1979, p. 71.)

Therapy is a social interaction where both client and therapist can exercise fate control. The therapist decides initially whether or not to work with a client. She or he develops a treatment plan for the client and makes interventions. While ideally made in the client's best interest, these are actions over which the client has no direct control and yet which affect her or his outcomes.

Clients also have fate control over the therapist. Regardless of the therapist's enthusiasm for and enjoyment of her or his work, the client's level of involvement in therapy can affect the therapist's outcomes; for instance, the client may miss appointments or terminate therapy prematurely. Clients' expressions of gratitude or their belief that therapy has made a difference in their lives are rewards for the therapist that the client controls.

In an extreme example of mutual behavioral control two persons gain something only by coordinating their actions (see Figure 3.2). In behavior control, one person can make it worthwhile for the other person to change her or his behavior. Thibaut and Kelley (1959) note that "A's behavior control is greater the more B stands to gain by adjusting his [or her] behavior in accord with A's behavioral choices" (p. 103). While fate control is based on one person's behavior influencing another's outcomes, behavior control is based on the combinations of both persons' behaviors affecting their respective outcomes (Kelley, 1979).

In the example of mutual behavior control presented in Figure 3.2, the therapist and client obtain positive outcomes if they both talk about the topic relevant to the client's problem or if both refrain from talking about the topic. On the other hand, they both obtain negative outcomes if one talks about the topic and the other doesn't. Thus, the pattern of outcomes in mutual behavior control makes it worthwhile for the individuals to coordinate their behaviors to insure positive outcomes.

There are a number of examples of behavior control in the psychotherapy interaction, where client and therapist must coordinate their behavior to maximize their outcomes. The client and therapist

	THERAPIST TALKS ABOUT THE TOPIC		THERAPIST DOESN'T TALK ABOUT THE TOPIC	
CLIENT TALKS ABOUT THE TOPIC	CLIENT'S OUTCOMES +	THERAPIST'S OUTCOMES +	CLIENT'S OUTCOMES −	THERAPIST'S OUTCOMES −
CLIENT DOESN'T TALK ABOUT THE TOPIC	CLIENT'S OUTCOMES −	THERAPIST'S OUTCOMES −	CLIENT'S OUTCOMES +	THERAPIST'S OUTCOMES +

FIGURE 3.2. An extreme example of mutual behavior control where outcomes depend on the combinations of both persons' behaviors.

who form an alliance in which they work together to overcome the client's problems provide an example of mutual behavioral control. Their respective outcomes are a function of the social interaction that occurs between them.

Consider a situation in which a client brings up a topic that has been bothering her or him. The client, say, refers to this issue indirectly at first, the therapist comments on it, and soon they are examining the issue intensively. Both client and therapist feel good about the interaction. Or perhaps the therapist does not make any reference to the issue, feeling that it is not yet time to pursue this particular topic, and the client feels relieved not to have to talk about it. Again both client and therapist are satisfied. These are examples of coordinated behavior. But what happens when the therapist makes some comment about the topic and the client does not respond to it and brings up another issue instead? The therapist may again try to raise the topic, but the client is not ready to talk about it. The therapist feels frustrated at the client's evasiveness; the client feels pressured and fears that the therapist disapproves. Or suppose the therapist ignores the client's oblique reference to the topic and asks a question about something else. The client answers the question halfheartedly but then returns to the previous issue. The therapist feels that the client is not fully engaged in the session; the client feels that the therapist has failed to understand what he or she is trying to say. In these two cases client and therapist behaviors are not coordinated, and neither client nor therapist is pleased with the outcome.

The therapy relationship, like any relationship, is generally a mixture of reflexive control, fate control, and behavior control. Clients may enter therapy having little capacity for reflexive control or behavior control. Clients' feelings of pleasure or displeasure may be at the mercy of what others do or do not do for them, and clients may similarly interact with others by trying to, or thinking that they can, control others' outcomes. In other words, clients' relationships may be a function of fate control, in which they believe that other persons control their (i.e., clients') fate and they have some control over others' fate. For instance, people who feel depressed and guilty may believe that other people's behavior has a negative effect on them and that things they have done have had a negative impact on the lives of others. These clients are likely to experience the relationship with the therapist in a similar fashion. By coordinating her or his behavior with the client, the therapist may provide examples of mutual behavior control. Also, by demonstrating to the client that her or his behavior cannot be controlled by the client, by communicating to the client that responsibility for the client's outcomes is her or his own, and by encouraging the client to take actions that will provide rewards for herself or himself, the therapist can enable the client to experience reflexive control.

Social Exchange and Responses to Dissatisfaction with Psychotherapy

How do clients and therapists cope with interpersonal problems and conflicts that might emerge between them in the course of psychotherapy? If one or the other is dissatisfied with how they interact, how will they handle this relationship problem? When are clients and therapists likely to end therapy due to dissatisfaction rather than attempt to discuss these interpersonal problems and try to seek solutions to them? On the other hand, what might make clients and therapists avoid discussing problems, hoping that things will improve (e.g., "giving things some time to work themselves out") and continuing to have faith in the partner and the relationship? Or, what might make clients and therapists refuse to discuss problems and perhaps chronically complain about the relationship without offering solutions to the problems?

Based on social exchange concepts, Rusbult (Rusbult, 1987; Rusbult et al., 1982) has developed a model of responses to dissatisfaction in personal relationships that may assist in understanding how clients and therapists might deal with dissatisfaction and interpersonal problems in the therapy relationship. Rusbult's analysis relies on three major social concepts to determine how individuals deal with present dissatisfaction with a relationship: (1) the degree of satisfaction with a relationship prior to the onset of interpersonal problems (or the degree to which outcomes are above the individual's comparison level); (2) the amount of resources that an individual has invested in the relationship (e.g., time, effort, money); and (3) the quality of outcomes that can be experienced in the best alternative relationship that might be available (i.e., the comparison level for alternatives). In general, prior satisfaction with one's relationship, a high investment of resources in a relationship, and an absence of a high-quality alternative to the present relationship should encourage constructive rather than destructive responses to dealing with relationship dissatisfaction.

Rusbult presents the following list of four major responses to the onset of dissatisfaction in a relationship:

1. *Exit*—threatening to end or actually ending the relationship. Examples might include getting a divorce to end a marriage, moving out of a residence that has been shared jointly, or, in the case of psychotherapy, the decision by a client or therapist to terminate the therapy.

2. *Voice*—expressing one's dissatisfaction with the relationship in a constructive manner with the aim of improving conditions in the relationship. Examples include, in the case of a marriage, the decision to seek help from a marriage counselor or to find compromises or, in the case of psychotherapy, discussing the problems in the therapy sessions.

3. *Loyalty*—being passive about problems in the relationship but hoping that matters will improve. Examples include hoping, on the part of the spouse or client or therapist, that the difficulties will somehow go away or praying that things will improve but not mentioning them to one's partner.

4. *Neglect*—being passive about solving problems in the relationship and contributing to the relationship's deterioration or dissolution. Examples include spending less time with the partner or having an extramarital affair in a marriage or, in the case of therapy, verbally abusing or criticizing the other person's comments in a manner that is unrelated to the real problem going on or missing or being consistently late for therapy sessions.

Rusbult emphasizes how these four responses to dissatisfaction in a relationship differ from one another along two dimensions (see Figure 3.3). The first dimension is constructiveness versus destructiveness. Voice and loyalty are responses that are intended to maintain or improve the relationship, whereas exit and neglect are responses that are intended to be destructive to the relationship. (It should be noted that a response that might be destructive to the future of a *relationship* may be either positive or negative for the *individual*.) The second dimension is activity versus passivity. Exit and voice are active behaviors because the individual is doing something about the problem whereas loyalty and neglect are more passive responses.

A high level of satisfaction with a relationship prior to the onset of interpersonal difficulties is expected to promote constructive, com-

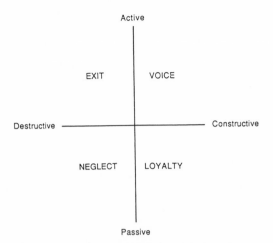

FIGURE 3.3. Rusbult's model of responses to dissatisfaction in a relationship. From "Responses to Dissatisfaction in Close Relationships: The Exit-Voice-Loyalty-Neglect Model" by C. E. Rusbult, 1987, in D. Perlman and S. Duck (Eds.), *Intimate Relationships: Development, Dynamics, and Deterioration* (p. 214), Newbury Park, CA: Sage Publications. Copyright 1987 by Sage Publications, Inc. Reprinted by permission.

pared to destructive, responses. It is likely that the individual in a relationship that has had a past history of rewarding interactions will try to restore or maintain the relationship in the belief that constructive responses are more likely to produce positive outcomes than are destructive responses. Hence, a high level of prior satisfaction will likely produce voice and loyalty responses and discourage exit and neglect responses.

A high level of investment in a relationship (e.g., spending money for therapy, time spent getting to the therapy sessions, effort associated with disclosing embarrassing personal information) is also expected to promote constructive responses and discourage destructive responses. Persons who have invested heavily in making the relationship successful stand to lose more than do persons who have invested little or nothing at all. A high level of investment will likely produce constructive voice and loyalty responses and decrease destructive exit and neglect responses.

The quality of outcomes in the best of one's available alternative relationships (or the comparison level for alternatives) will likely determine whether an individual responds in an active or passive way to the onset of dissatisfaction. The presence of good alternatives (for producing rewards at low costs) should give an individual a sense of personal control or power to deal with the interpersonal problem, according to Rusbult (by using either a voice or exit response). Thus, the individual who has an appealing alternative to the present relationship may either seek to find an active, constructive solution to the present relationship problem (i.e., voice) or may seek to end the relationship (i.e., exit). If the individual does not have an alternative, there may be a tendency to wait passively for matters to improve (i.e., loyalty) or to ignore the relationship and let it die (i.e., neglect).

Studies of opposite-sex romantic relationships provide general support for Rusbult's model (Rusbult et al., 1982; Rusbult, Johnson, & Morrow, 1986; see Rusbult, 1987, for a summary of this research). Voice and loyalty were more likely responses to the onset of relationship dissatisfaction if prior satisfaction was high. Voice and loyalty were also associated with high relationship investment, whereas exit and neglect were associated with a low investment. The presence of attractive alternatives to the current relationship tended to increase exit behavior and discourage loyalty responses. Rusbult's studies found no association between the attractiveness of relationship alternatives and voice or neglect as reactions to the onset of dissatisfaction, which Rusbult's model would have predicted.

Rusbult's model is useful in understanding how clients and therapists react to the onset of dissatisfaction with the course of psychotherapy. If the client and/or therapist perceive that the relationship has been unsatisfactory up to the present time, they will probably anticipate that the relationship has little chance of being successful in the future. Under these circumstances, they might do little or nothing to make the relationship work. On the other hand, if prior satisfaction was high, the individuals might continue to anticipate good outcomes in the future. Ensuring that clients experience good outcomes in their initial contacts may help clients develop confidence in the future of the therapy relationship and encourage constructive responses to therapy relationship problems. Therapists might also reinforce clients for voicing their concerns and frustrations with the course of psychotherapy, encouraging them to deal actively as well as constructively with conflict situations in therapy.

If the client or therapist has made a small investment in therapy, there is a decreased chance of therapy continuing productively after the onset of dissatisfaction. Rusbult's work indicates that it is a good idea for therapists to promote clients' investment and hence commitment to therapy. Techniques might include having the client pay part or all of the fee for treatment or having clients agree to attend a specific number of sessions. In a similar fashion, therapists' investment and likely commitment to working with clients may also be increased by having the therapist contract to see the client for a designated number of sessions.

The attractiveness of alternative relationships available to an individual affects whether her or his reactions to dissatisfaction will be active or passive. Rusbult's research indicates that the presence of attractive alternatives increases exit and inhibits loyalty responses. The correlations between quality of alternative relationships and voice and neglect responses to dissatisfaction are weak (Rusbult et al., 1982).

Though psychotherapy may traditionally be viewed as a dyadic relationship involving the therapist and client, the availability of high-quality alternatives (including relationships with family, friends, neighbors, colleagues at work, or solitude) may predict client termination of therapy when she or he is dissatisfied. Absence of an alternative or the availability of a poor alternative, on the other hand, may encourage a client to continue to have faith in the therapist and to hope that things will improve, but not to actively attempt to make the situation better, according to Rusbult's findings. Also, "alternative" clients available to the therapist (e.g., clients who are perceived as being easier to work with) may influence how the therapist deals with her or his dissatisfaction with a particular client. The presence of "good" alternative clients may encourage the therapist to terminate relatively quickly with an unsatisfactory client or attempt to pass the client on to a professional colleague.

What Are the Rules of Social Exchange in the Psychotherapy Relationship?

Social exchange theories traditionally assume that individuals are self-interested and will try to maximize their outcomes. However, based on research derived from equity theory (e.g., Adams, 1965; Homans, 1961; Lerner, 1977, 1982; Walster, Walster, & Berscheid, 1978) it is also assumed that in order to reach this goal individuals will conform to certain standards of justice in their interactions with others. A relationship is considered just or equitable if the ratios of outcomes to inputs for the participants in a relationship are equal; an individual who contributes more inputs to the relationship should receive better outcomes or benefits than an individual who contributes fewer inputs. Individuals who find themselves in an inequitable relationship will feel upset and will take steps to restore equity, actually or psychologically, by adjusting their own or their partner's inputs in the relationship.

Both the underbenefited and overbenefited persons feel distressed by an inequitable relationship, according to equity theory. If a person feels that she or he is on the giving end of a relationship (providing proportionately more inputs than benefits received), she or he may become resentful and angry. The individual on the receiving end of an inequitable relationship (providing proportionately fewer inputs but receiving many rewards) may also feel uncomfortable and perhaps guilty. The overbenefited person may feel that he or she is in debt to the other person and that the other person is being exploited. However, tolerance for inequity may be greater for the overbenefited compared to the underbenefited person in an inequitable relationship. The overbenefited person may feel less distress and be less eager to restore equity, compared to the underbenefited person, because he or she is benefiting materially (i.e., receiving proportionately more outputs) from the arrangement.

Consider the following example of an equity-based psychotherapy issue: A particular client held the belief that self-disclosure should be at least somewhat reciprocal in psychotherapy. He felt frustrated by providing the self-disclosure input during the therapy hour while the therapist listened and commented on what was said but never revealed anything about herself. The matching of self-disclosure may play a role in the formation and strengthening of friendships (see Altman & Taylor, 1973; Taylor & Altman, 1987): the reciprocal exchange of intimate information builds up bonds of intimacy and mutual trust between two friends. However, many therapists never reveal personal information about themselves to clients, and the failure of a therapist to reciprocate tit for tat (disclosure for disclosure) is the usual event and the standard rather than the exception in psychotherapy.

According to equity theory, clients (like the aforementioned client) may feel frustration and distress with what is an asymmetrical relationship, in which the client provides the self-disclosure input and the therapist does not reciprocate by sharing something equally intimate. Also, clients who have disclosed personal information may perceive that they have made an effort to establish a close relationship and that efforts are not being reciprocated by the therapist. Clients may ultimately accept that the therapeutic relationship is by its nature asymmetrical (e.g., the client discloses and pays for the therapist to listen and be supportive), but they may nevertheless wish for an enduring personal relationship with the therapist. The frustration and distress experienced by the client at the supposed inequity in the relationship could be used therapeutically to explore how the client tries to develop other relationships and how the client deals with frustrations in her or his other relationships. If the issue of inequity is not addressed, it may produce a lingering feeling in the client of not having gotten as much from therapy as she or he wished for or deserved.

Clients who are concerned about standards of fairness in the therapy relationship with respect to their self-disclosure input may not necessarily expect therapists to match them self-disclosure for self-disclosure. Other resources may be offered by the therapist after receiving an intimate disclosure in order to fulfill a standard of fairness. For instance, a therapist's display of concern or empathy after hearing a client's disclosure of an unpleasant experience may be preferred by the client over the therapist's reciprocal disclosure of personal information and may in fact be considered by the client to be more appropriate.

A study by Berg and Archer (1980) illustrates how a response that meets the needs of an initial disclosure may be preferred by a speaker even if the response doesn't reciprocate disclosure. College students who read a description of an initial meeting between two women reacted most favorably when there was a statement of concern by the second speaker whether the first speaker's disclosure input was nonintimate or intimate; the expression of concern was preferred over the reciprocity of disclosure. Berg and Archer suggest that expressing concern in this situation may have been considered the most appropriate or responsive act, since it best addressed the needs and wishes of the initial discloser. (See Chapter 5 for a discussion of the concept of responsiveness and its impact on the therapy relationship as well as for more details about Berg and Archer's study.)

In many, if not most relationships, equity is based on the exchange of nonidentical resources. Certainly in the therapy relationship, inputs and outcomes for clients and therapists will be quite different. Perceptions of equity should exist if the client's inputs (e.g., personal disclosures and fee payment) in relation to outcome (e.g., alleviation of symptoms) are balanced by the therapist's inputs (e.g., empathy and therapeutic interventions) in relation to outcome (e.g., receipt of fees). If the client feels that little improvement is occurring, she or he might experience inequity in the relationship. Or, if the client is a particularly demanding one (e.g., calling after hours or on weekends), the therapist might feel that she or he is putting more into the relationship than is fair.

How would client or therapist go about redressing a perceived inequity? A client might respond by missing payment of fees, requesting a reduction in fees, or participating less actively in therapy. The client might then feel that his or her inputs were more in line with outcomes. A therapist, perceiving the inequity in the therapy relationship, might also make efforts to correct the situation. Ideally, a therapist's behavior toward a client would be in the client's best interest and relatively independent of equity considerations. A burdensome client, however, might be treated differently from other clients. The therapist might be less empathic with the client, or she or he might try to increase the client's inputs into therapy by asking the client to self-disclose more or to engage in efforts at behavior change.

Equity theory is based on the assumption that partners maintain the same relative ratio of contributions (or inputs) to rewards (outcomes), but there are other rules of fairness that may influence client and therapist evaluations of their relationship (Leventhal, 1976). An equality rule requires an equal distribution of rewards (regardless of contributions) whereas a needs-based rule requires distribution of outcomes according to need. Clients and therapists may perceive that outcomes are being distributed equally (albeit not in identical benefits) if clients get symptom relief and therapists get a fee for service. On the other hand, using a needs-based rule, clients and therapists may perceive that the clients are rightfully receiving the major benefits of therapy (relief of symptoms, personality improvement, having someone listen attentively to what they have to say) because they have the presenting problem.

Equity theory's focus on the evaluation of fairness indicates one way that individuals can learn to coordinate their behaviors and maximize the satisfaction of both participants in a relationship. Another way that the client and therapist may learn to coordinate their behaviors may emerge from a greater sense of mutual involvement and caring in helping the client cope with her or his problems. A "we-feeling" may develop between the client and therapist so that they take account of one another's interests in deciding how to behave. This mutual concern provides a basis for maximizing the pair's joint outcomes and coordinating behavior.

Consider the matrix presented on the left in Figure 3.4. It presents the outcomes associated with mutual fate control, where one individual's outcomes are governed entirely by the other person's actions. This particular set of outcomes represents what is called the "given matrix" by Kelley and Thibaut (see Kelley, 1979; Kelley & Thibaut, 1978). According to Kelley (1979), "each outcome in the *given* matrix is determined independently, simply as a function of the direct consequences of the action or actions and what these consequences are, in rewards and costs, for each individual" (p. 69). The "given" matrix describes each individual's outcomes based on all the possible actions of the pair.

The "given matrix" does not consider how one person may respond to the outcomes another receives. Yet in much of human behavior our actions are, at least partially, determined by the effect we think they will have on others. In therapy much of the therapist's behavior is specifically designed to have particular effects on the client. Kelley (1979; Kelley & Thibaut, 1978) introduced the concept of transformation to account for the fact that people often consider others' outcomes in addition to their own when planning actions. One such transformation would be what is called a *max joint transformation,* in which a person is concerned with maximizing the total or joint outcomes of the pair of interactants. The results of applying such a transformation with the present example might be the "effective matrix" shown on the right in Figure 3.4. (A zero indicates a neutral point associated with the absence of both rewards and costs.) This illustration assumes that both client and therapist are responding to the sum total of their individual benefits (although in practice only one person might be making such a transformation). Because of the transformation, the pattern of interdependence is changed from what it was in the "given matrix," where neither the client nor therapist could influence his or her own outcomes. Yet when the other's outcomes also become one's own, as in this case, a basis for choosing among actions is provided. Notice that if the therapist is responding to the "effective matrix" (considering the client's outcomes as well as her or his own), the therapist receives a larger total benefit by choosing to discuss the topic. If the therapist were responding only to her or his own benefits (the given matrix), the therapist would have no basis for choosing whether

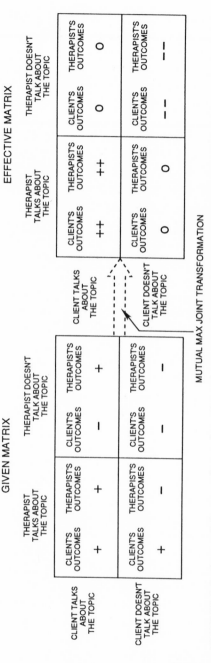

FIGURE 3.4. A max joint transformation of a "given" matrix associated with mutual fate control into an "effective" matrix where the client and the therapist are concerned with maximizing the total or joint outcomes of the pair.

to discuss the topic or not. A similar situation applies to the client if she or he has also made a max joint transformation. The client's outcomes in the "effective matrix" are better if she or he talks about the topic.

This description of a transformation matrix shows how an individual's behavior may be affected by taking account of the impact of one's actions on the other person's outcomes. When both client and therapist discuss the topic, benefits to both persons increase, given the use of the mutual max joint transformation. Mutual fate control, illustrated in the "given matrix," where the individuals were concerned only about their own self-interest, did not provide any certainty about outcomes and no basis for how to behave. But the mutual max joint transformation provides a basis for behavior that ensures good outcomes for both individuals (Kelley, 1979).

In the therapy relationship it isn't inevitable that the individuals' "effective" outcomes are influenced by a mutual concern for the partner's outcomes: for instance, whereas the therapist's behavior may be influenced by a max joint transformation strategy (seeking to maximize both persons' outcomes), the client's behavior may be determined only by self-interest.

We have discussed how the max joint transformation promotes joint outcomes and allows the client and therapist to coordinate their behavior. For a discussion of other types of outcome transformations and their implications for social interaction, see Kelley (1979) and Kelley and Thibaut (1978).

Conclusions

The therapy relationship basically involves an interaction between client and therapist in which each person's behavior has consequences for both. We have assumed that individuals are motivated to maximize their outcomes in social interactions and that a relationship is satisfactory to the extent that it accomplishes this goal. However, the impact of rewards and costs in the therapy relationship deserves further examination. Research on friendships indicates that rewards and costs *both* increase as a relationship progresses. Costs may reflect the effort incurred in making a relationship successful; those incurred in the past history of the relationship may also be viewed as investments that positively influence commitment.

A useful task for future study would be to examine the nature of the rewards and costs that clients and therapists perceive to occur in psychotherapy. It might also be possible to examine the expectancies that clients and therapists have about what kind of therapy relationship ought to exist between them. The role of alternative relationships that might be available to clients (e.g., with friends, neighbors, family) and therapists (e.g., with other clients, with one's family) in satisfaction and commitment to therapy should be considered.

The work of Rusbult on the impact of social exchange concepts affecting responses to dissatisfaction with psychotherapy has been examined. Her work indicates how prior satisfaction with the relationship, investment of resources, and the presence or absence of a high-quality alternative to the present relationship may encourage constructive, rather than destructive, responses to dealing with relationship dissatisfaction in psychotherapy.

The work of Kelley and Thibaut on the ways in which persons reconceptualize their outcomes (via cognitive transformations) suggests how clients and therapists may coordinate their behavior by means of a concern for the effects of one's actions on the other person.

There is relatively little research or theorizing about the therapy relationship based on exchange concepts. It is hoped that the current discussion about clients' and therapists' outcomes, and how these outcomes compare with what may be experienced in other possible relationships, will be useful in predicting how individuals become satisfied and committed to the psychotherapy process and, no less important, how they learn to successfully coordinate behavior in their respective roles.

A word of caution is necessary about the social exchange analysis of the client–therapist relationship. There is a tendency, when writing about social exchange theory, to make decision making about personal relationships sound overly rational (which is not surprising given the economic metaphor on which the social exchange idea is based). However, one can imagine that decisions by clients and therapists in psychotherapy may be far from rational and (especially in the case of clients) may be made under conditions of extreme stress and anxiety. Decision making under such circumstances may be the antithesis of rationality.

CHAPTER 4

Interpersonal Attraction in the Therapy Relationship

I am a female therapist, and I recently broached the subject of termination with a client whom I have been seeing in individual therapy for some time. The client is doing well, and both of us feel that the time has come for sessions to slow down and then cease altogether. The client says that she will miss me and asks about the possibility of the two of us getting together occasionally as "friends" when she is no longer in therapy. I really enjoy seeing this bright, verbal client—working with her has been like watching a flower unfold. I will miss her.

I am a male therapist. It is one week before Christmas, and one of my female clients brought me a Christmas gift—a tin of home-made peanut brittle. I feel a little uncomfortable about the time and effort that the client has expended on this gift. I typically maintain a warm but not "personal" relationship with all my clients.

A new client was referred to me. During our first session, I was aware of feeling uncomfortable with the client's apparent avoidance of interaction with me (e.g., keeping his coat on, frowning, avoiding eye contact). After the session was over, I felt very tired. I found that I was dreading the client's next session, which turned out to be just as uncomfortable as the first one had been.

Situations such as these occur every day to practicing therapists. They may be infrequent for any particular therapist, but all therapists have encountered such circumstances. And professionals who are not therapists have encountered similar situations with students and colleagues. One thread that ties all three situations together is attraction—or the lack of it. In the first example, the client likes and is attracted to the therapist and wants to initiate a personal friendship with the therapist. In the second example, the client expresses her positive feelings toward the therapist by bringing him a Christmas present. The third example involves a therapist's discomfort with (if not dislike of) a new client.

"Attraction" is such an everyday occurrence that we all probably have our own definition of what it means. Dictionaries emphasize the active qualities of attraction, the power of one person (or thing) to *draw* another to it. Social psychology has frequently defined attraction as liking for another, with disliking being the absence of attraction. Attraction can be defined as an attitude consisting of "an orientation toward or away from a person that may be described as having valence (positive, neutral, or negative). The orientation consists of a *cognitive* structure of beliefs and knowledge about the person, *affect* felt and expressed toward him or her, and *behavior tendencies* to approach or avoid that person" (C. Hendrick & Hendrick, 1983, p. 10, emphasis in the original). Such a definition captures the "motion" of attraction, emphasizing as it does the behavior that needs to follow both cognition and affect. This tripartite definition will be particularly useful as this chapter explores social psychological research on interpersonal attraction and its implications for psychotherapy relationships.

Both interpersonal attraction and the psychotherapy relationship are continua that may proceed from casual initial acquaintance to true interpersonal closeness. Attraction is not an event but, rather, a process that is embedded in the overarching process of relationship development. If we employ attraction as a synonym for liking, we immediately see its relevance for nearly all relationships. Just as certain relationship conditions (e.g., accurate empathy, unconditional positive regard) may be necessary conditions for effective therapy, so also may attraction be a necessary condition for relationship development. Liking is, of course, more or less important, depending on the nature of the relationship. Few of us would foster a friendship or a romantic relationship with someone whom we didn't like. Yet, many of us might retain a lawyer who is unlikable but very skilled. The importance of liking one's therapist may well fall somewhere in between, with the therapist being less than a friend and more than just a technically skillful professional (e.g., S. Hendrick, 1988).

In any case, attraction (in a broad-ranging sense) is a component of the therapy relationship, which is itself an essential component in psychotherapy (see Chapter 1). Although psychotherapy involves a professional relationship rather than a personal one (e.g., Reisman, 1986), that does not alter the utility of the personal relationship metaphor in the case of psychotherapy.

The interpersonal attraction and related personal relationships literatures have flourished in recent years, and they are directly relevant to the various aspects of attraction that occur between client and therapist. In the current chapter, we examine research on theories of interpersonal attraction and variables (such as similarity) that appear to influence attraction, weaving into the discussion research from psychotherapy that relates directly to the topics. We then apply attraction research specifically to psychotherapy, presenting therapy situations within a social psychological framework. Finally, we discuss therapist–client sexual involvement, a topic that is related to, yet set apart from, day-to-day interpersonal attraction in psychotherapy.

Research on Interpersonal Attraction

Theoretical Approaches to Attraction

There are at least four major approaches to interpersonal attraction (Perlman & Fehr, 1986): reinforcement, exchange, cognitive consistency, and developmental. We will briefly consider these four major paradigms and attempt to place some research findings within them.

Reinforcement theory in interpersonal attraction (e.g., Byrne, 1969; Lott & Lott, 1974) is premised on the idea that we like persons who provide us with rewards (e.g., reinforcements) and dislike people who engender too many costs (e.g., punishments). Such liking can be conditioned (e.g., an office supervisor who frequently praises a subordinate's work and, subsequently, becomes more liked) and can increase, based on the number and value of the rewards offered. For instance, if the aforementioned supervisor is known to be very exacting and difficult to please, the value of that supervisor's approval may increase, and liking for the supervisor may increase also, at least as long as the approval continues. If, however, the supervisor becomes more and more demanding (thus greatly increasing costs) or withdraws approval (thus decreasing rewards), liking may decrease.

Exchange theories (Thibaut & Kelley, 1959, discussed in detail in Chapter 3) go beyond simple unidirectional reward (such as the subordinate's liking for the supervisor) to explore reciprocal rewards (and punishments) in various relationships. Attraction may be influenced more by the *mutuality* of rewards than by the sheer number of rewards accruing to one person in a relationship. For instance, most of us would become extremely uncomfortable in a relationship in which we are getting all the rewards or, conversely, giving all the rewards. We feel best if there is some balance or equity to the distribution of rewards (e.g., Walster, Berscheid, & Walster, 1973, 1976). Even in the clinical situation there is some indication that mutual attunement, expressiveness, affirmation, and so on are required for a successful therapy relationship (Orlinsky & Howard, 1986).

Cognitive consistency theories (e.g., Heider, 1958) propose that people desire consistency and balance in their cognitions about ideas, individuals, or relationships. We want our world to make sense, to be ordered. We expect the sun to rise in the east, and we expect to be rewarded for our work efforts. Extending our need for consistency to relationships, we might say, "I like Mary, and I like John; I want them to like each other." Such a situation would represent balance in our relationships with Mary and John. However, many of our relationships do not balance so nicely. Often, we like Mary and we like John, but those two cannot stand each other. Much of the negotiation in human relationships may well be driven by a need for consistency (e.g., trying to get Mary and John to like each other more). However, all relationships must necessarily accommodate considerable inconsistency at times, and the therapy relationship is no exception (e.g., a therapist working with a couple trying to resolve their conflicts may like one partner more than the other; a client may like the therapist but dislike a particular intervention that the therapist feels is important).

Finally, the developmental or stage theories of attraction (e.g., Levinger & Snoek, 1972) focus on the chronological and behavioral sequences through which two people proceed as they develop a relationship. For instance, casual acquaintanceship is a beginning stage, whereas mutual intimacy occurs much later. People may first become aware of each other because each finds the other physically attractive. They introduce themselves to each other, find out that they share a number of attitudes and values, and then begin the process of spending time together, really getting to know each other, and letting their relationship develop. Within these stages of relationship development, different aspects of attraction (e.g., physical attractiveness) may be differentially important. The stage theories essentially state that there are logical, fairly predictable stages through which people proceed as they begin to develop a relationship. As we noted earlier, ongoing attraction is a process of movement, not just a single event.

Although the process of interpersonal attraction and relationship development has been approached in a number of different ways, certain variables affecting interpersonal attraction have received most of the attention. Several of the more important ones are described below.

Variables Influencing Attraction

Similarity. The hypothesis that two people who are similar on a wide variety of attributes are likely to be attracted to each other has received extensive research attention and support both in laboratory and field studies (e.g., Byrne, 1971). Why is similarity so important? Huston and Levinger (1978) note the following points: (1) similarity is directly reinforcing; (2) similarity confirms the positiveness of our own self-concept; (3) based on similarity, we assume that future interactions with another person will be positive; and (4) similarity and attraction are both correlates of some third variable, for example, positive affect. These explanations are certainly not mutually exclusive, and when taken together they provide some understanding of why similarity is so important.

An influential research program on similarity and attraction was developed by Byrne (1971), who essentially viewed similarity as a reward or reinforcement in a relationship or intended relationship. Most of the work has focused on similarity of attitudes, with results showing that (within some limits) greater similarity is related to greater attraction. Of course, similarity does not behave independently of other factors operating in a relationship at a given time. For instance, if a new relationship partner appears to be similar to us in nearly every way and then suddenly expresses a value that is the opposite of one we hold, we may well experience a sense of imbalance or disorder. To offer another example, an instance of similarity that might be rather meaningful at the beginning stage of a relationship (e.g., both partners drive the same model of foreign car) is likely to be unimportant as the relationship progresses. A recent study by Neimeyer and Mitchell (1988) assessed attitude, personality, value, and role construct similarities in pairs of subjects who interacted over the course of an 8-week period. Whereas similarity of general attitudes (art, literature, and so on) significantly predicted initial attraction, a similarity of somewhat "deeper" personality constructs and related cognitive constructs (measured by the 16PF [Cattell & Eber, 1966] and the Role Construct Repertory Grid [Kelly, 1955], respectively) predicted attraction after 8 weeks. Although these findings offer continuing support for similarity's influence on attraction, it is clear that people can be similar or dissimilar in a number of different ways, at a number of different points in time. Similarity on different dimensions thus influences attraction differentially at different relationship stages.

Recent research on similarity and attraction confirms a positive relation between the two constructs while seeking to uncover the causal mechanisms for this relation. Jellison and Oliver (1983) proposed that an implicit normative rule exists in which people believe that they ought to feel more attracted to similar others than to dissimilar others. In other words, if people are similar to us, we feel we should naturally like them (although sometimes we do not). This line of thinking suggests that in order to create a positive impression during a research study, research participants may feel constrained to follow this rule by expressing liking for others who are similar to them. In essence, they "know" that they are supposed to like someone who is similar to them, so they express liking whether or not they really feel it. Condon and Crano (1988) proposed that when we perceive another person as similar to us, we infer the possibility of a relationship that will be, in general, mutually rewarding. This might account for clients who appear very curious about a therapist's attitudes and values. Perhaps these clients are merely trying to establish the basis for what they believe will be a rewarding therapy relationship. Still other similarity research (Jamieson, Lydon, & Zanna, 1987) found the personality variable of self-monitoring (how much or how little we tailor our behavior to suit a particular person or situation) to be a moderating influence on the similarity–attraction relationship. Self-monitoring was particularly important when the basis for similarity was attitude versus activity preferences among recent acquaintances. Basically, high self-monitors responded more positively to activity preference similarities whereas low self-monitors preferred others with similar attitudes. Thus, considerable research has focused on additional variables that may mediate the relationship between similarity and attraction.

If we focus only on similarity and ignore dissimilarity, we neglect the latter's importance in relationship development. Certainly, disliking can be as potent an influence on relationships as liking. Rosenbaum (1986a) contends that similarity is not really as important as we think. Rather than viewing attitudinal similarity as leading to attraction, he posits that attitudinal dissimilarity leads to *repulsion*. Most people seek social validation in their interpersonal contacts, and similarity is one basis for such validation. When we encounter someone whose attitudes and values differ greatly from our own, we, rather than feeling validated, experience inconsistency between our perceptions and theirs, an inconsistency leading to distaste and perhaps dislike. Although a series of articles argued the various merits of the repulsion perspective (e.g., Byrne, Clore, & Smeaton, 1986; Rosenbaum, 1986a, 1986b), the importance of similarity to interpersonal attraction has not been seriously questioned. The basis of dissimilarity as a source of potential conflict between client and therapist cannot be ignored, however.

The various mechanisms by which similarity influences attraction (e.g., rewards, social validation, promise of future positive interaction) have major relevance for the psychotherapy relationship. Considerable research has examined the influence of similarity or difference of counselor gender on therapy process and outcome. Although in the past women have been underrepresented in such fields as counseling and clinical psychology, they now constitute a third of this group (e.g., Bernstein, Hofmann, & Wade, 1987). This represents an improvement over earlier years in which most clients were women and most psychologists men.

Proponents of such approaches to therapy as feminist therapy (e.g., Gilbert, 1980), while acknowledging that men can be feminist therapists, nevertheless present a therapeutic paradigm that may, at least currently, best be offered *by* women *for* women. Such a suggestion would seem to be a logical outgrowth of the research findings on the relationship between similarity and attraction (e.g., two people with specific and similar values may particularly like each other and thus work well together). For more general approaches to psychotherapy, however, the desirability of counselor–client gender similarity is less clear. As Bernstein et al. (1987) point out, some studies have found that male counselors are preferred and others that female counselors are preferred. These authors found that among those male and female subjects expressing a preference for counselor gender, male counselors were more often preferred than female counselors for all problem areas except sexual issues.

However, in other research (e.g., Blier, Atkinson, & Geer, 1987; Holland, Atkinson, & Johnson, 1987; Paradise, Conway, & Zweig, 1986), neither counselor gender nor client gender produced any significant effects. For the Blier et al. (1987) study, although the counselor's actual gender was not an issue, the counselor's gender *role* (traits that are traditionally considered appropriate for either males or females) was a significant variable; gender role was assessed with the Bem Sex Role Inventory (BSRI; S. Bem, 1974). Choosing between feminine, masculine, and androgynous (expressing strong feminine *and* masculine traits) counselors, subjects preferred to see a feminine (e.g., nurturing) counselor for personal concerns, a masculine (e.g., active) counselor for assertiveness concerns, and both masculine and androgynous counselors for academic concerns (p. 29). The authors proposed that more traditional (e.g., older, nonminority) subjects tended to favor masculine or androgynous counselors whereas no clear descriptive pattern emerged for those subjects who favored feminine counselors. These findings are consistent with personal relationship research showing gender role to differentiate more clearly among relationship attitudes than did actual subject gender (e.g., Bailey, Hendrick, & Hendrick, 1987). Thus, although similarity between client and therapist might be helpful in therapy, it is not yet clear what type of similarity should be sought. Should client and therapist be the same gender—or express the same gender role attitudes? Research that systematically varies both therapist and client gender and gender role attitudes and relates these to therapy satisfaction and outcome would be extremely useful.

The construct of similarity also has considerable relevance for the increasingly important topic of matching therapist with client in terms of racial and ethnic variables. As with the issue of gender matching, equivocal results have occurred from research exploring the effects of racially or ethnically similar therapist–client dyads on therapy effectiveness (e.g., Atkinson, Furlong, & Poston, 1986). However, research assessing black subjects' preferences for counselor race revealed consistent preferences by black subjects for black counselors (Atkinson et al., 1986). Other research showed that black clients expressed more general racial concerns than did white clients (Sue, 1988). The inconsistencies in the findings on client and therapist racial and ethnic matching have been attributed (e.g., Sue, 1988) to methodological problems such as nonrandom assignment of clients to therapists, studies with small numbers of subjects, confounding of racial and ethnic variables with other demographic factors such as social class, and instruments that may not be racially or ethnically sensitive.

In a recent commentary Sue (1988) proposed a reconceptualization of the whole argument concerning differential treatment outcomes based on therapist and client racial or ethnic matching. He suggested that availability of racially and ethnically similar counselors may be a valid political issue for minority clients in the sense that it represents freedom of choice. In other words, minority clients may, for political reasons, prefer a therapist who is racially or ethnically similar. However, when considering only the therapeutic issues involved, Sue argued that other types of matching, such as what he calls "cultural" matching (e.g., shared attitudes, values, and life experiences), may be more important for maximizing actual treatment outcome than either racial or ethnic matching. He noted that "ethnic mismatches do not necessarily imply cultural mismatches, because therapists and clients from different ethnic groups may share similar values, life-styles, and experiences" (p. 306). For example, a Hispanic woman seeking a divorce may be more likely to feel understood by an Anglo therapist who has herself experienced divorce than by a Hispanic therapist who has never married. A similar point of view was expressed by Ho (1987), who emphasized cultural awareness and appreciation rather than ethnic or racial matching in effective family therapy with minority clients. For both Ho and Sue, similarity between therapist and client is extremely important, but the similarity does not have to adhere to rigid racial or ethnic lines. This perspective was confirmed in a recent study (Atkinson, Poston, Furlong, & Mercado, 1989) in which similar attitudes, similar personality, more education, and greater age were counselor characteristics viewed as more important than counselor ethnicity. Subjects in this study were Asian-American, Mexican-American, and Caucasian-American students.

Physical Attractiveness. Another variable that appears to influence interpersonal attraction is physical attractiveness. Research consistently points to the conclusion that physically attractive people are responded to more favorably than unattractive people (e.g., Berscheid & Walster, 1974b; Hatfield & Sprecher, 1986). Although the literature indicates a strong tendency for people to prefer others who are highly attractive (no matter what one's own attractiveness level), some support has also been found for the following hypothesis: two people of similar attractiveness levels may be more likely to select one another as friends or to indicate a desire to see each other in the future (e.g., Cash & Derlega, 1978; Murstein, 1972; Murstein & Christy, 1976).

Additional research (e.g., Landy & Sigall, 1974) indicates that attractive people also tend to have other positive characteristics (for instance, intelligence) attributed to them, resulting, for example, in the conclusion that what is beautiful is good. Most of us could probably cite incidents where we have seen this particular norm in operation. For instance, all other things being equal, the physically attractive political candidate is the one who is likely to get elected. In a clinical situation it is possible that first impressions of both the therapist and client will be more positive if the two are physically attractive. According to the Landy and Sigall (1974) findings, a client might expect an attractive therapist to be more intelligent and able to help solve problems more quickly. In turn, a therapist might expect an attractive client to improve in therapy more quickly. In such a situation, a therapist may relate to the client more effectively, thus creating a self-fulfilling prophecy in which the client behaves in accord with these higher expectations and in fact progresses more quickly.

It is also possible that there are "different strokes for different folks," and that physical attractiveness in a partner is more important to some people than to others. For instance, Snyder, Berscheid, and Glick (1985) proposed that the personality characteristic of self-monitoring (tailoring behavior to the situation) might affect the importance of physical attractiveness in a dating partner, after the authors discovered that high self-monitoring men were more interested in physical attractiveness of a potential dating partner than were low self-monitoring men. This differential susceptibility of persons to the effects of physical attractiveness was supported in an analogue study by Vargas and Borkowski (1983), who found that subjects to whom physical attractiveness was more important (measured by subjects' self-report of how highly they were influenced by physical attractiveness in deciding on a potential date) perceived an unattractive counselor as less skillful than did clients to whom attractiveness in a potential date was less important. Thus, some clients may actually profit more from therapy when they are working with a therapist whom they consider to be physically attractive; for other clients, attractiveness will not be an issue.

 Proximity. Proximity is another variable important to attraction. Proximity, also sometimes referred to as propinquity, is typically used in attraction research to refer to spatial or geographic closeness and is one determinant of attraction. Several studies (e.g., Newcomb, 1961; Segal, 1974) found that proximity (e.g., being roommates, living on the same dormitory floor, sitting together in classes) was correlated with attraction or liking. Of course, the importance of proximity is not independent of other variables such as socioeconomic resources. Indeed, Palisi and Ransford (1987) concluded that proximity in voluntary friendships may be more important for lower-income people, who do not have the resources (such as transportation) to develop friendships outside their immediate neighborhood.

Proximity can be related to disliking as well as liking, as Ebbesen, Kjos, and Konecni (1976) discovered when they studied a condominium complex in southern California. Those whom residents most liked and most disliked all lived fairly close to the residents. It appears logical that we are more likely to interact with people who live closer to us, and in turn, our feelings (both positive and negative) are stronger for those with whom we interact a great deal. Proximity and disliking would seem unlikely to greatly affect a therapy dyad, however, because either partner can terminate the relationship (thus removing proximity) at any time.

An offshoot of the proximity idea is that of "mere exposure" (Zajonc, 1968), the idea that the more we see someone (or something), the more our attitude toward them will be enhanced. How many of us develop a favorite grocery store cashier or bank teller based on continued interaction over weeks or months? The expression "He kind of grows on you" is likely a common sense assessment of the mere exposure phenomenon. T. Hill and Lewicki (1991) propose that the mere exposure effect is one example of a more pervasive human tendency to develop unconscious patterns or structures for relationships between variables: in a therapeutic context, the client may begin to unconsciously associate the therapist with quiet, peacefulness, and the feeling of being understood. Thus, complex cognitive processes may operate within the phenomenon of mere exposure, with the end result being the client's increased attraction to the therapist.

Related to proximity is the whole area of nonverbal aspects of attraction, including personal space, body language, and visual interaction. Body language refers to the body, its clothing, and the way in which the clothed body communicates information. Thus, the body language medium may be anything from body posture to the jewelry one is wearing. For instance, a client who wears a lot of apparently expensive jewelry may communicate to the therapist that the client can easily afford therapy. On the other hand, if the therapist wears expensive jewelry, the client may begin thinking that the therapist's fees are too high.

The way we physically present ourselves to others has strong implications for how we may be evaluated, over and above sheer physical attractiveness. Scheflen (1965) described what he called "quasi-courtship behavior" in psychotherapy and other interaction situations, noting that when two people in conversation sit directly facing each other, lean forward, and screen other people out of awareness, it can signify courtship, a business deal, or psychotherapy. In the latter two situations, various "behavioral qualifiers," such as crossed arms or bodies at an angle rather than in direct alignment, modify the intensity of the interaction.

One important aspect of body language is visual interaction or "eye contact," which can be a significant mechanism for expressing dominance or hostility as well as intimate affection. One approach to eye contact (Argyle & Dean, 1965) posits that two people interacting seek to establish a comfortable degree of eye contact (as well as interaction distance, conversation intimacy, smiling, and so on) and when one factor such as eye contact changes, other factors will shift in order to maintain equilibrium in the encounter. Thus, if the therapist increases the intensity of the situation by asking the client intimate sexual questions, the therapist may correspondingly reduce eye contact.

Applications for Psychotherapy

The preceding review of theoretical bases of interpersonal attraction and variables influencing interpersonal attraction can be directly applied to psychotherapy.

Client-Therapist Interactions in an Attraction Context

First, let us reconsider the examples of client–therapist interactions that opened the chapter in the light of our social psychological analysis of interpersonal attraction. The situation of the client who is ready to end therapy and who wants to continue a friendship with the

therapist can be viewed within an attraction framework. It is important to note that the therapist in this situation also expresses considerable positiveness about the client. One of the contributors to attraction
in this situation may be gender similarity (both client and therapist are
women). Or perhaps gender role similarities are operating, and both
women have similar attitudes about the appropriate roles of men and
women in our society. *Both* gender and gender role may well be
influential, as may additional attitude and value similarities between
therapist and client. It could be that gender is actually less important
than a more general "cultural" (i.e., value, experience) similarity (e.g.,
Sue, 1988). In any case, it is difficult to ignore the importance of
similarity, whether it is similarity of gender, race, ethnicity, or some
other variable. It might also be the case that mere exposure of client to
therapist has led the client to associate very positive feelings with the
therapy hour—and with the therapist. The client may understandably
be reluctant to relinquish that experience.

If a therapist considers whether or not to have a personal relationship with a former client, attraction variables such as similarity, mere
exposure, and the like may all be involved. However, the choice the
therapist makes is governed by therapeutic orientation and ethical
considerations as well as issues of attraction/liking. Although some
therapists are simply not comfortable in any kind of personal posther-
apy relationship at any time, other therapists are open to them. What
seems most important in this situation is that the reason for establishing (or not establishing) a personal relationship be clearly understood
by both persons involved.

A very different example from the beginning of the chapter is the
unappealing client who avoids interaction with the therapist. Here
again is a situation comprehensible in attraction variable terms. This
may be a client who simply has poor skills in both body language and
general self-presentation. The person may be excessively shy or may
have grown up in a reserved, inexpressive family. Perhaps the client is
from a cultural or ethnic background in which eye contact is limited
and personal space is rigidly protected. Surely geography alone produces different norms. For instance, a client in cowboy boots and
Stetson hat is likely to look normal in El Paso, Texas, but somewhat
peculiar in Boston, Massachusetts. The client's mode of self-presentation could represent a case of extreme dissimilarity to the therapist—
an example of Rosenbaum's (1986b) "repulsion hypothesis," in which
dissimilar others are disliked. It could also represent a situation in

which there has been too little exposure by the therapist to people of other areas and cultures or where the therapist unconsciously associates client behaviors such as inexpressiveness with negative therapy outcomes (e.g., Hill & Lewicki, 1991). For example, the therapist may have had several inexpressive clients who appeared to be therapy failures. This client may actually be one whom a cognitive–behavioral therapist who employs psychoeducational and skill-building strategies would be able to help function more smoothly, both in therapy and in the wider society.

The gift-giving example in our introduction is common in therapy, particularly during the December holiday season. Therapists are of mixed minds on gift giving by clients. If attraction variables are governing the situation, the therapist and client may be similar in attitudes and tempo, and the client may give the gift to demonstrate liking. Perhaps the therapeutic relationship has continued for a long time (mere exposure), prompting the client to give a gift to someone who is very familiar. Perhaps the client routinely gives modest gifts to all friends and acquaintances in the local area during the holidays, and by virtue of proximity the therapist is included in that group. Gift giving may express liking behavior or simple role-governed behavior prompted by the holiday season. However, gift giving may also represent a client's attempt to become closer to the therapist, that is, to obtain the therapist's friendship.

For the therapist's part, the response to the gift may be related to attraction variables as well as to the therapist's theoretical orientation. One therapist might view gift giving as always appropriate, another as appropriate during the holiday period, and another as never appropriate. A therapist might feel that a particular client is trying to become inappropriately "special" to the therapist through giving gifts whereas the giving of a particular gift to the therapist by another client is considered perfectly acceptable. No two therapy situations are exactly alike.

An ability to separate "simple" attraction from other processes that occur during therapy (such as transference) can be aided by knowledge of attraction research as well as by understanding therapy dynamics. Viewing every instance of mutual attraction/affection between therapist and client as transference (emphasizing the past's influence on the present) is just as limiting as seeing it always as interpersonal attraction (emphasizing only the present). There are of course no absolute distinctions between transference and attraction.

Attraction is a complex phenomenon that can be viewed as a simple dependent variable, predicted by other psychological variables such as mere exposure, or as a causal agent influencing the development of therapy (and other) relationships. Attraction is both cause and effect, given that it occurs within the feedback loop that constitutes every type of personal relationship.

Brief Examples. Several therapy situations can be understood in light of the interpersonal attraction literature. An awkward aspect of therapy is sometimes the setting of and collection of fees. Little research has been done on fee payment and therapy process. However, Brigham and Brigham (1985) studied how raters (therapist trainees and undergraduates) evaluated videotapes of a therapist charging either a high, moderate, or low fee (there was also a "no fee mentioned" condition). An inverse relationship was obtained between positive evaluation of the therapist and fee amount; the therapist was less liked in the high-fee condition than in any of the other conditions and was also perceived as somewhat less trustworthy and expert. The raters attributed altruism (with altruism viewed as attraction-producing) to the therapist in the low- and moderate-fee conditions. On the other hand, similarity would provide an alternative explanation. Neither therapist trainees nor undergraduates are usually very affluent. The high-fee therapist ($70 per session) may have been perceived as dissimilar to the rater and hence less likable.

An intriguing example of the mere exposure phenomenon may be seen in the psychoanalytic practice of involving the client in from two to five therapy sessions per week (compared to "standard" practice of one session per week). Much client attrition in therapy occurs early in the process, before the client is fully committed to therapy. If an analyst succeeds initially in establishing a norm of multiple sessions per week, mere exposure of the client to the therapist may result in greater client attraction to or liking for the therapist simply on the basis of greater familiarity. As we have already discussed, sharing time and experiences with the therapist may increase the client's attraction to the therapist and perhaps foster greater commitment to therapy.

A final example concerns the importance of a therapist's choice of office secretary or receptionist and answering service. These choices are important because clients who may be in a psychological crisis state need to be treated carefully and responded to sympathetically. Another aspect may refer to the cognitive consistency theory of attraction, specifically Heider's (1958) Balance Theory. If, as a client, I like my therapist but dislike his or her abrupt office secretary or curt answering service, I will probably experience a sense of imbalance or disorder. To resolve the imbalance, I may try to develop more liking for the secretary or answering service (perhaps through continued exposure), or I may start to dislike the therapist. My ultimate resolution might be to find myself another therapist, whose demeanor, secretary, and answering service are all congruent. Of course, I could also choose to tell the therapist about my feelings concerning the secretary or answering service and hope that a mutually agreeable solution might be worked out.

Love Attitudes and Psychotherapy

In our application of various social psychological models of personal relationships to the therapy relationship, we now consider one rapidly developing area of personal relationships research that has provocative implications for psychotherapy: *love*. For our purposes, love may be considered as an expanded conception of attraction, and both attraction and love are bases of intimate relationships. Attraction and love are similar in emotion, but love seems to involve a deeper emotional commitment to a relationship (C. Hendrick & Hendrick, 1983). The possible role of love in the therapy relationship is an appropriate topic for our consideration.

Theoretical and empirical work on love has blossomed recently (e.g., Hazan & Shaver, 1987; C. Hendrick & Hendrick, 1986). A typology of love styles developed by Lee (1973) has been particularly productive in generating research. Lee proposed three primary love styles and three secondary ones. The primaries include *Eros* (passionate love), *Ludus* (game-playing love), and *Storge* (friendship-based love). The secondary styles, each a compound of two of the primaries, include *Pragma* (practical love, compound of Ludus and Storge), *Mania* (possessive, dependent love, compound of Eros and Ludus), and *Agape* (altrustic love, compound of Eros and Storge). Scales measuring each of the love styles have been developed (e.g., C. Hendrick & Hendrick, 1986, 1990; S. Hendrick & Hendrick, 1987; S. Hendrick, Hendrick, & Adler, 1988). Sample questionnaire items describing each love style are shown in Table 4.1.

Research has attempted to paint fuller portraits of the six love styles, exploring various demographic (e.g., gender, religiosity, ethnic background) differences and linking the love styles to interpersonal

TABLE 4.1. Sample Questionnaire Items Referring to Lee's (1973) Six Love Styles

Eros
1. My lover and I have the right physical "chemistry" between us.
2. Our lovemaking is very intense and satisfying.
3. I feel that my lover and I were meant for each other.

Ludus
4. I could get over my affair with my lover pretty easily and quickly.
5. My lover would get upset if he/she knew of some of the things I've done with other people.
6. When my lover gets too dependent on me, I want to back off a little.

Storge
7. To be genuine, our love first required *caring* for awhile.
8. I expect to always be friends with my lover.
9. Our love is really a deep friendship, not a mysterious, mystical emotion.

Pragma
10. I considered what my lover was going to become in life before I committed myself to him/her.
11. I tried to plan my life carefully before choosing my lover.
12. In choosing my lover, I believed it was best to love someone with a similar background.

Mania
13. Sometimes I get so excited about being in love with my lover that I can't sleep.
14. When my lover doesn't pay attention to me, I feel sick all over.
15. Since I've been in love with my lover, I've had trouble concentrating on anything else.

Agape
16. I try to always help my lover through difficult times.
17. I would rather suffer myself than let my lover suffer.
18. I cannot be happy unless I place my lover's happiness before my own.

Note. From "A Relationship-Specific Version of the Love Attitudes Scale" by C. Hendrick and S. S. Hendrick, 1990, *Journal of Social Behavior and Personality*, 5, 239–254. Reprinted by permission.

behaviors such as self-disclosure and personality characteristics such as sensation seeking (the need for variety and novelty in various experiences and persons). The applicability of the love styles to psychotherapy lies in their ability to help us conceptualize the therapist–client relationship in new ways.

In applying the first of the love styles to therapy, we might expect that an Eros-based (passionate) therapist–client relationship would be a quickly formed, intense therapeutic bond based in large measure on attraction/liking. Therapy might involve expression of emotion and considerable self-disclosure by both client and therapist. Gestalt therapy, which emphasizes present emotional and physical awareness and employs active techniques such as role-playing, or humanistic therapies, which emphasize the client's here-and-now experiencing of emotions, might both encompass some aspects of Eros.

Although Ludus is frequently characterized as a game-playing orientation to love, a more likely characteristic is distance/detachment by either one or both partners. In a Ludus type of therapy relationship, the therapist would remain rather distant, allowing the client to form his or her own subjective impressions of the therapist. There would be less emphasis on expression of feelings than would occur with Gestalt or humanistic therapies and more emphasis on affect combined with cognition (i.e., insight). Psychoanalytic approaches, which place the therapy relationship at the center of therapy as a means to explore the client's other relationships rather than as important in its own right, seem to come closest to the cool, studied qualities of Ludus.

A Storge (friendship) therapy relationship should be slow-moving and reality-based, with a firm undertone of acceptance and trust. Storge can be described as love through "evolution" rather than revolution," and as such, Rogerian client-centered therapy, which (as noted in Chapter 1) emphasizes an empathic, nonjudgmental, and trusting relationship between therapist and client, is an example.

Pragma (practical) therapy would seek to optimize the client's resources and use practical, realistic therapeutic strategies. Cognition rather than affect would be the bedrock of a pragmatic therapy approach. As discussed in Chapter 1, behavioral and cognitive–behavioral therapies, stressing the decrease of irrational thoughts and behaviors and the increase of adaptive, rational problem-solving approaches, fit almost perfectly within a pragmatic framework.

A Manic (possessive, dependent) therapist–client relationship is the most difficult to characterize because, by its very nature, Mania does not appear to be a very adaptive love style. Emotional ups and downs, self-doubts, and physical symptoms all haunt this love style. Perhaps Mania is represented less by a therapeutic orientation than by a therapeutic stage, in which a client is coping with a number of trying therapeutic issues or is beset by serious transference problems.

Finally, Agape, or altruistic therapy, would contain substantial therapist giving, little thought of any real returns from the client, and perhaps a focus on spiritual or philosophical issues. Therapeutic approaches typifying this style might include counseling offered in a religious setting, general supportive therapy, and perhaps in some cases, existential approaches that emphasize the human search for meaning in everyday existence.

Conceptualizing the therapy relationship in terms of orientations toward love links a social psychological approach to personal relationships with existing approaches to psychotherapy. One advantage to this process is a creative widening of our perspectives on therapy. Although love is only a general metaphor for therapy, using it may help us more easily view therapy relationships within the frameworks that apply to other intimate personal relationships. The final section of this chapter examines a controversial topic, that of sexual involvement between therapist and client, within the framework of interpersonal attraction.

Sexual Attraction and Involvement between Therapist and Client

Sexual Ethics

Although the American Psychological Association's (1981) "Ethical Principles of Psychologists" explicitly forbid sexual involvement between client and therapist, sexual attraction between the two and, to a lesser extent, sexual involvement do occur. Holroyd and Brodsky (1977) reported that 1.9% of female and 10.9% of male psychologists indicated incidences of erotic contact (e.g., kissing) with clients, and 0.6% of female and 5.5% of male psychologists indicated incidents of actual intercourse with clients. Similar results were obtained in other studies (e.g., Bouhoutsos, Holroyd, Lerman, Forer, & Greenberg, 1983; Pope et al., 1986).

Whether it is called sexual attraction or a manifestation of countertransference, many therapists experience romantic feelings for a particular client. The intimacy and intensity of the therapy context give rise to a wide range of emotions. However, therapists often do not have a full understanding of either the context of such feelings or ways in which to deal with them (e.g., Gilbert, 1987; Pope et al., 1986).

Attraction Explanations

There are various ways to employ social psychological research to conceptualize erotic/sexual involvement between therapist and client. One of the most interesting perspectives is drawn from Berscheid and

Walster's (1974a) work on passionate love. In applying a previously developed theory of emotion (e.g., Schachter, 1964; Schachter & Singer, 1962) to love, Berscheid and Walster stated that for an individual to experience passionate love, two things were required. First, the person must be intensely physiologically aroused and second, the person must respond to cues in the current situation by labeling the arousal as "passionate love" (see C. Hendrick & Hendrick, 1983, p. 105). For instance, an individual's heart rate and blood pressure may increase when he or she is in the presence of a very attractive person or one who is otherwise "special." This physiological arousal may then be labeled as attraction. It is not difficult to generalize this model to the therapy relationship and to understand that the emotional upheaval and psychological intensity that occur during periods of therapy generate a great deal of physiological arousal. Because of the interpersonal intimacy that characterizes the therapy relationship, such arousal may get labeled by one or both of the therapy partners as passionate love or sexual attraction.

Other theoretical models of interpersonal attraction that were presented earlier in this chapter are applicable to client–therapist sexual attraction. Sexual attraction might occur when one (or both) therapy partner becomes such a significant reinforcer of the other that the rewards offered are greater than those offered by relationships outside of therapy (see Chapter 3); the significant persons in a client's life will seldom be able to react to the client as nonjudgmentally, for instance, as does the therapist. In addition, the very intensity of the therapy relationship can make other relationships pale by comparison: it is not possible to maintain the focused intimacy of the therapy hour on a 24-hour basis.

According to a developmental or stage theory approach to the phenomenon of sexual attraction, the client and therapist may be more likely to become attracted to each other at some points in therapy than at others. For instance, physical attractiveness may be more salient at an early stage of therapy, and therapist and client who find each other physically attractive may thus feel more sexually attracted as the relationship begins; as therapy progresses, physical attractiveness may be a less influential variable. For another therapist and client dyad, however, variables such as time spent together (e.g., mere exposure) may precipitate sexual attraction at a later stage of therapy.

In terms of the variables that influence attraction, all might play a part in fostering sexual attraction between therapist and client. As we just noted, physical attractiveness may be a factor, as may the phenomenon of mere exposure. Similarity may be a more or less potent variable, depending on the needs of the client and therapist. If feelings of isolation and inadequacy have characterized a particular client and the client feels accepted and understood by the therapist, the client may tend to exaggerate the importance of similarities between himself or herself and the therapist and may use these apparent similarities as a basis for sexual attraction. Because of the intimacy and intensity of the therapy relationship, a client may blur the boundaries between a professional and a personal relationship. In this situation it is desirable if such feelings can be disclosed to the therapist, allowing therapist and client to clarify the feelings and put them in a perspective that can facilitate rather than impede therapy.

Something that goes beyond mere exposure in the therapy situation is the general issue of proximity. When two people spend many hours together, sharing intimate conversation and becoming part of each other's ongoing lives as well as part of each other's history, they become in some sense part of each other. They share time, space, emotions, and both verbal and nonverbal communications. It is not difficult to understand how such intimacy can lead to feelings of romantic and perhaps sexual attraction. Understood in this light, sexual attraction may be an extreme form of the interpersonal attraction that occurs in most, if not all, therapy relationships. However, although the sexual feelings are understandable, acting on those feelings can be devastating for the client and therapist. Several studies have reported adverse psychological consequences (such as negative feelings about the self or negative effects on other close relationships) for clients who have had sexual involvement with their therapists (e.g., Bouhoutsos et al., 1983; Pope et al., 1986). Understanding sexual attraction does not mean condoning sexual involvement.

Conclusions

This chapter has been concerned with the process of interpersonal attraction and the part it plays in the development of relationships, particularly the relationship between therapist and client. As viewed from the reinforcement, exchange, cognitive consistency, and stage/developmental theoretical perspectives, attraction in a relationship is not static. It is influenced by a number of different variables, including the length of time the relationship has existed. Similarity between partners is a potent force in interpersonal attraction and hence in relationship development. In the client–therapist relationship (as in other relationships), similarity of one type (e.g., gender) may be less important to some people than similarity of another type (e.g., ethnicity). To some persons the only similarity that is important may be similarity of life experience: the client may want to know that the therapist has "been there." Another variable influencing attraction is proximity and, linked with it, mere exposure. The effects of these variables would seem to be particularly important in psychotherapy, where therapist and client are often together for many hours over long periods of time.

A novel way of conceptualizing various therapy approaches is to fit them within a love styles framework. Such an approach underlines the differences between theoretical approaches (e.g., use of affect versus use of behavior strategies) as well as the similarities (e.g., all are dyadic therapies oriented toward the health of the client). Although we can extend the attraction paradigm into the realm of sexual attraction and involvement between therapist and client, that is an ethically complex area that requires specialized attention.

Current social psychological research on attraction in relationships has useful explanatory power for a number of situations that occur in psychotherapy and fits in well with psychotherapy research. However, ongoing research on interpersonal attraction in psychotherapy is clearly important. We need to know how the physical attractiveness and body language of the therapist affect client attitudes toward therapy. Is an attractive, well-dressed therapist more likely to be perceived as expert and in turn more likely to facilitate change in the client? Is there a point at which a therapist can become *too* physically attractive or *too* well-dressed, thus intimidating the client into either terminating therapy or continuing treatment with outward compliance and inward resistance? What kinds of similarity are important to a client? And how much similarity is too much similarity, with a therapist so allied with the client that he or she is unable to be confrontational? Much of the existing social psychological findings on attraction have been based on first encounter studies rather than on ongoing relationships. However, they offer a useful starting point for research on attraction in therapy.

If there is one overarching concept that traditional attraction research can offer to psychotherapy, it is that a number of different individual variables (such as proximity) influence the development of attraction in relationships. In turn, psychotherapy research illuminates for those who study other personal relationships the importance of interpersonal variables (such as cooperation and mutual affirmation) in relationship development. If future research takes account of both these perspectives, as well as of the dynamic nature of attraction across time, useful and exciting knowledge is likely to result.

CHAPTER 5

Development of
the Therapy Relationship

Throughout this book we attempt to apply concepts drawn from work on interpersonal relationships to the relationship between therapist and client. In this chapter we will examine how the therapist–client relationship develops and factors that can facilitate or impede its development. Does a working relationship between therapist and client develop gradually over numerous hours of therapy, or can an effective therapist–client relationship be detected at an early point in therapy? Which factors are important in determining the speed with which a therapeutic relationship develops? We will draw upon theory and research on the development of personal relationships as well as other social psychological research to understand how the therapist–client relationship evolves.

Although virtually all psychotherapies and therapists acknowledge the importance of the relationship between therapist and client, substantial differences exist concerning the nature of the relationship and its centrality to therapeutic progress, as reviewed in Chapter 1. An extreme behavioral view conceptualizes relationship factors as nonspecific variables that are important for enhancing the social influence of the therapist in his or her task of eliciting behavior change (G. Wilson & Evans, 1977). At the other extreme is the view of Rogers and his colleagues that the relationship is central to the therapeutic process (e.g., Rogers, 1957). Although it may not be the case, as Rogers asserts, that the relationship alone can provide the necessary and sufficient condition for change, it is likely that the relationship permeates and affects all other aspects of therapy from setting goals to evaluating outcomes (Orlinsky & Howard, 1986; Saltzman, Luetgert, Roth, Creaser, & Howard, 1976).

In addition to factors such as attraction, exchange, and privacy, the type of relationship that develops between a therapist and client will be affected by their goals in therapy, their resources and perceptions of each other's resources, and their expectations about one another. Equally important will be the way the goals, characteristics, and expectations of the therapist and client fit with each other. Before addressing the time course of the relationship directly, we will briefly consider how the therapist–client relationship might be affected by goals, personal characteristics, and expectations.

Goals of Therapy

Mahrer (1967) presents views on the goals of therapy from authors with diverse theoretical orientations. Across the various theoretical orientations, considerable diversity appears regarding what the goals of psychotherapy are. Some believe the goals of therapy should be very specific (e.g., reduction in anxiety, learning more adaptive habits or social skills) while others express broad general goals (e.g., gaining insight, self-actualization). Because a person's goals will greatly affect her or his interpersonal behavior (Miller & Read, 1989), the practice of clients and therapists agreeing on the goals of therapy at an early point is important for the development of the therapeutic relationship. The particular goals for therapy will partially define what the therapist–client relationship will be like. For example, if the goal is to reduce symptoms, a drug treatment program or a program of systematic desensitization may be adopted. The therapist's role in the relationship may then be more directive and come to resemble that of a physician with a patient. At the other end of the continuum is the case where the goal of therapy is the client's self-actualization. Here the therapist may adopt a very nondirective role similar to that of a best friend and confidant.

The goals of therapy (and hence the therapist–client relationship) will be affected by the internal characteristics of the therapist (e.g., theoretical orientation, training, personality), the internal characteristics of the client (e.g., nature of problem, previous knowledge or experience with therapy), and the match or "fit" of therapist and client personalities, cognitive styles, and feelings about each other and about therapy (Sullivan, 1953; Yalom & Elkin, 1974).

In addition, factors that are external or beyond the control of either therapist or client may exert a strong influence on the goals of therapy and the therapist–client relationship. Perhaps chief among the external factors is the time available for therapy. If therapy will be relatively short-term, the primary objective is likely to be relief or reduction of distress. If the therapist is working in a context that requires him or her to see a large number of clients or if geographical or financial constraints mean the client can stay in therapy for only a brief time, short-term therapy may be necessitated. In fact, the prevailing current view of therapy seems to favor relatively brief therapies, due to their presumed cost-effectiveness. If short-term therapy is necessitated by external constraints on the therapist, does the client understand this? If clients initially expect therapy to last a relatively long time, does learning it may be brief cause them to reevaluate their condition? Does it lead to the expectation by clients that the therapist will provide quick answers to the clients' problems instead of the therapist assisting clients to work out their own problems gradually? How crucial is it for therapists and clients to initially agree on goals?

Horn-George and Anchor (1982) studied the goals of both therapists and clients in dyads expected to be long-term (more than 20 sessions anticipated) and in dyads expected to be short-term (fewer than 15 sessions anticipated). In both types of dyads, independent assessments of therapists' and clients' perceptions of goals, behaviors, feelings about one another, and satisfaction were obtained after the fourth, sixth, eighth, and tenth sessions. Although overall there was greater agreement between therapists' and clients' views of goals in later sessions than in earlier ones, there was significantly greater agreement between those in dyads expected to be long-term. Individuals in these pairs showed greater agreement about the goals of therapy, their perceptions of what occurred in therapy sessions, and their feelings about each other. As noted in Chapter 4, such increased similarity has been consistently found to increase interpersonal attraction and further relationship development. Horn-George and Anchor found that in many cases, greater phenomenological consensus between the client and therapist (i.e., agreement about what happened in the therapy relationship) was present from the beginning of therapy in the long-term pairs. The fact that the same therapists were used in both the long- and short-term conditions suggests that the greater consensus in the long-term pairs resulted primarily from clients' goals, expectations, and perceptions being more consistent with those of long-term therapy.

If a major goal of brief psychotherapy is reduction of current distress, participants should value various interpersonal behaviors differently in short-term therapy than in long-term therapy. Consistent with such a view is Horn-George and Anchor's (1982) finding that short-term therapy dyads placed greater value on support and conformity than did long-term dyads. Support from the therapist and conformity to the therapist's recommendations may be particularly effective ways of reducing immediate distress. Independence was found to become increasingly valued over time. This is reasonable, since after the acute crises are dealt with, goals may shift. The fact that support and conformity are more valued in brief therapy may again suggest that therapeutic techniques will be more directive early in therapy or in short-term therapy. Horn-George and Anchor's results also suggest that to the extent congruence between therapist and client is necessary for effective therapy, attempts to match clients and therapists may be more important when brief therapy is anticipated.

In addition to this external factor of time, the goals of participants and their perceptions and feelings about one another also seem likely to be affected by the match between their cognitive styles. Because social perception is largely a process of cognitive categorization, a relationship should be facilitated if therapist and client use similar cognitive categories. Having similar cognitive styles and categories should also facilitate achieving consensus about goals and treatment procedures. Consequently, one would anticipate that similarity in the cognitive styles of clients and therapists will facilitate treatment. Consistent with this line of reasoning, both Carr (1970) and Hunt et al. (1985) found that the less therapist and client perceptions correlated with one another, the more likely premature termination of therapy became. In addition, the rate of improvement among clients who remained in therapy was slower in those who showed less cognitive agreement with their therapists. One interpretation of these results is that a certain degree of similarity in the perception of goals and behaviors is essential for the therapeutic process to be successful. When the perceptions of therapists and clients are too dissimilar, a period of time is needed for consensus to develop before therapy can succeed; if consensus is not achieved, therapy may be terminated.

Resources of Therapists and Clients

If we consider the resources that therapists and clients bring to the relationship, we encounter additional examples of its asymmetry. The therapist has knowledge and skills the client may lack. The fact that a person voluntarily seeks therapy implicitly acknowledges the fact that he or she lacks important supports or needs resources or knowledge. This asymmetry is recognized and may even be welcomed by clients as they attempt to find things out about a therapist prior to beginning therapy, as revealed in questions such as "How long has she been practicing?" and "Does he deal with problems like mine often?"

Part of therapy may thus involve clients acquiring new skills or learning new ways of applying or mobilizing the resources and skills they have. The difference in knowledge between therapist and client creates an initial difference in the social power available to them. In terms of French and Raven's (1959) bases of social power, the therapist has more expert, informational, and legitimate power. Since close relationships usually involve reciprocity and mutuality, such differences in social power may pose an initial barrier to the relationship between therapist and client.

By conveying empathy, respect, and concern for a client, the therapist may attempt to overcome the barrier posed by differences in social power. When clients feel respected and understood, they are less hesitant to become involved in therapy than if they feel powerless and dependent on another (the therapist) to make their decisions for them. Several studies demonstrate the positive effect of these factors on clients' satisfaction with therapy (e.g., Rudy, McLemore, & Gorsuch, 1985; Strupp, Fox, & Lessler, 1969). In their reviews of research relating therapist qualities to outcomes of therapy, Orlinsky and Howard (1978, 1986) found a positive relationship between clients' perceptions of therapist empathy, caring, and genuineness and treatment outcomes in a majority of studies.

Personal characteristics of the client, including his or her commitment to work with a therapist (Gomes-Schwartz, 1978), the ability to experience and express emotions in therapy, and willingness to engage in self-disclosure and self-exploration (Truax & Carkhuff, 1965), affect the development of a therapeutic relationship. Moreover, just as characteristics of the therapist may affect the likelihood that the client will behave in certain ways, so too can characteristics of a client influence the likelihood of various therapist behaviors. Although characteristics of both therapists and clients (or at least their expression) can be modified in the course of therapy, their presence at the beginning of therapy will influence the course of therapy and the development of the therapeutic relationship.

Expectations of Therapists and Clients

The way in which clients and therapists view each other, their relationship, and therapy will be influenced by the expectations and hypotheses they have about one another and about therapy (see also Chapter 3). A substantial literature exists demonstrating that therapeutic outcome may be positively or negatively affected by expectations of both clients and therapists regarding these outcomes (e.g., Kirsch, Tennen, Wickless, Saccone, & Cody, 1983; Shapiro, 1981).

What concerns us here is the manner in which expectations can influence the interpersonal behavior of therapists and clients and the relationship that develops between them. Recently, social psychologists have addressed the question of how beliefs and expectations about another can affect one's behavior toward the other in such a way that even erroneous beliefs are subsequently confirmed by the other's actions (see Snyder, 1984, for a review). Such behavioral confirmation of even erroneous beliefs involves the fact that people use their beliefs and expectations to set goals for their interactions and to plan and guide their behavior. Plans and behaviors are generally designed in a way that increases the likelihood they will elicit responses from another that confirm the original beliefs and expectations. This process has been demonstrated for both beliefs about another (e.g., Snyder & Swann, 1978) and beliefs about oneself (e.g., Swann & Read, 1981).

For an example of such a process consider an experiment conducted by Snyder, Tanke, and Berscheid (1977) based on the premise, discussed earlier, that physical attractiveness results in increased attraction. In their experiment, Snyder et al. had pairs of men and women engage in a telephone conversation. Prior to the conversation, males were shown a photograph of either an attractive or unattractive woman and told it was a picture of the woman they would be speaking with. The men who expected an attractive partner expected her to be more sociable, poised, humorous, and socially adept. Given the widespread nature of a physical attractiveness stereotype (Berscheid & Walster, 1974b; Dion, Berscheid, & Walster, 1972), it is reasonable to believe that both clients and therapists form similarly positive expectations on the basis of physical appearance. Judges who heard only the males' portion of the conversation rated men expecting an attractive partner as showing greater warmth, friendliness, and admiration for the other than those expecting an unattractive partner. Other naive judges, who heard only the women's portion of the conversation, rated her as friendlier, more likable, and more sociable when she had been speaking to a man who believed she was attractive. Thus, even though expectations about a partner's attractiveness were unrelated to the partner's actual attractiveness, they led subjects to behave in ways that subsequently confirmed the initial expectations.

A study by Piner and Berg (1987) suggests that beliefs and expectations about another's similarity may also influence dyadic behavior. Piner and Berg led pairs of subjects, prior to engaging in a conversation, to believe that they were similar or dissimilar in attitudes and values. Besides increasing attraction, anticipating interaction with a similar other should create the expectation that the other will understand and reciprocate one's behaviors. Consistent with this, subjects who believed they were similar reciprocated intimate disclosures more than those who thought their partner was dissimilar. In addition to intimacy, each subject's verbalizations were coded using Stiles's (1978) Verbal Response Modes for three indices of verbal familiarity: presumptiveness (e.g., advising and interpreting), attentiveness (e.g., questioning and acknowledging), and acquiescence (e.g., reflecting and confirming). Partners who believed they were similar matched one another more closely on all three familiarity indices compared to those who thought they were dissimilar, suggesting their interaction was more reciprocal, an important characteristic of close relationships. The implication for therapy is that if clients or therapists believe the other is similar, their conversations in therapy may also show greater reciprocity. Moreover, since reciprocity may be crucial to establishing a relationship, such behaviors can again contribute to initial beliefs about how similar the therapist and client are, as well as how well they will get along, becoming self-fulfilling.

Development of the Therapy Relationship

How might the various factors discussed in this book come together in the development of a relationship between therapist and client? If we examine various theories of relationship formation and development we find that almost all view development as a gradual process. For example, according to Levinger and Snoek (1972), intimate relationships arise as shared experiences and increasing degrees of mutuality develop. The implication is that such mutuality develops gradually over many encounters and interactions. That development of a relationship is a gradual process is also implied by filter theories (Kerckhoff & Davis, 1962; Murstein, 1970). According to these views, people pass through a succession of "filters" in forming a relationship. Initially, external characteristics such as appearance and proximity will be maximally important. If individuals pass this filter, issues such as attitudinal similarity and value consensus become paramount; finally, questions involving complementarity and role fit become central. Again, the implication is that relationship development is a gradual process.

Recently, an alternative approach was outlined by Berg and Clark (1986) suggesting that relationships that will become close may be distinguished from those that will not at a very early point in their development. Berg and Clark noted instances where persons who would develop a close relationship could be distinguished from those who would not from the first hour of interaction on. We will examine this idea in greater detail after discussing the most articulated of the gradual approaches to relationship development, namely, social penetration theory.

Social Penetration Theory: A "Gradual" Approach to Development

Social penetration theory (Altman & Taylor, 1973; Taylor & Altman, 1987) is the most complete example of a traditional approach to relationship development. Social penetration theory explicitly holds that the development of a relationship is gradual: "Social penetration processes proceed in a gradual and orderly fashion from superficial to intimate levels of exchange" (Taylor & Altman, 1987, p. 259). Moreover, the process may not be monotonic, since any desires for penetration and intimacy must be continually balanced against desires for privacy and control of another's access to highly personal information (see Altman, Vinsel, & Brown, 1981, and Chapter 7, this volume).

To understand the hypothesized developmental process, one must first understand the view of personality taken by social penetration theory. First, the theory views personality as encompassing all those categories of subjects relevant to the self (e.g., one's views and feelings about family, work, or relations with the opposite sex). Within each category, information about the self is arranged in a hierarchical fashion. At the periphery is information that is easily visible, common to many people, and socially acceptable. More intimate information is more central to the personality, less visible, and more unique to a particular person and often represents something the person considers a vulnerability and less socially desirable. For these reasons and because it is more affectively charged, intimate information is not generally disclosed to others unless one has a close relationship with them.

For example, consider information about family. It may be known immediately from one's accent where one's family lives and where one grew up. Similarly, it may be learned very quickly and rather easily how many brothers and sisters one has and one's current marital status. A person is less likely to divulge immediately what it was like growing up as the only child in a single-parent household and would probably have to have a close relationship before revealing that the reason for feeling happy at the death of a father was the memory of abuse during childhood. And it might take years for a person to disclose sexual feelings about her or his own children. The basic point is that in any topic area, information of different degrees of intimacy exists, and the process of relationship formation involves two people gradually penetrating these levels.

The process of penetration can be divided into four stages (Altman & Taylor, 1973; Taylor & Altman, 1987). In the initial stage of this process, *orientation*, interaction occurs at the periphery: individuals make little of themselves accessible to another. The information they reveal tends to be public, the interaction, tentative; they strive to avoid conflict and emotionality.

During the next stage, *exploratory affective exchange*, communication occurs involving peripheral aspects of self in many areas. Interactions are less formal and friendlier, and movement toward interactions of intermediate intimacy begins in one or two areas.

Relationships at the next stage, *affective exchange*, involve heightened activity at the intermediate intimacy levels. Although participants are cautious, there is relatively little resistance to revealing more intimate levels and aspects of self. Barriers are being broken down and participants are learning a great deal about one another.

At the final stage, *stable exchange*, relationships are characterized by openness across all aspects of personality and levels of intimacy. Participants know each other very well and can reliably predict each other's feelings and behavior.

Again, movement through these stages is hypothesized to be a gradual process. At all points, participants are evaluating the rewards and costs of interaction and making predictions about the rewards and costs of future interactions at the same or other levels of intimacy. If the forecast reward–cost ratio is favorable, the decision is made to continue interactions at the present or higher levels of intimacy. If the forecast reward–cost ratio is unfavorable, a person will reduce interaction intimacy or take steps to terminate the relationship. Although direct evidence on the point is lacking, it is tempting to hypothesize that these forecasts may operate in the self-fulfilling manner we saw earlier for other beliefs and expectations. For example, consider a client who is initially pleased during his or her early meetings with a therapist and believes the therapist has been supportive and helpful. This person is likely also to hypothesize that the therapist will continue to be a source of help. Expecting this, the client becomes more willing to disclose to the therapist, shows less resistance, and becomes increasingly likely to comply with any of the therapist's recommendations. Doing these things is likely to result in more successful outcomes, thus confirming the client's belief that such outcomes were forthcoming.

Attempting to apply social penetration theory to development of the relationship between client and therapist is complicated by several fundamental differences between this and other close relationships. Perhaps the most obvious of these differences is that in therapy disclosure is often not reciprocal: the client discloses much more and much more intimately than the therapist. For the therapy relationship, then, it seems less appropriate to talk about mutual penetration or the exchange of disclosures. Indeed, some clients may be sensitive to this asymmetry, saying to a therapist, "You know everything about me, but I don't know anything about you." Earlier in this chapter we noted other asymmetries (power and resources) that exist. In contrast, behavior, power, and resources are typically more symmetrical in the development of other close relationships.

One solution to the problem posed by asymmetry may involve therapist responsiveness (see Chapter 6). Although he or she may not self-disclose and may have more resources and greater power, the therapist can still try to convey to a client an interest in and an understanding of him or her. If the therapist succeeds, the client may perceive that a close relationship exists and begin acting in ways he or she would with a close friend (e.g., increased openness and accessibility). This implies that, to a degree, the development of a relationship is a phenomenon that occurs in the mind of the client. Anything a therapist can do to facilitate this perception should then facilitate therapy.

A second important difference between development of the client–therapist relationship and that of other close relationships is that in therapy clients will often reveal intimate information within the first hours of therapy. The stages of orientation and exploratory exchange that social penetration theory posits would appear to be lacking or at least greatly truncated in the case of therapy. This is not to say a client will disclose everything immediately. Highly sensitive information (e.g., homosexuality) may not be revealed until a therapist has convinced the client that she or he is accepted, respected, and understood. Qualities of the therapist and therapist responsiveness will again be important. The point we wish to emphasize now, however, is that in many cases, a relationship between therapist and client develops more rapidly than might be expected from application of social penetration or other traditional theories of relationship development.

The Impact of Schemata: A "Rapid" Approach to Development

An alternative to the view of gradual relationship development suggested by social penetration and other traditional theories was proposed by Berg and Clark (1986). In marked contrast to other theorists, Berg and Clark hypothesized that relationships that will become close can be distinguished from those that will not at a very early point in their development, sometimes within the first hour. In other words, people may know or decide at a very early point that they want a relationship to be a close one or that they do not want it to become close. If a close relationship is anticipated, they begin almost immediately to behave in ways that are characteristic of close relationships. At this early point, they begin to disclose more, disclose more intimately, show more concern with the other's needs, show decreased concern with reciprocity, and feel more positive toward the other (e.g., Berg, 1984; Berg & McQuinn, 1986; Clark & Mills, 1979; Clark, Mills, & Powell, 1986; Hays, 1984, 1985). Such a view would appear to explain the early appearance of intimate disclosure in therapy and the asymmetry of the therapist–client relationship better than that suggested by the traditional theories.

Berg and Clark (1986) suggest a possible rationale for early-appearing differences between dyads who will become close friends and those that will not: people may have scripts or schemata for relationships. A schema is a cognitive structure containing a person's organized knowledge about a particular situation or type of person; incoming information is referred to schemata. In social perception this process allows the individual to quickly identify a situation, know what events to expect and look for in that situation, make plans for obtaining new information, and plan actions and behavior (cf. Taylor & Crocker, 1981).

A particular schema or script may be applied because some aspect(s) of a current situation or interaction resembles central aspects of that schema. When a schema is evoked, it is applied in full, and all the aspects contained in the schema are assumed to be true in the present situation, regardless of whether or not the person has actually observed them. The person then begins acting as if all these attributes were in fact present. Note how such a process can underlie the effects of expectations that we noted earlier.

Schemata have been found to exist for love, commitment, and different kinds of relationships (K. Davis & Todd, 1985; Fehr, 1988). It is reasonable to expect that both therapists and clients have a schematic representation of psychotherapy. The therapist's schema will be more developed and differentiated than that of the client, because of her or his increased knowledge and experience. Nevertheless, the client's schema may be just as important in guiding goal setting, perceptions, expectations, and behaviors. It seems quite possible that the reason behind Horn-George and Anchor's (1982) finding that progress was slower when therapists and clients had different goals and Hunt and associates' (1985) finding on the importance of similar cognitive styles is that therapists and clients may have initially different schematic views of therapy and each other. Until such differences are reconciled it is unlikely that there could be much therapeutic progress, since schemata guide perceptions and actions. Consistent with the hypothesis that clients' schemata are less developed is a finding by Benbenishity (1988): greater discrepancies initially existed between expectations and perceptions of clients than of therapists (these initial discrepancies subsequently decreased). One interpretation of these findings would be that therapists' schemata are more developed, and initial discrepancies between expectations and perceptions are consequently smaller. Clients, on the other hand, may be in the process of developing a schema of therapy. (See also Chapter 2 on clients' and therapists' views of their roles in therapy.) There may be a large initial gap between expectations and perceptions, but as this schema develops, it begins to exert more influence, thus narrowing the gap.

An approach emphasizing rapid development would expect to find differences almost immediately between relationships that will become close and those that will not. Berg and Clark (1986) review a number of both experimental studies and longitudinal surveys of developing relationships that support this view of rapid differentiation. For example, Berg (1984), Berg and McQuinn (1986), and Hays (1984, 1985) all found greater disclosure at a very early point in dyads that later became close than in dyads that did not become close. Persons expecting a close relationship are more responsive to indications of a partner's sadness (Clark, Ouellette, Powell, & Milberg, 1987), more concerned with the other's needs (Clark et al., 1987), and less concerned with reciprocity (Clark & Mills, 1979) than those not expecting to become close.

The schemata of both therapists and clients for therapy seem likely to contain the same elements. For instance, they may include expectations that the client will disclose intimately and that the therapist will be concerned with the client's needs and responsive to his or her emotional state. Thus, when the client begins to disclose and the therapist is perceived as empathic, concerned, and responsive, intimate disclosure by the client may quickly follow. The therapist's response and the client's continued intimate disclosure are likely to reinforce the schematic view of both.

An approach emphasizing rapid relationship development would expect to find differences very early between client–therapist dyads that will be successful and those that will not. It would also expect that both clients and therapists will "know" that the relationship is going well or not at an early point.

Theories suggesting both gradual and rapid development recognize the central importance of self-disclosure, intimacy, rewards, and costs. Before attempting to describe the development of the therapist–client relationship further, we will briefly review the influence of these factors on the development of close relationships. At the same time, we will suggest both similarities and differences with their probable operation in the development of the therapy relationship.

Self-Disclosure and Intimacy

Because self-disclosure (at least by clients) is likely to be a central element of both therapists' and clients' schemata and because it also plays a central role in all theories of relationship development, a brief discussion of the role of disclosure in a developing therapist–client relationship is in order. Readers are also referred to discussions of self-disclosure in Chapters 6 and 7.

Social penetration theory emphasizes the role of reciprocity and changes in reciprocity when discussing the role of self-disclosure in relationship development. In initial encounters the *norm of reciprocity* is viewed as governing disclosures. This norm predicts that when a person receives disclosure from another, he or she feels obligated to return disclosure of a comparable amount and intimacy. Reciprocity is hypothesized to vary as a function of both the intimacy of disclosure topics and the stage of the relationship (Altman, 1973).

For topics of low intimacy, reciprocity is hypothesized to be maximal at the beginning of a relationship and to decrease thereafter. For intimate subjects, a curvilinear pattern is predicted: reciprocity is hypothesized to be maximal during the middle stages of relationship development as participants are developing trust in each other. Before this time, disclosure of intimate information is seen as inappropriate and is avoided. At later stages trust has already developed, so the recipient of intimate disclosure need not return intimate disclosure to discharge obligations and demonstrate her or his own trust. Altman (1973) suggests that late in a relationship's development the disclosure recipient becomes more likely to design his or her response specifically to issues raised by the discloser rather than reply with a new disclosure of his or her own.

Although studies of naturally occurring relationships have found patterns of disclosure that are generally consistent with this view (Derlega, Wilson, & Chaikin, 1976; Won-Doornick, 1979, 1985), in the case of the therapist–client relationship a quite different pattern may apply. Here, the position/role of the therapist and the total situation surrounding therapy imply that the therapist can be trusted and make reciprocity unnecessary to demonstrate the therapist's trustworthiness. Also, it may be important to therapeutic success to both encourage client disclosure and keep attention focused directly on the client and the issues she or he has raised. As noted in Chapter 6, a more appropriate way for doing this may be through demonstrating responsiveness rather than through reciprocal disclosure.

Studies that have demonstrated beneficial effects of therapist disclosure (e.g., Berg & Wright-Buckley, 1988; Bundza & Simonson, 1973; Jourard, 1971; Murphy & Strong, 1972) generally expose subjects to a disclosing or nondisclosing therapist *before* the subject discloses. Such initial disclosure by the therapist may function as a model of appropriate behavior, reduce ambiguity for the client, and increase initial trust in a therapist. However, if such initial disclosure by a therapist is too intimate, it may both not fit with a client's schema of therapy and violate his or her expectations of appropriate therapist behavior. Negative perceptions of the therapist with negative implications for therapy then result (Derlega, Lovell, & Chaikin, 1976; Simonson & Bahr, 1974).

One dyad member generally takes the lead in establishing the rate at which disclosure intimacy develops. This person discloses at a higher level of intimacy, and the other then reciprocates (J. Davis, 1976). In heterosexual relationships it is generally males who take the role of setting the pace (J. Davis, 1978; Derlega, Winstead, Wong, & Hunter, 1985), presumably because of social norms and expectations. In the case of therapy, the therapist will play a role in determining the rate at which intimate disclosure occurs. We noted earlier that the therapist will have greater social power and knowledge and that the schemata of both clients and counselors are likely to assign this role to the therapist because of his or her position and assumed knowledge. While therapists may not reciprocally disclose, they may use their disclosure to model desired behavior for a client or to set a tone for interaction. Most important, therapists can question the client and use responses to client verbalizations to reinforce disclosure on certain topics or of certain levels of intimacy (see Chapters 6 and 7).

M. Patterson's (1976) model of intimacy suggests a therapist's response to a client's disclosure may influence development of intimacy. According to Patterson, changes in intimacy produce changes in arousal. It is relatively easy to see how increases in arousal can accompany increases in the intimacy of clients' disclosures. If the arousal is negatively labeled (e.g., anxiety), attempts are made to reduce this negative emotional state (e.g., disclosing less or even terminating therapy). If a positive level is given (e.g., relief), further intimacy is facilitated. It is primarily the response of the therapist that will determine the label the client applies. In this regard we refer again to Horn-George and Anchor's (1982) finding that support was a particularly valued response early in therapy. It is at an early point that a client is likely to be most aroused when disclosing. A supportive response by the therapist increases the chances of this arousal being positively labeled.

Rewards, Costs, and Development

Anticipated benefits provide the motivation for attempting to develop relationships with others (see Chapter 3). Expanding on Thibaut and Kelley's (1959) exchange theory, social penetration theory considers five separate aspects of rewards and costs. First is the reward–cost ratio, or the balance of positive and negative events. If there are more rewards than costs and the magnitude of rewards exceeds the magnitude of costs, the relationship will be satisfying. The greater the size of rewards relative to costs, the faster relationship development is hypothesized to be. Although intimate self-disclosure is important for the formation of close relationships and particularly in the therapeutic relationship, Rosenfeld (1979) notes that it may often be perceived as a cost by the discloser; intimate information often involves a weakness that is undesirable and that disclosers feel makes them different. Embarrassment or even potential future harm could follow (see Chapter 7).

In therapy, it will be the reaction of the therapist to client disclosure that primarily determines whether disclosure is viewed as a cost or not. Given other costs of the clients, a therapist's response may thus have a substantial effect on the reward–cost ratio and the speed with which the therapeutic relationship develops.

A second dimension to rewards and costs noted by social penetration theory is their *absolute magnitude*. Given equivalent numbers of rewards and costs in alternative relationships, a person will prefer the relationship that provides the largest amount of reward. The reward–cost ratio and the absolute magnitude of rewards appear to be relatively straightforward applications of Thibaut and Kelley's views regarding the comparison level and comparison level for alternatives (see Chapter 3).

Social penetration theory also distinguishes between *immediately experienced* and *delayed* rewards and costs. In therapy a client will often experience some costs (e.g., expenditure of effort and money, embarrassment) almost immediately. Rewards, at least in terms of a reduction in symptoms or distress, however, may not be experienced for some time. The apparently negative reward–cost ratio that results for the client may be offset by the therapist offering support and acting in a responsive fashion (see Chapter 6). By conveying interest and understanding, the therapist provides the client with immediate rewards that can motivate him or her to continue the therapeutic process. The immediacy of rewards appears especially important at the start of a relationship (McLaughlin, Cody, & Rosenstein, 1983). If so, the immediacy of rewards would be another reason behind Horn-George and Anchor's (1982) finding that supportive behaviors are particularly valued early in therapy.

Forecasts or *predicted rewards and costs* provide a fourth aspect of rewards and costs. According to social penetration theory it is the anticipation of future rewards that motivates people to increase the intimacy of their interactions and self-disclosures. Presumably, such forecasts are made on the basis of rewards and costs previously experienced in the relationship. A more schematic view might hold that once a relationship is identified as a particular type, the schema for that type of relationship specifies both the amounts and types of rewards and costs one will experience and when one will experience them. By deciding to enter into that type of relationship, the person is implicitly agreeing to the rewards and costs specified; the continuous process of evaluating rewards and costs and, on this basis, continually assessing whether or not to increase interaction intimacy would be eliminated. Instead, the decision would be made early that this kind of relationship, involving these rewards and costs, is desired. Once the decision to pursue this kind of relationship is made, the person begins to follow her or his script for that type of relationship. Unless something occurs that causes the person to question use of the script (e.g., an unexpected amount of effort is required or another's actions depart from what is expected), there is no need to repeatedly revise expectations and forecasts (cf. Langer, 1978). A view like the one we have just described would underscore the value of therapists and clients agreeing on goals and establishing expectations at the outset of therapy.

The *cumulative aspect of rewards and costs* is the final one distinguished by social penetration theory. The cumulative aspect represent the history of reward–cost experiences in a relationship. If a person has previously experienced a surplus of rewards in a relationship, present experiences in which costs outweight rewards will have less of a detrimental effect, because a reserve of positive experiences is available to draw on. Because there is no such history in the therapist–client relationship until later in therapy, this may be another reason for supportive behaviors of the therapist being particularly valued early in therapy.

An additional aspect to rewards is suggested by the work of Clark and her colleagues (e.g., Clark, 1984; Clark et al., 1986, 1987; Clark & Mills, 1979; Mills & Clark, 1982). Clark's research indicates that those who desire a close relationship will be less concerned with keeping track of individual outcomes and more concerned with meeting the other person's needs. Although studies of naturally occurring friendships suggest provision of needed or highly desired resources may not occur until later in a relationship (Berg, 1984; Berg & McQuinn, 1986), a study by L. Miller, Berg, and Rugs (1983) suggests this may be the case because time is often required to learn exactly what resources a partner most needs or wants. In the case of therapy, however, the knowledge and experience of a therapist may allow him or her to know early in therapy what resources a client needs. Providing these needed resources or the means by which the client can obtain them raises the reward–cost ratio of the client, increases his or her absolute amount of reward, and is most likely consistent with what he or she has expected to gain from therapy. Providing the client with access to needed rewards not only furthers the development of a therapist–client relationship, it is precisely the purpose of therapy.

Consider the following scenario of the operation of rewards and costs in therapy: A male client at the outset of therapy is experiencing a negative reward–cost ratio in life. The amount of reward he is receiving is so low that he decides to seek help. Although he may express this in different terms, the fact that his costs have been in excess of rewards is what leads him to seek therapy. Based on his goals, perceptions of therapy, and expectations, he elects to see a therapist. At the beginning the client's perceptions and expectations are probably based primarily on stereotypic views of therapy, on information from others he knows who have been in therapy, and on initial impressions derived from seeing the clinic and interactions with an appointment secretary. It is likely that these expectations include anticipating that he will have to disclose intimately, thus incurring possible costs of embarrassment in addition to the expenditure of time and money. The client also expects that a therapist will provide rewards that offset these costs by being supportive and helping him cope with difficulties. In the therapy relationship, in contrast to most relationships, disclosure depth may precede disclosure breadth. Within the first therapy session, the client may be disclosing relatively intimate information that he rarely tells others. This intimacy may correspond to what would normally occur only when the affective exchange stage of relationship development is reached. The risks of such disclosure are lessened because of the nature of the therapy situation and its assured confidentiality. In addition, the client's schema of therapy leads him to anticipate intimate disclosure. Because the therapist's knowledge and experience may include a great deal of information about clients with a similar type of problem, the therapist can know much about the client and be able to accurately and quickly predict his reactions. Such knowledge and ability to predict a partner's reactions corresponds to the final stage of social relationship development, according to social penetration theory (stable exchange). In our scenario of a therapy situation this stage has been achieved very quickly.

When a therapist responds to client disclosures by conveying empathy and understanding, clients experience rewards and are encouraged to continue to explore intimate aspects of the disclosure topic and of other topics. While the client may make initial tests to see whether a therapist is likely to be supportive before she or he brings up the subject that actually brought her or him to therapy, the point is that in the therapy situation intimate disclosure about an issue comes before increased breadth. The phenomenon that depth precedes breadth of disclosure early in therapy is contrary to what is proposed by theories that view relationship formation as gradual. Such a phenomenon would, however, fit with theories that view relationships as forming rapidly or as a result of applying schemata.

Early Indications of a Viable Therapeutic Relationship

If theories viewing relationship development as a process that occurs relatively quickly are accurate, it should be possible to find differences between more and less successful therapist–client pairs early in the process of therapy. This does not imply, however, that *all* relevant differences are present full-blown at the start of treatment. Initially, both therapists and clients may engage in a forecasting process, trying to evaluate each other and their relationship. Given the tendency of hypotheses to be self-fulfilling (as discussed earlier), subsequent effects of these forecasts and evaluations on perceptions and affect should appear. It should also be possible to detect differences in the personal characteristics and behaviors of both therapists and clients in more and less successful dyads early in therapy. These differences should correspond to factors that are theoretically important in relationship formation.

One factor we would expect to influence early development of a client–therapist relationship is the schema of therapy of both the client and the therapist. While studies exist that have examined the effects of clients' and therapists' expectations, we do not know of work that has attempted to directly apply the theories and methods of social cognition to the therapy relationship. Research examining the schemata of therapists and clients and the effects of these schemata on the therapy process would be useful.

Malan (1976) holds that establishment of a strong therapeutic relationship early in therapy will be crucial for a successful outcome (particularly in brief therapies). If this is true, it should then be possible to identify factors that are predictive of either a positive or negative outcome at a very early point in the therapeutic process.

Luborsky, McLellan, Woody, O'Brien, and Auerbach (1985) performed just such a study investigating early-appearing indications of therapeutic success. This study investigated two general therapist characteristics relevant to forming a viable therapeutic relationship—interest in helping people and psychological health and skill—and a number of client demographic factors (e.g., age and education). Therapists' and clients' assessments of the therapeutic relationship (e.g., degree to which therapy and therapist have been helpful) were obtained after the third therapy session. Three treatments or therapies were also studied: therapy focusing on specific needs and contacting providers of services to meet these needs, psychodynamic therapy focusing on supportiveness and working through of underlying problems, and cognitive–behavioral therapy. In addition, ratings were made of the extent to which therapists consistently applied a given therapy (purity). Clients were drawn from a drug treatment program and had no pretreatment diagnosis of organic brain damage or psychosis. Outcomes were assessed 7 months following the conclusion of treatment.

Consider the relevance of these factors to development of a therapeutic relationship. First, the therapist characteristics—interest in helping others and adjustment and skill—should increase the likelihood that a relationship will form. Demographic characteristics of clients should exert much less influence on relationship formation. If the therapist–client relationship forms relatively quickly and is essential to success, assessments of it following the third therapy session, if valid, should be predictive of outcomes. Among the various therapies studied by Luborsky et al., one would expect that relationships should be more likely to form in either the psychodynamic treatment or the cognitive–behavioral therapy than in therapy in which attention is focused primarily on specific needs and services. The first two approaches should thus show higher correlations with outcome than the third. Finally, if a client's schema for therapy is poorly developed initially, the consistency or purity of a therapist's application of a particular technique should facilitate the client's formation of a schema similar to that of the therapist and should thus be predictive of outcome. Although the mediating processes we propose were not assessed, the correlations with outcome were consistent with all the aforementioned expectations.

The variable of client involvement in the first three therapy sessions has been explored by O'Malley, Suh, and Strupp (1983) and rated from tapes of those sessions. Although client involvement in the first session was not strongly related to outcome as rated by therapists, clients, or an outside clinician, involvement was significantly related to all three ratings of outcome by the third session. So while these results suggest that a client's willingness to participate in therapy can be an important determinant of outcome, they also suggest that it is not the pretherapy willingness of the client that is crucial. Rather, it is the way this develops in the course of therapy, presumably as a function of the therapist. Note, however, that the important development, client involvement, appears to have occurred rather quickly.

Just as factors associated with either the client, the therapist, or their interaction may be predictive of a positive relationship and good outcomes, other aspects of the client, the therapist, or their interaction will impede relationship development and be predictive of poor outcomes. For example, Hadley and Strupp (1976) found poor motivation and low ego strength to be commonly cited negative client factors. Negative therapist factors include such things as excessive need to make people change and hostility. In addition, there may be what Sachs (1983) refers to as errors in treatment (e.g., presentation of poorly timed or destructive interventions and passive acceptance of problematic aspects of clients' behavior or attitudes).

Sachs (1983) investigated the influence of negative factors during the early stages of therapy. From audiotapes of the first three therapy sessions of 18 college students seen by one of seven professional therapists, judges rated negative client factors, negative therapist factors, errors in treatment, and deficiencies in the client–therapist relationship and interaction. These ratings were made for each of the first three therapy sessions and correlated with an overall improvement score formed from posttherapy ratings of therapists, clients, and a clinical observer. For ratings from the first session, only errors in treatment had a significant negative correlation with outcome. By the third session negative client characteristics and deficiencies in interaction had also come to show a significant negative relation to outcome.

As in Sachs's (1983) study, differences between more and less successful therapy dyads appear quite early. The fact that errors in treatment were predictive of poor outcomes from the first session on and the fact that client and relationship factors came to be predictive soon after make it tempting to speculate on a causal mechanism. Perhaps errors in treatment (deficiencies in the therapist's application of resources) impeded establishment of a therapeutic relationship, which then led to a decline in client involvement and motivation. This also seems consistent with Luborsky and associates' (1985) finding on the relationship between outcomes and the consistency with which a therapeutic technique is applied.

Saltzman et al. (1976) investigated therapists' and clients' feelings and their perceptions of a number of factors relevant to a therapist–client relationship and related these to the likelihood that a client would continue in therapy versus terminate prematurely. Reports obtained immediately following the first, third, and fifth therapy sessions are considered. At different times, different factors were found to distinguish maximally those who dropped out of therapy from those who remained. Clients who dropped out after the first session reported significantly *less* anxiety than those who continued. Saltzman et al. (1976) suggest that those dropping out so early were relatively apathetic or had strong defenses against anxiety. In either case, it seems unlikely these low-anxiety clients would forecast the rewards available in therapy to be higher than those available elsewhere.

The greatest number of dropouts in the Saltzman et al. study were found following the third session. At that point client reports indicated that those who dropped out compared to remainers felt that (1) the therapist respected them less as a person, (2) they had less understanding of what the therapist was trying to convey, (3) they could disclose less, (4) they were less confident of the therapist's ability and commitment, (5) the therapeutic relationship was no different from other relationships, (6) they were not involved in a continuing relationship and thought less about it outside of therapy sessions (continuity), and (7) they were not making progress in solving their problem. Rather than immediately dismissing these findings ("If this is how they felt, no wonder they left"), consider for a moment that these feelings and perceptions did not distinguish the session one dropouts from those who remained in therapy. Rather, these feelings and perceptions appeared *after* a relatively *short* amount of interaction with the therapist. Apparently, these clients revised their initial forecasts very quickly and then acted. Although there were far fewer dropouts after the fifth session, those who did leave reported feeling less respect from the therapist and thought less about therapy outside of the therapy sessions.

Therapists' reports following the first session also distinguished dropouts from continuers. Therapists of clients who dropped out at this time felt less concern for the client, felt the client relied on them less, and felt the client was less able to make progress. Remembering that clients who left at this point reported less anxiety, one can only speculate on whether a lower than average amount of client anxiety led to these therapist feelings or whether clients used increased defense mechanisms to combat anxiety when a therapist was not showing as much concern as they expected.

After the third session therapists' ratings of dropouts compared to remainers were lower on therapist respect, therapist understanding, openness, involvement, and continuity. In addition, therapists reported feeling fewer emotions and felt the client had a poorer prognosis. After the fifth session dropouts were distinguished by lower therapist reports of respect, involvement, and continuity. Again, we can only speculate on the degree these perceptions of the therapist may have had causal influence on a client's perceptions and vice versa. The important point here is that we not only have very quickly appearing differences for both client and therapist but also evidence that the differences may be related to each other in a conceptually meaningful way that allows us to see the interdependence of clients and therapists. It is very likely that the client feelings we described may impact on the therapist to produce the differences in therapist feelings and perceptions about clients who drop out versus those who remain in therapy that were noted. Similarly, the therapist differences can impact on clients to produce their feelings.

Conclusions

Two general approaches to relationship development appear in the literature. The traditional approach, best exemplified by social penetration theory, views the development of a relationship as a gradual process. A more recent alternative holds that relationships that will become close can be identified and distinguished from relationships that will not become close at a very early point. Some evidence can be found in the relationship literature supporting both approaches (cf. Berg & Clark, 1986, and Taylor & Altman, 1987).

The gradual approach emphasizes the repeated evaluation and forecasting of future rewards and costs together with reciprocity and the gradual development of trust. An approach favoring rapid differentiation emphasizes the existence of cognitive schemata or scripts for relationships. When aspects of interaction evoke a script for a particular type of relationship, a person quickly begins to act as if the present interaction were that type of relationship.

This chapter reviewed research on counseling and therapy that indicates successful therapist–client pairs can be distinguished from less successful ones at an early point in therapy. Such evidence is more consistent with the view of relationship development that emphasizes rapid differentiation.

What is it about therapy that might evoke a client's schema for a close relationship? The client will certainly have expectations when entering therapy. Although these may be based only on movies or books, they are likely to lead the client to expect talking about very personal things and to expect the therapist to be concerned with him or her. Personal disclosure and concern for another's needs are two factors that distinguish close relationships. A therapist's response to a client can reinforce these initial expectations. When the client perceives that the therapist accepts, understands, and respects him or her, more of the factors that distinguish close relationships are present in the therapy interaction. Although the therapist does not reciprocally disclose, concern with reciprocity is *not* a characteristic of close relationships.

The therapy relationship thus contains a number of factors that characterize other close relationships. Upon experiencing these factors, a client is likely to view her or his relationship with the therapist as similar to other close relationships and begin treating it like a close one.

Although empirical evidence is lacking, we would be remiss if we did not at least mention what might elicit a schema for a therapist. We do not think it is uncommon for a therapist to think after spending only a little time with a client either "This will be a tough one" or "I can really help here." Both responses imply the therapist has certain expectations for the relationship. Perhaps when a client appears defensive or resistant or seems reluctant to disclose, a therapist expects the client to be difficult to deal with. Likewise, the therapist could form positive hypotheses on the basis of a client's initial behavior. Regardless of their valence, such hypotheses may become self-fulfilling in the manner described earlier.

The lesson to be derived from this discussion is the importance of what occurs in early therapy sessions for the ultimate success of therapy. Future investigations of counseling and psychotherapy could profitably devote increased attention to attempts to directly relate client and therapist behaviors that occur early in therapy to client and therapist perceptions of their relationship and to ultimate therapy outcomes. Work is also needed that demonstrates empirically what the contents of clients' and therapists' schemata for therapy include and that applies the theories of social cognition to therapy more directly than have past studies.

CHAPTER 6

Responsiveness in the Therapy Relationship

In other chapters in this book we have addressed the influence of attraction, exchange, privacy, and development of relationships between therapists and clients. Underlying all these issues is a very basic question: How do therapists and clients communicate their feelings about one another? If it is important for the client to perceive the therapist as genuine, understanding, and concerned with her or him as a person, how are such perceptions fostered? Similarly, how do clients demonstrate that they understand what the therapist is attempting to communicate? It is questions like these that concern us in this chapter.

In recent years, several investigators in the area of personal relationships have applied the concept of responsiveness to the communications and social exchange behaviors of those who are in the process of developing a close relationship. Because we view the relationship that develops between clients and therapists as a special example of a close relationship, we believe responsiveness on the part of both clients and therapists will be equally important for this relationship. In exploring the applicability of the concept of responsiveness to therapy, we will first discuss the various ways the concept has been used by those studying close relationships and the consequences that have been shown to follow from responsive actions. Then we will employ the concept of responsiveness to understand and integrate findings drawn directly from the literature on counseling and psychotherapy and suggest directions for future investigation.

What Is Responsiveness?

Kelley (1979) and Kelley and Thibaut (1978) hypothesized that one of the primary characteristics of a close relationship is that those involved in such a relationship are responsive to one another's outcomes. By this is meant that when planning actions, people will be concerned not only with the rewards they are likely to receive but also with the rewards the partner will receive. In the earlier discussion of social exchange (see Chapter 3), we noted how clients and therapists might apply a *max joint transformation* to the pattern of rewards and costs in their relationship. When this happens, one person receives rewards whenever the other is benefited. We noted that when this happens, the partners "transform" their pattern of interdependency. Actions are then based on what is likely to provide the greatest reward for them as a pair rather than for each as an individual. By doing this, therapist and client show themselves to be responsive to the other's outcomes. Such a max joint transformation can facilitate the development of a therapy relationship.

In an extensive series of studies investigating communal and exchange relationships (e.g., Clark, 1984; Clark & Mills, 1979; Clark, Mills, & Powell, 1986; Clark, Ouellette, Powell, & Milberg, 1987; Mills & Clark, 1982), Clark and her colleagues have employed the term *responsiveness* in a similar fashion. To summarize Clark's conclusions briefly, communal relationships correspond to what are generally viewed as close relationships such as those that exist between close friends or family members. These relationships operate according to a norm of mutual responsiveness. Each participant is obligated to attempt to meet the other person's needs without an expectation that he or she will be compensated directly for these efforts. In a communal relationship, receiving a benefit from another does not impose any new obligation on the recipient to repay or return a comparable resource; the obligation of a recipient remains the same as before. She or he is obligated to attempt to meet the other's needs when they occur. Also, since communal relationships are expected to be continuing ones where participants care about each other, it is easier to disclose one's feelings and needs to another when one has a communal relationship with the partner. Since in a communal relationship the other is sensitive to one's feelings, monitors one's needs, and is concerned with trying to meet them, it is likely the sought-for aid will be willingly provided.

In contrast, exchange relationships (which correspond to business relationships or relationships between casual acquaintances) operate according to the norm of reciprocity. They are expected to be of relatively short duration, participants are not concerned with the other's needs, and receiving any benefit obligates the recipient to quickly return a resource to repay his or her benefactor.

Psychotherapy occupies a unique position because it contains some elements of both communal and exchange relationships. On one hand, it has been our premise throughout this book that much of the therapy process can be described and understood through applying constructs drawn from the literature on close relationships. The therapy relationship appears similar in many ways to Clark's communal relationship. The therapist is by definition concerned with monitoring clients' needs and providing conditions that will enable clients to meet their own needs. The therapist's concern about the client's welfare is not necessarily linked to being paid for providing the service. Clients in successful therapy relationships often care about the therapist and what the therapist thinks of them, and they are able to disclose personal feelings and needs. All of these are characteristic features of communal relationships. On the other hand, therapy is often understood from the outset to be of a fixed and relatively short duration. In addition, it cannot be denied that it contains elements of a business relationship, since clients exchange money in return for the therapist's services. These latter features are clearly more characteristic of exchange relationships.

It seems that some aspects of communal relationships will be essential if therapy is to be effective. Since exchange issues such as fees and duration are likely to be salient at the outset of therapy, therapists need to find a way to increase the likelihood clients will act in communal, rather than exchange, ways. This is complicated by the fact that often it is difficulty attempting to form or maintain close relationships that has led the client to seek therapy. Some indications of how therapists may help clients come to view the therapy relationship as close and communal are suggested in the work of D. Davis and Perkowitz (1979) and L. Miller and Berg (1984) on responsiveness.

In their investigation of communication in the acquaintanceship process, D. Davis and Perkowitz (1979) define *responsiveness* as the extent that a reply to another's communication meets three implicit demands of conversation: (1) that a response be given; (2) that this response address the content of the preceding communication; and

(3) that the response be of a degree of elaboration appropriate to the situation and the original speaker. To these, D. Davis and Holtgraves (1984) added a fourth condition: (4) that the time elapsing between the initial communication and the reply be appropriate. This is very similar to L. Miller and Berg's (1984) concept of *conversational responsiveness*, which is defined as behaviors made by the recipient of communication through which that recipient demonstrates interest in and understanding of the other. L. Miller and Berg note that perceptions of responsiveness will be based on three separate aspects of a response. The first is content (what is said); this satisfies the demands for a respone that addresses previous communicative content and is of appropriate elaboration (D. Davis & Perkowitz, 1979). Also, it is crucial for a person to indicate interest in and understanding of another through what he or she says. While this might be done by discussing the same topic the initial speaker raised, it may be done in other ways, too. For example, one might express concern for the other or disclose at a comparable level of intimacy. By doing these, a person is responding to the latent content of the other's communication. One can sometimes indicate understanding of another by bringing up a topic one has reason to believe the other is interested in but is reluctant to raise. A therapist who provides an insightful interpretation for the client may also be demonstrating responsiveness (i.e., understanding) along the content dimension.

The second aspect of a response that will affect perceptions of responsiveness is the style of action (how something is done). This would include all those signals commonly called "listener cues" as well as nonverbal and paraverbal aspects of conversation. In fact, these may influence a listener's impression of a speaker more than what a person says (Gladis, 1985; Mehrabian, 1972). The third aspect of a response to influence judgments of responsiveness is the timing of an action, that is, when it occurs in relation to the action of another. In general, the longer the delay, the less responsive an act is likely to be.

While there appears to be relatively little conflict between the elaborations of responsiveness made by D. Davis and Perkowitz (1979) and L. Miller and Berg (1984), they do emphasize different aspects of the concept. D. Davis and Perkowitz emphasize the relationship of a response's content to another's previous behaviors. L. Miller and Berg emphasize that a response should convey interest or understanding of the other in order to be responsive. D. Davis and Perkowitz appear to be concerned primarily with the actual behaviors offered in reply to another, whereas L. Miller and Berg focus more on the intentions of the person giving the response, that is, whether she or he expresses interest and concern.

D. Davis (1982) and Berg (1987) have noted several effects expected to follow from responsive statements that are important for the therapy process. Among these effects are the following: (1) the continuation of interactions, (2) the maintenance of interaction focus; (3) a reduction in stress for the initial speaker; (4) facilitation of more self-disclosure by the initial speaker; (5) increased attraction for the respondent; and (6) an increased probability that the two persons will develop a close relationship. All of these are factors that we have discussed throughout this book and that we believe are crucial to an effective therapist–client relationship and successful therapy. The following section will review research on responsiveness in reference to L. Miller and Berg's (1984) definition of responsiveness, which includes content, style, and timing.

Review of Research on Responsiveness

Responsive Content

The vast majority of research on responsiveness is concerned with the content dimension. D. Davis and Perkowitz (1979) varied the proportion of times a confederate chose to answer a question after subjects had answered one and the proportion of times the confederate chose to answer the same question the subject had as opposed to a different one. In this way they varied both the probability that a communication recipient would make a response and the degree that the response would address the content of a preceding communication. D. Davis and Perkowitz found that as the proportion both of trials on which the confederate chose to answer a question and of trials on which the same question was answered increased, so did subjects' attraction to the confederate and their feeling of having a relationship with the confederate.

D. Davis and Holtgraves (1984) had subjects view a political debate in which the responsiveness of a candidate's answers was varied by manipulating the question that preceded the answer. Half the time the eliciting question was such that the candidate's remarks directly addressed it (more responsive) and half the time the question was such that the same answer addressed it only indirectly (less responsive). As predicted, subjects' impressions of the candidate were more positive in the former case.

Berg and Archer (1980) manipulated the responsiveness of a reply's content in a different way. Their subjects read a description of a first encounter in which the recipient of a self-disclosure replied by making either a reciprocal or nonreciprocal disclosure of her own or by expressing concern for the discloser and willingness to listen if she wished to say more about the issue she had raised. The expression of concern and willingness to listen was the clearest indication of interest in the discloser and understanding of her feelings; thus, it was the most responsive of the replies. The next most responsive was a disclosure of comparable intimacy but on a different topic, and least responsive was a reply in which neither topic nor intimacy was similar to that of the discloser. In line with the expectations noted earlier, subjects were most attracted to the respondent and rated her as warmer, more adjusted, and more trustworthy when she expressed concern. Next in terms of favorability was the respondent who made a return disclosure of matching intimacy but on a different topic. This response matched the emotional, if not the manifest, content of the first speaker's remarks. The least favorable impressions were formed by the respondent who made a disclosure of disparate intimacy on a different topic (the least responsive reply). In a related study Berg and Archer (1983) found that intimate disclosure led to more attraction than nonintimate disclosure only when it dealt with the same topic as a subject's previous disclosure. Finally, Berg and Archer (1982) found that when subjects were given the goal of maximizing their attractiveness to another subject, they showed the greatest degree of responsiveness, matching both the topical content and the intimacy of the other's communication.

The results of all these studies dealing with responsive content clearly warn against the stereotypic image of the silent psychotherapist who listens and accepts everything but says little. Instead, they suggest that development of a therapeutic relationship requires that a therapist demonstrate interest and understanding of both the manifest and emotional issues raised by a client.

Responsive Style

Responsive style can involve the use of eye contact, smiles, and head nods, as well as other nonverbal signals typically classified under the heading of "listener cues." For a speaker, responsive style involves modulations in the paraverbal aspects of speech, the affect that is expressed, and the use of questions. Although no direct investigations of responsive style have been done, indirect evidence on the importance of this class of variables comes from several sources. L. Miller, Berg, and Archer (1983) developed the Opener Scale to identify individuals who were best able to elicit disclosure from others. Persons who score high on this scale report greater interest in listening to others and encouraging others to talk and the ability to make others feel relaxed and trusting. In an analogue of interviewing, persons who scored either above or below the median on the Opener Scale asked a series of five questions to other subjects who had been classified as either dispositionally high or low self-disclosers. In examining the intimacy of the interviewees' answers to these questions, an interaction between the Opener Scale status of the interviewer and the disclosure status of the interviewee was found. If the interviewee was a dispositionally high self-discloser, she disclosed at the same level regardless of the Opener Scale status of the interviewer. However, when the interviewee was a low self-discloser, she disclosed more intimately when the interviewer was one who scored high on the Opener Scale. In this circumstance, the low self-discloser was just as intimate as the interviewee who was typically a high discloser. In a second study L. Miller et al. (1983) found that high scorers on the Opener Scale were better liked and more likely to be disclosed to by others in natural settings. These findings may have particular relevance for the therapy process. Not only is client disclosure essential to successful therapy, but deficits in the ability or opportunity to disclose to others or receive confidences from them may have contributed to the problems that led the person to seek therapy. If the therapist has the skills of one who scores high on the Opener Scale, he or she will be more likely to receive disclosures even if the client normally has difficulty disclosing. For clients with difficulty developing and/or maintaining relationships, learning such social skills from the therapist may also be beneficial.

Stylistic differences between low and high scorers on the Opener Scale must have accounted for the results found by L. Miller et al. (1983) because all interviewers asked the same five questions. Differences could only have resulted from the order in which low compared to high scorers on the Opener Scale chose to ask these questions and/ or their use of the various "listener cues." More direct evidence of differences in conversational style between low and high scorers on the

Opener Scale is provided by Purvis, Dabbs, and Hopper (1984). These investigators videotaped low and high scorers who were conversing. Judges who watched videotapes without sound reported that high scorers nonverbally displayed more enjoyment, comfort, and attentiveness while talking to their partner. Male subjects who scored high on the Opener Scale also used more "simultaneous speech" than did male low scorers; that is, they interjected a brief sound while the partner is talking (e.g., saying "Uh huh"). These stylistic skills contribute to how a listener demonstrates interest in and understanding of a speaker and, thus, are responsive behaviors.

Timing and Responsiveness

The third aspect of responsiveness noted by L. Miller and Berg (1984) is timing. An experiment by Piner, Berg, and Miller (1986) is the only study to date that has attempted to investigate the effects of timing of a reply on perceptions of responsiveness. The researchers hypothesized that timing would intensify differences between responsive and unresponsive content. In other words, an unresponsive statement will appear particularly unresponsive and responsive content will appear even more responsive when they immediately follow another's communication than when a period of time intervenes between the initial communication and the reply. Piner et al. (1986) tested this prediction by having subjects read about an interaction in which a woman initially revealed that her father was an alcoholic and implied that he abused her. The recipient of this disclosure made either a more responsive reply (expressed concern and a willingness to listen if the revealer wanted to talk) or a less responsive statement (asked if the discloser wanted to see a movie with her). These responses were reported to have been made either immediately following the discloser's statement or after a period of time.

The expression of concern and willingness to listen was viewed as more responsive and as indicating more interest in and understanding of the discloser's feelings when it was made immediately than when time intervened between the original communication and the reply. Just the opposite pattern was found when the less responsive reply was made. Asking the discloser if she wanted to see a movie was viewed as less responsive and indicating less interest and understanding when it

was made immediately instead of after a delay. In addition, the immediate responsive statement led subjects to infer that the respondent had
the goal of helping the discloser and produced a more positive impression and greater attraction. Although no experimental evidence exists,
we hypothesize that timing will have a similar effect in intensifying
stylistic indicators of responsiveness. For instance, nonverbal displays
of concern and attentiveness (as in Purvis and associates' 1984 study)
will be greeted most favorably when they occur concurrently or immediately after the partner speaks than if some time intervenes.

Consequences of Responsiveness and Therapist Behavior

When a client perceives a therapist to be responsive, the effects
that follow are precisely those necessary for effective therapy and the
client should come to see the relationship with the therapist as more of
a communal and less of an exchange relationship. The effects that
follow from responsive actions have been described in the literature
(e.g., Berg, 1987; D. Davis, 1982; D. Davis & Perkowitz, 1979). Most
important for the therapy relationship are the following consequences
of responsive acts by the therapist: (1) a maintenance of interaction and
interaction focus, (2) a reduction in stress for the client, (3) increased
attraction to the therapist, (4) facilitation of disclosure by the client,
and (5) an increased perception that therapist and client have a close
relationship. If therapy is to be effective, a therapeutic relationship
must be established and the client must self-disclose. Because such
disclosures are likely to be stressful and/or embarrassing for clients, it
is important for the therapist to reduce interaction stress and help the
client focus on his or her problems. By acting in a responsive manner
the therapist will be able to accomplish these goals.

Since the effects that follow from responsive action are also therapeutic goals, therapists should be motivated to act in a responsive
manner, and one should find numerous examples in the clinical
literature in which therapist qualities and behaviors that facilitate
therapy can be explained in terms of responsiveness. In this section, we
will reexamine therapist variables in terms of their relation to responsiveness. What therapist behaviors and characteristics are most likely
to convey responsiveness? To what extent can responsiveness encompass and explain different findings about therapist behaviors?

Self-Disclosing and Self-Involving Statements

An extensive body of work exists dealing with how therapists can use self-disclosure to facilitate self-disclosure by clients (see Chapter 7, this volume, as well as Doster & Nesbitt, 1979, and S. Hendrick, 1987, for reviews). As S. Hendrick (1987) notes, the question at present concerns not whether therapists should or should not disclose to clients but, rather, when and how much they should self-disclose.

Experiments investigating the effects of therapist disclosure (often based on analogue techniques) have almost always exposed subjects to a disclosing or nondisclosing therapist prior to or at the start of a therapy session. Many studies (e.g., Anchor & Sandler, 1976; Berg & Wright-Buckley, 1988; Bundza & Simonson, 1973; Carkhuff & Pierce, 1967; Doster & Brooks, 1974; Graff, 1970; Halverson & Shore, 1969; Jourard, 1971; Mayo, 1968; Murphy & Strong, 1972; Truax & Carkhuff, 1965) have found therapist disclosure will increase attraction for a therapist and will foster perceptions of him or her as friendly, warm, and expert. Therapist disclosure has also been shown to facilitate client disclosure and perhaps influence therapeutic outcome.

Several different factors have been hypothesized to contribute to the beneficial effects of therapist disclosure. First, such disclosure may function as a model that clients then imitate. It can thus help in reducing ambiguities and stress for clients. Through its influence on impressions and attraction, disclosure may lead clients to view a therapist as more approachable and so facilitate clients' motivation to become involved in therapy.

While the bulk of experimental evidence supports the belief that disclosure by a therapist will facilitate therapy, therapist disclosure has *not* always been found to be beneficial. Reports are found of disclosing therapists being rated as less relaxed, less emotionally stable, and less professional (e.g., Dies, 1973; Dies & Cohen, 1976; Weigel, Dinges, Dyer, & Straumfjord, 1972; Weigel & Warnath, 1968). In attempting to understand cases in which therapist disclosure has negative effects, recall what we said earlier about schemata for therapy (see Chapter 5). Although clients' schemata probably lead them to expect a therapist to be open and warm, it is also likely to contain the expectation that interactions will be focused on the client and his or her problems. Thus, when a therapist discloses too much, too intimately, or on an issue the client is not concerned with, this expectation is violated, with the result that therapy is impeded. (See the section on "Therapist Self-

Disclosure" in Chapter 7 for a discussion of the pros and cons of therapist self-disclosure based on a privacy regulation perspective.)

The effect of client expectations regarding therapist disclosure can be seen in a study by VandeCreek and Angstadt (1985), who found that subjects expecting high disclosure from a therapist had more positive reactions to a disclosing therapist than those expecting little therapist disclosure. Perhaps even more important are studies by Derlega, Lovell, and Chaikin (1976) and Simonson and Bahr (1974), both of which found evidence consistent with the hypothesis that when therapist disclosure violated client expectations, therapy was impeded.

The concept of responsiveness may help us understand when therapist disclosure will and when it will not be beneficial, even though studies of therapist disclosure have most often had therapists disclosing before the client does. To understand this, recall that the key aspect of L. Miller and Berg's (1984) concept of responsiveness is the conveying of interest in and understanding of another through the communication. In an actual therapy situation a therapist will have at least some knowledge of the client and her or his reason for seeking therapy. The therapist will also have knowledge of clients who have had similar problems in the past, and perhaps the therapist may have dealt with this problem personally. Disclosing information and experiences of this kind would directly address content that is of concern to the client and would, by definition, be responsive. If the content of the therapist's initial disclosure is not of concern to the client, the disclosure would not be responsive and, as in the Berg and Archer (1983) study, would not be expected to lead to positive effects. Thus, in addition to the factors hypothesized earlier to underlie the beneficial effects of therapist disclosure, we would add the following qualification: Therapist disclosure will be of benefit primarily when the disclosure is responsive to the client's concerns. An analogous explanation has been offered by clinical researchers who recommend a therapist disclosure of information similar to that revealed by the client (Hoffman-Graff, 1977; Hoffman & Spencer, 1977). What makes an explanation in terms of responsiveness more appealing than one based on similarity of content is that the possible beneficial effects of therapist disclosure are precisely the effects that have been shown to follow responsive actions.

The clearest evidence on the effects of responsive therapist behavior is found in those studies investigating "self-involving" therapist remarks. In distinguishing self-involving from self-disclosing statements, Danish, D'Augelli, and Brock (1976) define a *self-disclosure* as "a statement of factual information on the part of the helper about himself or herself" and a *self-involving statement* as "a statement of the helper's personal response to statements made by the helpee" (p. 261). McCarthy (1979) notes that while self-disclosing statements refer to past behaviors or personal experiences of therapists, self-involving statements are direct expressions of the therapist's present feelings about and reactions to the statements and/or behaviors of the client. Because self-involving statements directly address a client's past actions, they are by definition responsive (D. Davis & Perkowitz, 1979). This is in contrast to a self-disclosing statement, which may or may not be responsive, depending on its content and its relation to the client's concerns.

Self-involving statements can vary in terms of their negativity-positivity. A positive self-involving statement involves direct personal expression of a therapist's positive feelings about or reactions to a client's statement or behavior (e.g., "I'm glad to see that you're trying to do X"). A negative self-involving statement is a direct personal expression of negative feelings about or reactions to a client's statement or behavior (e.g., "It frustrates me to hear you talk about manipulating people"). Anderson and Anderson (1985) and Remer, Roffey, and Buckholtz (1983) presented subjects with an excerpt from a therapy session in which the therapist made either positive or negative self-involving statements. Subjects expressed more favorable impressions of and were more willing to see the therapist who made positive remarks. What is more important to our present purpose, however, is a study by Reynolds and Fischer (1983) that compared both positive and negative self-involving statements to self-disclosing statements. Therapists using both types of self-involving statements were rated as more trustworthy and expert than the one using the self-disclosures. This finding clearly supports a responsiveness interpretation.

McCarthy and Betz (1978) and McCarthy (1979) compared positive self-involving and self-disclosing statements. Both studies found that therapists using self-involving statements were viewed as more trustworthy, expert, and attractive than therapists using self-disclosing statements. In addition, the self-involving statements by therapists fostered greater self-exploration in clients, and these findings held across all possible therapist–client gender pairings.

The overall pattern of results in all studies investigating self-involving and self-disclosing statements may be interpreted in the following manner: First, therapist self-disclosure may facilitate impressions of a therapist, enhance attraction for him or her, and increase client self-disclosure when it addresses issues that are of concern to the client. However, because both positive and negative self-involving statements directly address the content of clients' communications (D. Davis & Perkowitz, 1979) and immediately follow them, they are likely to be viewed as more responsive than self-disclosing statements, with the result being that perceptions of the therapist and subsequent self-exploration by the client are facilitated more than with self-disclosing statements. Finally, it seems likely that clients will feel that a therapist who makes a positive, as compared to a negative, self-involving statement is more interested in them and understands them more (L. Miller & Berg, 1984). Thus, further studies comparing positive and negative types of self-involving statements would be expected to find results favoring the positive ones.

Another difference between self-involving and self-disclosing statements, at least as the latter were operationalized in the preceding studies, is that the self-involving statements were all moderately intimate because they expressed a feeling. Morton (1978) has termed such expression of feelings "evaluative intimacy." In contrast, the self-disclosing statements did not reveal intimate factual information (descriptive intimacy). McCarthy (1982) compared client reactions to self-involving therapists with reactions to both high- and low-disclosing therapists. Her operationalization of low-intimacy disclosures involved the therapist agreeing with the client's previously expressed experience (e.g., "I remember having to make it on my own when I was growing up"). The high-disclosing statement both agreed with the client's experience and expressed an emotion the client had not yet identified (e.g., "I remember having to make it on my own when I was growing up and it was so lonely"). As in her other studies, McCarthy's self-involving statements expressed the therapist's feelings about the client's behavior (e.g., "I appreciate the way you are relating to me right now"). Notice that all three types of responses address the content of previous communication and so would be considered responsive (D. Davis & Perkowitz, 1979). The high-disclosing and self-involving statements, but not the low-disclosing response, are evaluatively intimate. It has been proposed that increased intimacy will lead to attraction and favorable impressions only when it occurs in conjunction with a responsive action (Berg, 1987; Berg & Archer, 1983). From this perspective, both the high-disclosing and self-involving therapists should be more favorably viewed than the low-disclosing therapist, and this is precisely what McCarthy (1982) found.

No study to date has compared self-involving statements (evaluative intimacy) with disclosures that are only descriptively intimate or descriptively nonintimate in a therapy context. Berg and Archer (1982) compared subjects' attraction for a disclosure recipient who replied with a statement high in evaluative intimacy with that for a person who replied with high descriptive intimacy and found the former response led to greater attraction. In discussing the development of intimacy in close relationships Clark and Reis (1988) predict that the expression of feelings will be more important than the revelation of private facts. To the extent that developing a sense of intimacy is important for the therapist–client relationship, the judicial use of evaluatively intimate, self-involving statements by the therapist may be therapeutic.

While therapists often self-disclose or make self-involving statements of the kind discussed here, therapists must exercise caution about what they say based on knowledge about the client's problems, the stage of therapy, how the client seems to be feeling at the particular moment, and the anticipated effect of the therapist's self-statement on the client. An analysis of the therapy relationship as a communal relationship reveals one potential problem with certain therapist self-disclosures. In a communal relationship the client will feel an obligation to respond to the needs expressed directly or indirectly by the therapist. Therapists generally avoid direct expressions of need, but therapist self-disclosures may suggest to the client that the therapist does have particular needs. The client may try to meet these needs by talking more or less about certain topics in therapy or by behaving in ways intended to help the therapist. The therapist may be unaware of the client's efforts to help him or her, but therapy has been impeded because the client is no longer working on his or her problems only. Issues associated with therapist self-disclosure are discussed again in the next chapter on privacy and self-disclosure in the therapy relationship.

Stylistic Aspects of Therapist Behavior

In this section we briefly discuss work that has examined nonverbal aspects of therapist behavior and the effects of the interaction style of the therapist on responsiveness. Therapist qualities such as warmth, empathy, and respect will be communicated to clients through both verbal and stylistic means, and the manner in which a therapist structures and conducts a therapy session will be largely a function of the therapist's style. The climate and tone of a situation and its perceived intimacy is determined by the total set of verbal and stylistic behaviors, and these two types of variables exist in an equilibrium with each other (Argyle & Dean, 1965; M. Patterson, 1976, 1982).

The most obvious nonverbal variable is the use of touch. Views on therapists touching clients range from an absolute prohibition against it (e.g., Render & Weiss, 1959; Menninger, 1958) to acceptance of it as a highly effective aid in establishing a relationship with clients and encouraging self-disclosure (e.g., Fromm-Reichmann, 1950; J. Wilson, 1982). Our view, while not an absolute prohibition, is that it should generally be avoided. First, it is likely to be an invasion of a client's personal space and privacy (Altman, 1975; Hall, 1966). Obviously, such an invasion of personal space would not be a responsive behavior. Second, the message conveyed by touch is a very ambiguous one. While touch may signal warmth or affection (Nguyen, Heslin, & Nguyen, 1975), it can also be a signal of sexual desire (Derlega, Lewis, Harrison, Winstead, & Costanza, 1989; Gutek, Nakamura, Gahart, Handschumacher, & Russell, 1980) or interpersonal dominance (Henley, 1977; Whitehurst & Derlega, 1985), both of which would be disastrous for a therapeutic relationship. Other nonverbal behaviors, such as the use of distance, facial expressions, and eye contact, may effectively convey a therapist's feelings toward the client and his or her view of their relationship as close without the problems associated with touch.

Even with these less intrusive behaviors, however, there is no simple rule (such as the less distance or the more eye contact, the better). Although Jourard and Friedman (1970) found that interviewees' self-disclosure increased at closer interviewer distances and Altman and Taylor (1973) report that people with closer relationships will interact at a close range, a therapist must attend to and be able to respond to cues from a client that personal space is being invaded. Only in this way can a therapist regulate his or her nonverbal behavior in a responsive manner. In a similar fashion, although Ellsworth and Ross (1975) found that subjects disclosed more when an interviewer gazed at them, other work (e.g., Ellsworth, Carlsmith, & Henson, 1972) indicates that being looked at can also be aversive and a stimulus for flight. Again, in order to use nonverbal (stylistic) behaviors in a responsive manner, a therapist must be sensitive to client reactions and changes in these reactions.

In addition, studies of nonverbal behavior suggest that individuals tend to have a preferred level for interaction intimacy. When something occurs that disturbs this traditional level (e.g., someone makes or receives a disclosure of very high intimacy; a partner gazes at a person more or positions himself or herself closer), arousal will be experienced and attempts made to restore interaction intimacy to its traditional level (e.g., by reducing eye contact or increasing distance). In the case of therapy, it is likely that clients will have a lower traditional level of interaction intimacy than the therapist. What one may be likely to observe at an initial therapy session, then, is a client revealing a quite personal problem but sitting in a rigid closed posture while the therapist assumes a more relaxed open position and attempts to maintain eye contact.

If a client's traditional level of interaction intimacy is often disrupted during therapy, he or she may experience arousal; how that arousal is labeled may have profound implications for the therapy process and the client–therapist relationship. Do clients label their arousal as relief or the result of finally getting something "off their chests"? Is the arousal seen as resulting from feelings of embarrassment or disgust with oneself and one's weaknesses? Here, both the verbal and nonverbal behavior of the therapist may be crucial. Through the use of self-involving and interpretive statements the therapist may give feedback and explicitly provide a label. Therapists' behaviors can tell clients that they are still accepted and valued.

What happens if verbal and nonverbal signals emitted by a therapist do not agree with each other? When such nonverbal leakage occurs, it is the nonverbal rather than the verbal messages that are more likely to be believed, because nonverbal behavior is felt to give a more accurate reflection of the individual's true feelings. Consider this in light of the preceding remarks about therapist disclosure. One of the advantages of such disclosure is believed to be the fact that it makes a therapist seem more authentic and open to a client. However, if the therapist's nonverbal signals are indicating discomfort or rejection, for example, through a formal vocal tone or rigid posture, nonverbal messages will be believed and it is unlikely that the therapist's verbal disclosure will produce positive effects. We suggested earlier that therapist disclosure could at times be negative because it might lead the client to focus on the therapist's problem rather than on her or his own. This may be even more likely when the therapist's stylistic behaviors suggest discomfort or distress because of the high apparent validity of such nonverbal cues.

Therapist "authenticity" has been considered important by some writers (e.g., Kaslow, Cooper, & Linsenberg, 1979; C. Patterson, 1985). Although stylistic behaviors will be important in conveying authenticity, one must recognize that behavioral style is not a gimmick and no specific set of behaviors can be specified that will invariably convey authenticity. Authenticity requires a therapist to be active, spontaneous, and flexible. She or he must be open and nondefensive, sometimes questioning, sometimes interpreting, able and willing to reveal her or his own experiences when appropriate, but always concerned more with the immediate here-and-now relationship with the client than with any specific technique. Although it is important that the therapist express confidence in the eventual outcome of therapy, the therapist should not be afraid to admit that she or he is occasionally playing a hunch and doesn't "know" the answer.

If specific stylistic behaviors that would always indicate responsiveness cannot be identified, an alternative is to consider general interaction styles that make it more likely an individual will act in responsive ways. We noted one of these earlier, namely the constellation of behaviors characteristic of subjects who earn high scores on the Opener Scale (Miller et al., 1983). Future work is needed that would apply the Opener Scale directly to a therapy context. We would predict that therapists will, in general, score higher on the Opener Scale than persons in other fields. And we would expect positive relationships between Opener Scale scores and therapists' use of eye contact, facial expressions, and other paraverbal and nonverbal signals indicating interest and understanding. We would also expect a positive relation between scores on the Opener Scale and ratings of both the therapist and of therapeutic outcome.

Previous work demonstrating the positive effects of therapist empathy (e.g., C. Patterson, 1985) deals with a second personality variable important for responsive behavior. By definition, empathy involves the ability to feel with others and to take their perspective. Indicating that one is doing this will, by definition, involve responsive action. Future studies need to describe the verbal and nonverbal behaviors of more empathic therapists in greater detail, rather than merely relating therapist empathy scores to client disclosure or therapeutic outcome. We would predict that therapists higher in empathy would employ more evaluative self-disclosure and self-involving statements, maintain more eye contact, and display by their nonverbal behavior more interest in and attention to their clients. At the same time, we would also expect empathic therapists to be more sensitive to both verbal and nonverbal indications that a client is distressed or anxious and to be better able to adjust their interaction style in response to such distress and anxiety.

Responsiveness as a Client Variable

The responsiveness of the client's behavior will be important for several reasons. First, since the classic writings of Harry Stack Sullivan (1953, 1954), it has been recognized that deficits in interpersonal relationships will underlie many of the psychological problems leading an individual to seek therapy. Work reviewed earlier in this chapter and reviews of responsiveness (Berg, 1987; D. Davis, 1982) suggest that deficiencies in interpersonal relationships may often result from problems in enacting responsive behaviors. For example, Berg and Peplau (1982) correlated students' loneliness scores with scores on the Opener Scale (L. Miller et al., 1983). If the Opener Scale measures a person's interest in listening to other people and her or his tendency to exhibit responsiveness, as we have suggested, a substantial negative relationship with loneliness would be expected, and the negative correlation of .57 between Opener Scale scores and loneliness that Berg and Peplau found confirms this. In a similar vein, Berg (1987) argued that disclosure reciprocity (i.e., matching an initial disclosure offering with a similar level of disclosure output) results in part from attempts by a disclosure recipient to demonstrate responsiveness; numerous studies have shown that deficits in disclosure reciprocity are exhibited by lonely individuals (e.g., Berg & McQuinn, 1989; Franzoi & Davis, 1985; Solano, Batten, & Parish, 1982). Other work suggests that distressed individuals may not be using disclosure in responsive ways. For example, Chelune, Sultan, Vosk, Ogden, and Waring (1984) found that distressed individuals elaborated less on their disclosures and showed less congruence between the verbal content of these disclosures and the affective manner in which the content was presented. Jones, Hobbs, and Hockenbury (1982) noted that lonely individuals were less attentive to a conversation partner and exhibited fewer responsive listener cues than did nonlonely individuals. All such characteristics would make an individual's conversational behavior less responsive.

Similar findings have been obtained by those studying distressed and nondistressed marital couples. These studies demonstrate that marital satisfaction is related to reciprocal disclosure to the spouse, to the ability to encode and decode the spouse's nonverbal behaviors, and to other skills and deficits in responsive communication patterns (see Cleaver, 1987; Davidson, Balswick, & Halverson, 1983; Emmelkamp, Van Linden Van den Heuvell, Ruphan, & Sanderman, 1988; Glander, Locke, & Leonard, 1987; S. Hendrick, 1981; Levinger & Senn, 1967; Noller, 1981).

If a client's inability to form or maintain close relationships is, as Sullivan (1953, 1954) suggests, a cause as well as a sign of psychological distress and if, as other work we have noted suggests, the ability to disclose and communicate responsively is crucial to the formation and maintenance of close relationships, then one of the chief tasks in therapy will be to teach clients more responsive communication patterns. Evidence that this is often the case can be found in the extensive literature on training individuals in the use of communication skills. For example, both Waldo (1989) and Sollie and Scott (1983) have developd methods for teaching expressive communication and empathic listening. After showing that lonely individuals exhibited deficits in responsive listener cues and conversational behaviors Jones et al. (1982) not only demonstrated that such deficits could be overcome through training but found that the loneliness of subjects given such training subsequently declined. Therapists working with distressed couples have also found improvements in marital satisfaction following training in communication skills (e.g., Cleaver, 1987; Emmelkamp et al., 1988; Glander et al., 1987).

The work dealing with teaching communication skills has come out of a largely behavioral tradition focusing on specific behaviors. Other work dealing with distressed and nondistressed populations has found that the deficiency suffered by distressed individuals may be related to more global personality traits. For example, Jones, Freemon and Goswick (1981) report that lonely individuals experience more social anxiety when interacting with others and show distrust and even dislike of others and decreased interest in them. Prager (1986) notes that individuals low in intimacy motivation fail to vary the intimacy of their disclosures to individuals of different degrees of closeness. All of these more global characteristics inhibit responsive action. If deficits in responsiveness and psychological distress stem from these or other more global characteristics, one would expect that more would be necessary for therapy than if the deficits were simply due to a lack of specific skills.

A second way a client's responsiveness will be important is in terms of the interest and understanding she or he demonstrates to the therapist and what the therapist is saying. As Kiesler (1979) reminds us, a client's pattern of verbal and nonverbal behavior towards a therapist will reflect the pattern she or he typically displays towards others. Thus, therapists can and do use their observations of client communication behaviors to help in both diagnosis and treatment of clients' problems. What therapists may not be aware of, however, is the effects these client behaviors have on them and their relationship with the client.

There is no reason to expect that therapists will be any less likely than others to experience increased attraction toward and more favorable impressions of another who acts responsively. In fact "contrast effects," resulting from often dealing with clients showing deficits in responsiveness, may lead to even more positive effects when a client does act responsively. Such effects could occur during the initial therapy session. An effective way for a client to demonstrate interest in and understanding of a therapist at this point would be to consider and perhaps comply with requests, techniques, or recommendations made by the therapist. Recall from our earlier discussion in Chapter 5 on the development of therapist–client relationships that compliance with therapists' recommendations may be particularly valued in the early stages of therapy (Horn-George & Anchor, 1982). Recall too from Chapter 5 how what occurs in these early sessions will have an enormous effect on the client–therapist relationship. Future research is needed to investigate therapists' impressions of more and less responsive clients. For example, do therapists form more favorable impressions of clients rated as more responsive? Do responsive clients maintain greater eye contact with the therapist? What results do these behaviors have on the client–therapist relationship and the outcome of therapy?

Conclusions

The concept of responsiveness appears to encompass previously diverse findings in the therapy literature. For example, it suggests a reason why therapist disclosure sometimes is and sometimes is not effective and why self-involving statements by a therapist and therapist empathy may have beneficial effects in the therapist–client interaction. At the same time, the concept of responsiveness points to a factor that is likely to be a chief cause of a client's distress and reason for seeking therapy and suggests linkages with behavioral research on communication skills.

To date, research directly investigating responsiveness has been confined to the social psychological and personal relationship literature. An important and exciting direction for future research will be more direct investigations of responsiveness in clinical settings; this chapter suggests some preliminary directions and hypotheses for such work.

CHAPTER 7

A Privacy Model of Self-Disclosure in the Therapy Relationship

Individuals are inherently social. Not only are our individual behaviors influenced by social forces but our interactions and relationships with other people are a critical feature of human experience. Interactions with other people involve different kinds of social exchanges, including sharing pleasantries (e.g., "Hello, how are you?"), physical contact (e.g., a handshake or a hug), problem-solving conversation (e.g., "Have you figured out how to use the new software program?"), and expressing pleasure (e.g., "Your newborn baby is a pleasure to hold in my arms!"). Individuals frequently talk to one another about their personal problems: after some small talk, strangers seated next to one another on a cross-country flight often share personal experiences, for example, about difficult adolescents; a man talks occasionally over lunch with a male colleague about difficulties in his marriage; a male college student tells a girlfriend about his fears and anxieties concerning possible failure to complete the course work in a premedical program; a woman describes to her neighbor how she has been physically abused by her husband but says she is afraid to report him to the police or even to tell their families.

As we have just described, most of the time individuals who have problems or pressures they can't adjust to approach a friend, spouse, family member, or acquaintance for advice or support. Sometimes they even confide in a stranger. Occasionally, because of the unavailability of a confidant or because their problems are severe or persistent, individuals may seek help from a psychotherapist.

Basically, when a person seeks psychotherapy, her or his role is to disclose personal thoughts and feelings as well as to undergo the short-term psychological and financial costs of therapy. In return, the therapist, by her or his warmth, acceptance, understanding, interpretation, and/or advice, will help the client to acquire new skills in dealing with personal problems and in understanding himself or herself. Asymmetry of client–therapist disclosure is a common characteristic of most forms of psychotherapy, but it is in contrast to the mutual self-disclosure that is a common, though not universal, feature of relationships between close friends and spouses (Derlega, Margulis, & Winstead, 1987; Winstead, Derlega, Lewis, & Margulis, 1988).

Because of the centrality of client self-disclosure in psychotherapy (Derlega et al., 1987; S. Hendrick, 1987; Stiles, 1987), this chapter focuses on its impact on the client–therapist relationship. The chapter adopts a "privacy" approach to understanding individuals' decisions to disclose or not disclose information about themselves in therapy. Self-disclosure is conceptualized as a form of boundary adjustment in the maintenance of privacy. This framework will be used to enhance our understanding of the role of self-disclosure in the therapy relationship.

The first section of this chapter focuses on a social psychological analysis of the functions of self-disclosure and examines its implications for individual psychotherapy. The second section describes the privacy regulation model of self-disclosure (Derlega & Chaikin, 1977) and how the regulation of two boundaries are involved in self-disclosure: the "dyadic boundary," which separates the discloser and the person disclosed to from all others, and the "self boundary," which separates the self from the potential recipient of disclosures. We will describe how adjustments in the self boundary (based on the disclosure or concealment of information) may affect clients' self-concepts and their attitudes about the therapy relationship. Pathological verbalizations by schizophrenic patients in personal interviews will illustrate an extreme example of a closed self boundary. We will also consider how clients' concerns about confidentiality, and their trust in the therapist, affect their decisions to disclose or not to disclose. The third section of this chapter examines therapist self-disclosure, including its effects on both clients' and therapists' reactions to the therapy process. This last section will examine how therapist disclosure may assist in the creation of rapport between the client and therapist as well as aid the client to explore suppressed feelings.

A Functional Model of Self-Disclosure Applied to Therapy

The term *self-disclosure* has been used to describe the degree to which individuals reveal information about their thoughts, feelings, and experiences to another. According to a definition used by Derlega and Grzelak (1979), self-disclosure involves *"any information exchange that refers to the self including personal states, dispositions, events in the past, and plans for the future.* It can be operationally defined as any verbal message that formally begins with the word 'I' (e.g., 'I think,' 'I feel') or any other verbal message about the self"* (p. 152, emphasis in the original). Self-disclosure involves decisions about whether to reveal one's thoughts, feelings, or past experiences to another, about the level of the intimacy at which to reveal personal information, and about the appropriate time, place, and target person for disclosure.

The aforementioned definition of self-disclosure does not specify whether self-disclosure is limited to intentionally planned disclosures or whether it can be inferred (e.g., through a listener's interpretation of a slip of the tongue). For the purposes of this chapter we are focusing on verbal self-disclosures that are intentional.

On the basis of a functional approach to self-disclosure (Derlega & Grzelak, 1979; Derlega et al., 1987), one can consider the expressive value and/or the instrumental effectiveness of self-disclosure in therapy as seen by the discloser and the disclosure recipient. A self-disclosure can be viewed as serving one or more of five functions, described in the following paragraphs.

Expressive Function

During self-expression clients seek to ventilate their feelings by talking with someone. For instance, anguish or grief associated with the death of a family member may be ventilated by talking with the therapist. Breuer and Freud's (1895/1966) early work stressed that memories surrounding a traumatic event might be suppressed while the emotion associated with it continues in consciousness in the form of anxiety. The cathartic method, as developed by Freud (1904/1954) in the so-called "talking cure," allowed the forgotten memories to be remembered and linked to the anxiety. A client's hysterical symptoms were likely to disappear when the events were remembered and described in detail.

In a series of studies, Pennebaker (e.g., Pennebaker & Hoover, 1986; Pennebaker & O'Heeron, 1984) found that the failure to discuss a traumatic event (e.g., child abuse, rape, spousal death) with another person may have serious health consequences. For instance, Pennebaker (1985) found that college students who had had at least one upsetting trauma that they had not confided to others were more likely to go to the university health center, report symptoms and diseases, and take more over-the-counter medications than were students who had not had traumas or who had had them but shared the experience with others. Interestingly, this pattern held regardless of the number of very close friends.

Pennebaker and Beall (1986) have also found that writing about a traumatic event—specifically, about the emotions associated with it— may serve the same function as talking about it. Undergraduates who wrote about personally traumatic events for 15 minutes each day for 4 consecutive days and addressed either (1) the facts and the associated emotions, (2) only the emotions, or (3) only the facts were compared to control subjects who wrote about trivial topics. Initially, the subjects who addressed either facts and emotions or only emotions experienced increased blood pressure and negative moods, but in the long term they reported reductions in health problems compared to those who wrote about only facts or trivial topics. Writing only about the facts of traumatic events, however, was similar in its effects to writing about trivial topics: subjects in this group did not report being upset and were not physiologically aroused by the experience of writing, but there were no long-term benefits. Pennebaker's findings underscore the importance of putting into words the emotions associated with personal traumas.

Self-Clarification

Self-disclosure may be beneficial when used to increase self-awareness. Clients who disclose or who anticipate disclosing information may be able to clarify self-knowledge and feelings. According to Duval and Wicklund's (1972) theory of objective self-awareness, the anticipation of speaking about themselves may cause individuals to focus on themselves instead of on the environment, thereby increasing their attention to the consistency and integration of their ideas. Thus, clients may find that they understand themselves better simply because they have "prepared" a talk about their problems and in the process discovered causes and consequences of their behavior of which they were previously unaware.

A person's current feeling state is also magnified in self-awareness, according to Duval and Wicklund. If a person is feeling somewhat negative, increased self-awareness may lower self-esteem. Because disclosure in psychotherapy tends to focus on personal problems and perceived weaknesses, the expectation of such disclosure occurs in a social context such as in the presence of a psychotherapist, self-awareness should increase and in turn lead to greater negative affect. This prediction has been supported in an experiment by Archer, Hormuth, and Berg (1982). Subjects who were assigned to talk about intimate topics (which could include making negative comments about self, e.g., "my ups and downs in mood") under conditions that increases self-awareness (facing a large mirror) enjoyed the task least, took longer to begin talking about the topics, were rated as finding the experiment most unpleasant, and were rated as having produced the least complete self-descriptions. (Subjects in the "intimate topic–mirror" condition were compared to subjects who talked about nonintimate topics in front of a mirror as well as to subjects who talked about nonintimate or intimate topics in a room that did not have a mirror.)

This analysis suggests that although self-disclosure in psychotherapy may be positive by increasing self-clarification, it can also be unpleasant because self-awareness intensifies the impact of negative thoughts and feelings that clients may have about themselves. Some clients may even abandon therapy after one or a few sessions because they are not ready to disclose highly intimate material. These clients' problems may be aggravated by disclosing too much information too quickly. On the other hand, clients who disclose little or nothing about themselves may also terminate early because they do not provide themselves the opportunity for self-clarification and feedback.

Social Validation

According to Leon Festinger's (1954) theory of social comparison, people look to social reality to obtain feedback and ultimately to validate their self-concepts. Talking with others about personal problems may help individuals decide on an appropriate course of action. Also, properly selected others can help individuals define the appropriateness of their attitudes, beliefs, and feelings.

Individuals who seek help from a therapist are likely to be experiencing negative feelings about themselves, others, and/or life circumstances. Clients' self-disclosure of personal problems to the therapist may elicit from the therapist acceptance and validation for the client's sense of worth (see Chapter 8 on social support). Clients seek confirmation for their self-worth in terms of their mental health (e.g., "I am not crazy, am I?") and their personal and moral worth (e.g., "I am basically a good person, aren't I?"; "It wasn't my fault, was it?").

Clients often also expect to receive feedback on how they are viewed by others, and some therapies advocate providing this feedback. Group therapy, rather than individual psychotherapy, may be recommended for clients who are perceived as needing to receive direct feedback from others. The interaction among group members provides more opportunities for social validation and feedback than is likely to occur in individual psychotherapy.

The validation that can result from disclosing to a therapist derives in part from the therapist's being identified by clients as an expert or authority figure who has special knowledge by virtue of the fact that the therapist knows clients better than they can know themselves and treats many people with problems; thus, clients feel reassured that their problems aren't unique and that they can be treated. Although personal relationships with a spouse, lover, relative, coworker, or friend may also function to validate one's self-concept, the relationship with the psychotherapist may be given more weight because of the therapist's perceived professional expertise.

Relationship Development

Self-disclosure may be used to reflect the level of intimacy in a personal relationship: more intimate disclosures may be expected to occur as a relationship progresses. The disclosure of information serves as a barometer of the state of the relationship and as a way to sample the kinds of outcomes one can expect (see the description of social exchange theory in Chapter 3).

The potential value of the therapy relationship is first explored by the client and therapist in the initial sessions. The client may reveal something about her or his personal problems, using these interactions to sample and forecast the possible outcomes in the relationship. Similar assessment processes may occur at different steps in the therapy relationship, as the client tests the therapist to determine how much she or he can be trusted and what sorts of disclosures are acceptable.

As an illustration, at some point in therapy clients may make comments about the therapist or the therapy process. These events serve as a test for the client of how much the therapist can be trusted. The client may criticize the therapy or therapist and assess how the therapist reacts. One client we talked to accused her therapist of distracting her by playing with his watch, an accusation he vigorously denied. On later occasions the client was aware of thoughts and feelings about the therapist but was unwilling to talk about them. Although in principle a client may be encouraged to speak freely about the therapy process, how the therapist handles the client's comments on this matter (e.g., by being defensive, self-conscious, or embarrassed instead of nonjudgmental, attentive, and empathic) affects the client's willingness to disclose.

As clients discover that the therapy session provides a supportive atmosphere for talking openly, they may divulge previously hidden information that has been shared with few (if any) others. According to Daryl Bem's (1972) theory of self-perception processes, the act of self-disclosing may itself affect how much clients like and trust the therapist. Bem's analysis assumes that we rely on the same kind of cues that are available to an outside observer in order to explain our own behavior. Individuals usually think of intimate disclosures as being exchanged between close friends or confidants, that is, between persons who like and trust one another (Chaikin & Derlega, 1974; Derlega, Winstead, Wong, & Greenspan, 1987). According to the self-perception explanation, clients who divulge intimate information to the therapist may infer that they like and trust the therapist, since such disclosure is ordinarily limited to liked and trusted others. This attribution should make the client more comfortable about disclosing to the therapist in future sessions and should increase the client's commitment to working with the therapist. The belief in the specialness of the client–therapist relationship may be undermined, however, by the realization that the client shares the therapist with other clients. The knowledge that the therapist talks to many clients during a typical week may lead to the inference that the therapist doesn't care about any particular client and that the relationship is "only business."

Social Control

Clients may selectively disclose information about themselves with the goal of creating a desired impression on the therapist. For instance, a male client may disclose certain "negative" aspects of the self (e.g., promiscuity) that, in the client's view, convey his sexual attractiveness and manliness. However, he may hide other aspects (e.g., adolescent homosexual thoughts or experiences) that he feels might threaten his image as a man. In this example, the client, afraid of losing the therapist's positive regard through what he feels is a discreditable disclosure, may hope to gain greater regard through a self-enhancing disclosure.

Clients may simply avoid disclosing certain information or even lie when they feel ashamed of what they have felt or done. A teenage girl reported to a therapist that she had been treated for depression but didn't admit (and even denied when asked) that she had occasionally engaged in binge-eating episodes that were followed by vomiting and laxative use. A male client reported concealing "undesirable" information:

> There were a few times when I didn't tell the therapist the truth because I was so ashamed. I just didn't want him to know about it. Afterwards I would go home and say, "Why the hell did I lie? Here I am paying this guy all this money." I knew if I lied that it wouldn't help, so I resolved to tell the truth the next time I went. But I didn't. (Derlega & Chaikin, 1975, p. 93)

Clients may thus engage in a form of impression management or self-presentation through selective disclosure of personal information to control what happens in the therapy relationship (e.g., to make a favorable impression on the therapist or avoid feeling uncomfortable talking about an embarrassing topic).

Clients may also selectively reveal unfavorable information about themselves as a tool to control their relationship with the therapist. For instance, a husband in family therapy may tell the therapist about affairs he has had. However, the client may ask for reassurance that the therapist will not give away this "secret" to the wife. If the therapist agrees to keep the husband's secret, he or she is in effect colluding to keep information away from the betrayed wife. The errant husband may be relieved that he has confessed and, at the same time, has avoided having to face his wife's anger or his own shame and guilt in her presence. In such instances the therapist might avoid taking sides by insisting on full disclosure of information between the partners.

Privacy Regulation Model of Self-Disclosure

If clients are to obtain the benefits of self-disclosure, they must make available to the therapist information that may not ordinarily be known to others. For instance, if a client feels she is not adequately understood as a person, self-disclosure to the therapist can assist in validating her self-concept if the therapist sees her in the way she sees herself (Kelvin, 1977). However, there are risks in sharing personal information: the client may fear that the therapist will distort what was said (e.g., the therapist may select an interpretation for what the client says that is at odds with what the client "knows" or wants to hear about herself); the client may fear rejection by the therapist (e.g., a client may have lied about material divulged earlier in therapy and be concerned that the therapist won't trust what he says now); or the client may worry about the therapist betraying information that was supposedly told in confidence (e.g., a client may describe physically abusing her children and fear that the therapist will inform the police about it).

In this section, a *privacy model* of self-disclosure is presented to explain why clients (and therapists) may or may not disclose personal information about themselves. The disclosure of personal feelings and information potentially makes one vulnerable to being hurt in a close relationship, and the decision to disclose depends on the perception that the information is safe with the recipient. As Kelvin (1977) has noted, "The disclosure of areas of privacy reveals the underlying causes and motives of the individual's behavior: this potentially gives those to whom they are disclosed power over him; and in doing so, disclosures make him vulnerable to exploitation" (p. 367). Individuals may have a lurking fear of being hurt and betrayed if they make themselves known and understood. Clients may hold back intimate information because they are afraid of what the therapist would do with the information;

disclosure of information depends on the perception that disclosure is safe.

In our view, privacy represents control over the amount and kind of information exchange persons choose to have with others. If individuals can voluntarily choose how much or how little to divulge about themselves to another, privacy is maintained. If others can influence how much information persons divulge about themselves, a lower level of privacy exists (Derlega & Chaikin, 1977; Derlega & Margulis, 1982; Margulis, 1979).

Altman (1975) has proposed the following approach to understanding privacy, emphasizing the opening and closing of "boundaries":

> Privacy is conceived as an *interpersonal boundary process* by which a person or group regulates interaction with others. By altering the degree of openness of the self to others, a hypothetical personal boundary is more or less receptive to social interaction with others. Privacy is, therefore, a dynamic process involving selective control over a self-boundary either by an individual or by a group. (p. 6, emphasis in the original)

Self-disclosure, the verbal transmission of information about oneself, contributes to the boundary regulation process. Adjustment in self-disclosure outputs and inputs is an example of boundary regulation, and the extent of control one maintains over this exchange of information contributes to the amount of privacy one has in a social relationship.

While self-disclosure is an example of boundary regulation, it is useful to note that the regulation of at least two major boundaries is involved in self-disclosure (Derlega & Chaikin, 1977; see Figure 7.1). One boundary, the "dyadic boundary," ensures the discloser's safety from leakage of information to uninvited third parties; this boundary establishes the precondition for self-disclosure. It is perceived by the individual as the boundary within which it is safe to disclose to the invited recipient and across which the self-disclosure will not pass; that is, the discloser believes the disclosure is safe with the recipient. The client's expectation of confidentiality in the therapy relationship is an example of a closed dyadic boundary. The second boundary is the "self boundary" around the person; it is modified by self-disclosure. Persons maintain a barrier around themselves that is based on nondis-

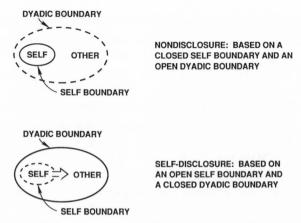

FIGURE 7.1. Self-disclosure as a function of self and dyadic boundary adjustments. From "Privacy and Self-Disclosure in Social Relationships" by V. J. Derlega and A. L. Chaikin, 1977, *Journal of Social Issues, 33*(3), 102–115. Copyright 1977 by The Society for the Psychological Study of Social Issues. Reprinted by permission.

closure. This barrier is opened when persons self-disclose. Decisions about how to adjust the self boundary enable clients to control the kind of relationship they have with the therapist. Also, how clients regulate self boundary control mechanisms may influence their sense of vulnerability, autonomy, and worth in the therapy relationship.

Disclosure versus Concealment of Information and the Self-Concept

Individuals may make adjustments in self-disclosure outputs (represented as changes in the personal or self boundary) depending on the content area of disclosure, the social relationship, and the personality characteristics of the discloser and the disclosure recipient. Persons may maintain relatively closed self boundaries in content areas that relate to anxiety-provoking personal problems while maintaining an open exchange in areas that do not provoke anxiety and stress. The act of closing or opening the self boundary (by concealing or disclosing information about the self) may, however, influence how the information is evaluated by the discloser as well as how individuals feel about themselves.

Consider the case of clients who have not disclosed to others what they themselves perceive to be important information (e.g., about alleged transgressions, psychological problems, or personal difficulties). They may come to therapy with the tendency to assume that the previously hidden information represents something "bad and shameful" about themselves. A beneficial effect of disclosure in therapy may be to assist clients to see themselves more positively *because* they have divulged information.

Fishbein and Laird (1979) conducted an experiment that demonstrated how concealing or disclosing information about oneself influences how it is evaluated. Research participants first completed a series of tasks that were described as measures of "social and nonsocial intelligence." They were then given an ambiguous score of "4.6," which supposedly represented their performance. Research participants were then asked to discuss the experiment with another subject (who was actually a confederate of the experimenter). In the "conceal condition" subjects were instructed not to divulge their score to the confederate whereas in the "disclose condition" subjects were asked to make sure that they divulged their score. The subjects engaged in a 5-minute conversation with the confederate and followed the instructions they had been given. Subsequently, subjects completed a questionnaire including an item about how satisfied they were with their performance on the tasks. As predicted, subjects in the disclose condition (who divulged their score to the confederate during their discussion) were more satisfied with the alleged intelligence test results than subjects who were asked to conceal the information.

Fishbein and Laird's (1979) results suggest that a major contribution of self-disclosure to therapy can be in helping clients feel good about themselves. The act of self-disclosure may relieve anxiety and guilt over nonexistent or actual difficulties that clients have kept hidden. However, if clients in therapy persist in concealing information out of a fear of being embarrassed or hurt in the therapy relationship, the conscious decision to withhold the information may make them feel worse. For instance, a depressed client who has been sexually abused as a child by her father may have concealed this information from her family. The decision to hide this information from the therapist may compound the client's sense of guilt. She may think "I must have really done something wrong if I can't even tell this information to the therapist. A really good person would have done something about what happened, or at least would have told her family—or her therapist." (For a related discussion of these issues, see Mowrer, 1968, who sees suppression, a conscious decision to withhold the truth about oneself from others, as a "pathogenic act.")

Pathological Verbalizations and the Avoidance of Intimacy

The self boundary around the client is modified by self-disclosure, and a boundary is established between the client and therapist based on nondisclosure. The maintenance of a closed self boundary for the client can take several forms, including failing to disclose "undesirable" information, lying (which includes concealing certain items while still providing ostensibly veridical information), and "acting out" in an inappropriate manner to distract attention from a sensitive topic area.

An experiment (Shimkunas, 1972) conducted with schizophrenics illustrates in an extreme manner how some clients might use bizarre behavior to prevent others from finding out information about them. An interviewer talked individually to paranoid schizophrenic, non-paranoid schizophrenic, and nonpsychotic psychiatric patients about emotion-laden topics in either an intimate style (divulging personal feelings) or a superficial style (avoiding disclosure of personal feelings about certain events, making detached generalizations about experiences being talked about). Patients were next asked to give their feelings and experiences about the same topics in the same manner the interviewer had used. It was predicted that schizophrenic patients would avoid an intense social interaction, defined as making intimate self-disclosures. The schizophrenics, who heard an interviewer reveal personal information, were expected to avoid personal disclosures and to engage in delusional and autistic verbalizations to escape an intimate interaction.

Results indicated that the nonpsychotic group disclosed more intimately in the personal than in the nonpersonal disclosure conditions. Both the paranoid schizophrenics and nonparanoid schizophrenics showed a low level of personal disclosure in both the personal and nonpersonal disclosure conditions. The schizophrenic patients also used bizarre behaviors in the personal disclosure condition. On a measure of autistic behavior (based on the occurrence of illogical and tangential associations and thought sequences that were virtually impossible to understand), paranoid and nonparanoid schizophrenics were more "autistic" in the personal than in the nonpersonal disclosure condition. The nonpsychotic patients maintained a low level of autistic behavior in both the personal and nonpersonal disclosure conditions. Paranoids in the personal disclosure condition demonstrated more delusional thinking than any other group of patients in the personal or nonpersonal disclosure conditions. Examples of delusional thinking included references to plots to do the patient in or control him or her and statements that the patient was an important or famous person.

Shimkunas's (1972) research indicates how schizophrenics may create barriers to intimacy by engaging in peculiar and bizarre behavior. In response to the request to establish a personal relationship with the interviewer by divulging intimate information about themselves, the paranoid and nonparanoid schizophrenics used more inappropriate behavior than the paranoid and nonparanoid schizophrenics who were asked to develop a superficial interview relationship.

It is not possible to draw simple comparisons between the bizarre behavior of schizophrenic patients in a psychiatric hospital and the behavior of clients in an outpatient psychotherapy facility. However, clients may display unusual behaviors (serving to close the personal or self boundary) to reduce a sense of vulnerability and threat in therapy associated with having to disclose personal information.

Dyadic Boundary Regulation in Therapy

If client self-disclosure depends on an open self boundary, relationship intimacy between the client and therapist depends on the client's perception of a closed dyadic boundary that ensures confidentiality and protection of the divulged information. A secure dyadic boundary is the client's basis for believing that no personal information will be divulged to others. A closed dyadic boundary places an imaginary fence around both the client and therapist that separates them from other persons. This boundary emphasizes the specialness of the relationship, because the client and therapist share information which might not be known by anyone else; the client and therapist form a personal relationship that is based in part on knowing the client's secrets. By protecting the client's self-disclosures, the therapist maintains the client's trust and safeguards their relationship. We will consider how the therapist's success or failure in maintaining confidentiality affects the therapy relationship.

In therapy the perception of a closed dyadic boundary is rooted in the principle of confidentiality "wherein the self-disclosures or confidences of a client may not be revealed without the authorization of the client" (Rubanowitz, 1987, p. 613). Protecting the confidentiality of client information is considered essential in promoting client trust in the therapy process. The obligation of therapists to protect clients from unauthorized release of confidential information is also consistent with professional ethical guidelines. According to Principle 6 of the American Psychological Association's ethical guidelines:

> Psychologists have a primary obligation to respect the confidentiality of information obtained from persons in the course of their work as psychologists. They reveal such information to others only with the consent of the person or the person's legal representative, except in the unusual circumstances in which not to do so would result in clear danger to the person or to others. (American Psychological Association, 1981, pp. 635–636)

Also, based on the "General Guidelines for Providers of Psychological Services":

> Psychologists do not release confidential information, except with the written consent of the user involved, or of his or her legal representative, guardian, or other holder of the privilege on behalf of the user, and only after the user has been assisted to understand the implications of the release. (American Psychological Association, 1987, p. 717)

Psychotherapists are reluctant to reveal information without the client's consent (Baird & Rupert, 1987). However, clients may be unrealistic to expect that the therapist will inevitably help in maintaining barriers in disclosures to others. For instance, psychologists interviewed in seven states indicated a willingness to divulge confidential information to consult with a professional colleague about a client or if a client was judged to be imminently dangerous. In consulting a colleague about the client's case, 60% indicated they would do so without the client's knowledge or consent, 12% indicated they would require the client's knowledge, and 26% stated they would need both the client's consent and knowledge. In the case of a dangerous client, 64% indicated they would divulge this information without necessarily getting consent but with the client's knowledge whereas 34% would divulge this information without the client's consent or knowledge.

A survey of 456 members of Division 29 (Psychotherapy) of the American Psychological Association confirms that therapists are willing to break confidentiality to prevent harm (Pope, Tabachnick, & Keith-Spiegel, 1987). A large majority indicated that it was ethical for the therapist to breach confidentiality without the client's consent in selected circumstances, including cases in which the client is homicidal (88%), suicidal (81%), or involved in child abuse (85.7%). Breaking confidentiality under such dangerous circumstances is a part of the usual practice for therapists. For instance, 58.1% reported actually having broken confidentiality when a client was homicidal, 78.5% when a client was suicidal, and 62.2% in cases involving child abuse. However, a majority of the therapists also reported that they had disclosed information unintentionally or informally about clients even though most identified their behavior as unethical or as ethical only under rare circumstances. For instance, 61.9% reported having unintentionally disclosed confidential data and 76.4% reported having discussed clients (without names) with friends. (Only 8.1% reported discussing a client by name with friends; this behavior was considered clearly unethical by 94.5% of the sample.) Almost half of the therapists (49.3%) reported having used a collection agency to collect late fees, and 32.2% reported using a lawsuit to collect fees from clients (both practices break confidentiality).

Clients may not ordinarily be concerned about the leakage of information in therapy, but they may withhold information or discontinue therapy if there is a risk of confidentiality being breached. For instance, a study of public attitudes about confidentiality in therapy (D. Miller & Thelen, 1986) found that 97% of those surveyed wanted to know if within the rules of confidentiality there were "special situations" that might be discussed that are not considered confidential by therapists. Forty-six percent wanted to be told that a situation or topic was not confidential before therapy begins, 4% at the first session, 18% when the particular situation was discussed, and 29% on each of these occasions. However, these persons were asked what their reaction would be "If they were told before the first session that certain information is not confidential?" Forty-two percent indicated that this information would have a negative effect (e.g., "I would find it difficult to talk with the therapist"), 27% indicated they would have ambivalent feelings (e.g., "It might make one feel hesitant at first . . . I don't know''), 2% stated that they would react positively (e.g., "I would feel that the therapist was being honest"), and 10% said they would automatically discontinue therapy. Individuals in Miller and Thelen's (1986) study were asked if they would discuss information that was not considered confidential. While 15% said they would discuss information that was not considered confidential, 41% said they would not discuss such information, and 44% said they didn't know how they would react.

Consistent with the survey information discussed above, therapists report a reluctance by clients to divulge information if they believe that the therapist may break confidentiality. Consider the effects of the precedent-setting case in California of *Tarasoff v. Board of Regents of the University of California* (1974): The California Supreme Court held that therapists had a legal duty to warn an intended victim if they learned that a client intended to seriously harm that person. One year after the *Tarasoff* decision, about one-quarter (24.5%) of California therapists who were surveyed (Wise, 1978) indicated observing a reluctance in clients to discuss violent tendencies when told of the possibility of an exception to absolute confidentiality, although 47.5% of the therapists indicated that they had not noticed such reluctance and 27.9% did not respond. Most of the therapists (79.1%) also answered yes to the following question: "Once a patient is aware you might have to discuss his [or her] case with someone else, do you think that the patient is less likely to divulge certain information to the therapist?" Also, 25.7% of these therapists answered yes to the question "Have you ever lost a patient because he [or she] feared a breach of confidentiality?"

Therapists, in their desire to protect the confidentiality of the therapy relationship, may avoid probing into sensitive areas that would require them to report the client to legal authorities. The survey of therapists in California conducted by Wise (1978) on the impact of the *Tarasoff* decision found that 16% of the respondents felt the decision had "led them to feel tempted to avoid probing into some areas (i.e., those relating to dangerousness)."

Therapists might subtly forewarn clients about what *not* to say so that the legal duty to report a law violation will not interfere with the therapy relationship. For instance, a therapist who ran a treatment program for legal offenders informed her clients at the first visit about the limits of their confidentiality, namely, that she was legally required to report any current incidents of child abuse that the client disclosed to her. She said, "I'm sure there's child molestation I'm not aware of. If I were trickier, maybe I'd find out about it. But I'm trying to prevent many child molestations through treatment" (quoted in Denton, 1987, p. 22).

In order to maintain confidentiality, therapists may also ignore laws requiring them to report clients who may be dangerous to others. For instance, a survey of mental health practitioners (including psychologists, social workers, and psychiatrists) in Nebraska presented respondents with a hypothetical case of child abuse by the father in a family that presented itself for treatment. Even among the practitioners who were aware of the law requiring the reporting of child abuse, 63% indicated that they would not have reported the child abuse in the hypothetical case (Swoboda, Elwork, Sales, & Levine, 1978).

Most clients probably don't worry about confidentiality being violated by the therapist because of a legal matter or about casual remarks by the therapist to friends. They also may accept that therapists consult with other professionals occasionally (Rubanowitz, 1987). However, an obvious breach in client confidentiality involves the detailed information therapists must submit about clients to insurance companies. Although clients agree to this practice in order to have insurance coverage for therapy fees, having reports sent to insurance companies may inhibit client self-disclosure and disrupt the therapy relationship. Robert Langs (1979), in his book *The Therapeutic Environment*, has argued that any third-party payment destroys the client–therapist reationship because of the breach in confidentiality. The following anecdote illustrates a client's conflicts about having information concerning his therapy passed along to the insurance company:

My wife wouldn't let me come here for therapy unless the insurance covered most of the fee, and she made the calls to check it all out. I was very upset because I have a sensitive job now, and I'm concerned that somebody else would be reading my diagnosis and other information about me. There are some who think that people who go to therapists are crazy. I work in insurance and I don't know what will happen. I hadn't even realized that my wife had called up the insurance company, and she wondered if other insurance companies could get hold of the information. They told her that they don't release such information, and I guess I have to believe that because I need treatment desperately. (Langs, 1979, p. 505)

Clients whose livelihoods or personal relationships may be affected by others knowing they are in therapy may experience stress over the disclosure to insurers that they are or have been a participant in therapy. The information provided by the therapist in exercising third-party payment options may then become a source of conflict in the client–therapist relationship. It is possible that clients who are unwilling to submit information to insurance companies may end the therapy prematurely or (if financial resources are adequate) pay for the therapy themselves.

Therapist Skills in Safeguarding Confidentiality

Most clients assume that they can disclose personal material in therapy without the fear that the therapist will communicate this information to others. Therapists in general are probably successful in upholding the principle of client–therapist confidentiality, with the possible exception of breaching confidentiality in order to prevent danger or consult with professional colleagues. However, it is also the case that therapists often unintentionally break confidentiality by talking about clients with coworkers, friends, and their own spouses (Pope et al., 1987). The 19th-century sociologist Georg Simmel noted how people often can't resist the impulse to gossip and tell secrets. He advised that "it is necessary, above all, to learn how to be silent, before silence regarding any particular item may be expected" (Simmel, 1950, p. 349). While therapists seek to draw a "curtain of strict confidentiality" (Wise, 1978, p. 165) around the disclosures of their clients, many therapists unintentionally violate this principle themselves. Therapists acknowledge the importance of confidentiality in client–therapist communications but need to refine their skills in safeguarding clients' secrets.

Therapist Self-Disclosure

Personal relationships are for the most part symmetrical. The parenters in a relationship are usually mutually dependent (though perhaps not to the same degree), they serve to satisfy one another's important needs, and they exchange self-disclosures. Thus, each is vulnerable to being hurt or exploited by the other. On the other hand, the therapy relationship is asymmetric. Though there may be senti-ments that are felt by the both client and therapist, these feelings are usually expressed only by the client to the therapist. Client and thera-pist must deal with the particular ground rules for therapy: the client provides the self-disclosure input and the therapist listens and com-ments. Clients are expected to maintain an open self boundary by disclosing content relevant to their personal problems, while thera-pists are expected to maintain a closed self boundary by divulging little or nothing about themselves.

The early psychoanalytic view held that therapists may never reveal personal information about themselves to the client. The thera-pist, according to Sigmund Freud (1912/1956, p. 331), should be "im-penetrable to the patient; and like a mirror, reflecting nothing but what is shown to him." This approach encourages the transference relationship, and it is supposed to protect the therapist from becoming emotionally involved.

Despite the traditional psychoanalytic view that the therapist should appear as a neutral observer and remain uninvolved (Reich, 1951, p. 25; 1960, p. 391), this version of the therapist as a "blank screen" is not maintained by most practicing psychologists. The sur-vey by Pope et al. (1987) of psychotherapists (affiliated with Division 29 of the American Psychological Association) found that over 90% (on rare occasions or more often) reported both "using self-disclosure as a therapy technique" and "telling a client . . . [when] angry at him or her."

As noted in the preceding chapter on therapist and client respon-siveness, there are several reasons why selective use of self-disclosure by the therapist (particularly about her or his reactions to the therapy process) can be helpful. For instance, therapist self-disclosure may be a useful device to promote client self-disclosure and to strengthen rap-port between therapist and client. Also, clients may feel that their behavior is not so unusual if the therapist has had similar feelings and experiences.

Therapist self-disclosure may be particularly useful in making clients aware of how they come across to others in interpersonal interactions. Clients may be doing to the therapist what they have frequently done to other people. Also, when clients' behavior elicits certain reactions in the therapist and the therapist discloses how she or he feels, clients may be reassured that their behavior has real and not imagined consequences. For instance, Gorkin (1987) describes how the disclosure of his feelings of anger to a borderline man helped the client become more comfortable in exploring his own feelings of hostility and anger. The therapist's self-disclosure also helped the client see the impact of his angry behavior:

> The patient had told me a good deal about himself and seemed to value coming for treatment, although he would frequently attempt to provoke me with some sort of personal attack. For the most part, I was unbothered by his remarks. One evening, however, his remarks were unusually vitriolic and did annoy me; what was even more irritating was his punctuating that evening by storming out of the session, flinging open the door and allowing the winter wind to blow through the office. The following session I inadvertently locked him out. When I did let him in, he commented dryly, "You want to keep me out tonight." He then continued in a low-key voice to speak of various rejections he had experienced that day at work. When he finished, I immediately returned to his initial comments and told him that, while I had not locked him out intentionally, in a way he was correct in thinking that I wanted to keep him out that night. I also told him why, stating, "Your unusually sharp remarks last session did annoy me. But what got to me even more was your taking out your anger by flinging the door open when you left. *That* really got me sore!" I then added, "I am sorry, though, that I evidently have taken out my anger by locking you out." (Gorkin, 1987, pp. 89–90)

In talking to the patient about his reactions, Gorkin (1987) acknowledged feelings (anger) and his mistake (locking the patient out) and, in this case, helped the patient feel freer to explore his own feelings of anger.

This example suggests how therapist self-disclosure may be a useful therapeutic technique. However, it may not be appropriate for the therapist to divulge other personal information about reactions to the client or about his or her own life history, family relationships, or problems. For instance, therapists might have sexual fantasies and feelings for certain clients. It might be useful for therapists to acknowledge to themselves that these sexual fantasies and feelings exist so that the danger of acting out or the stress of trying to hide them from oneself is reduced (Gorkin, 1987). But the disclosure of these sexual fantasies to clients may not be helpful and in fact may burden them, forcing them to cope with sexual issues that may overwhelm them or causing them to become absorbed in the therapist's emotional problems rather than focusing on their own.

Clients who expect therapists to maintain some "psychological distance" may react negatively to therapists who attempt to divulge personal information about themselves. The therapist's self-disclosure input, when it is seen as inappropriate or unusual, may be perceived as an annoyance or a threat to the client. Gorkin (1987) gives an example of a situation in which he wished to share with his client, a well-liked and respected woman who was moving to another city, his disappointment and frustration at losing her. Gorkin (1987, p. 279) writes: "Her response, blunt as it was, snapped me into an awareness of what I was doing. 'This may seem strange, Dr. Gorkin,' she said, 'but right now I don't want to know anything about you. I only want to think about me!'"

How Potential Clients Evaluate Therapist Disclosure

There is some evidence about *what* clients might want therapists to talk about, based on results from analogue studies. For instance, S. Hendrick (1988) developed a 32-item questionnaire (the Counselor Disclosure Scale) to measure the level of therapist/counselor self-disclosure desired by potential clients in six major areas: (1) professional issues such as the counselor's training and professional experience; (2) the counselor's success rate; (3) the counselor's interpersonal relationships with spouse and close friends; (4) the counselor's health, religious beliefs, and personal tastes in art, music, literature, and so forth; (5) the counselor's fears and other personal feelings; (6) sexual issues, including the counselor's sexual practices and orientation and whether the counselor is attracted to the client.

The Counselor Disclosure Scale was administered to college students who were asked to imagine that they were clients going to see a counselor. Results indicated that the students—in the role of potential clients—were most interested in the therapist's answers to questions about professional issues, for example, the extent of the therapist's expertise and how the counselor would diagnose the client's problem. On the other hand, they were least interested in the therapist talking about sexual issues, which they may have found personally threatening.

Research on group psychotherapy also found that potential clients have strong opinions about what therapists should and should not say about themselves. Dies and Cohen (1976) asked college under-graduates to evaluate a set of statements that might be made by a leader during a group therapy discussion; ratings were based on how helpful or harmful subjects felt it would be for the therapist to disclose on each topic. Individuals indicated they would react more favorably to a leader who revealed information about her or his "positive strivings (personal and professional goals) and normal emotional experiences (e.g., loneliness, sadness, anger, worries, and anxieties)" (p. 85). Items that were considered helpful for the group leader to disclose included the following: "The kind of person he'd like to be"; "His professional goals"; and "One of the worst things that ever happened to him." In contrast, items that were considered harmful focused on information that represented either a personal attack on group members (e.g., the group teacher's anger, prejudice, or distrust of group members) or lack of confidence about his or her professional skills (e.g., feeling anxious about leadership skills, being currently in therapy, failing as a thera-pist in the past).

Dies and Cohen (1976) also found that self-disclosure by a group therapist may be viewed as more helpful later in the therapy than in the beginning. Disclosure by the group therapist was rated harmful on 54 of 65 possible statements during the first session of the therapy, on 38 of 65 items for the eight session, and on 20 of 65 items for the 15th session. Thus, as the sessions progressed, the content of therapist self-disclosures was less likely to be rated as potentially harmful, and the therapist was allowed more latitude to share personal information. However, even with 15 sessions, some items were still considered harm-ful: those that would either threaten group members (e.g., sexual attraction towards a member of a group) or undermine group members' confidence in the therapist's abilities (e.g., anxiety about his or her professional abilities, being in therapy). Such results are quite consistent with those of S. Hendrick (1988).

It is probably impossible to make a general statement about the usefulness of therapist self-disclosure, since it will depend on its tim-ing, the specific problem of the client, and the content of the disclo-sure. However, at least from the perspective of the potential client, therapist disclosure of "normal" concerns may be more appropriate in later stages than at the beginning of therapy. But it may be that clients never consider therapist disclosure of professional insecurities or se-vere psychological problems helpful because of the heavy emotional demands they place on the client.

Conclusions and Implications

Self-disclosure mediates several therapy functions, including expression, clarification, social validation, relationship development, and social control. However, at the outset of therapy and perhaps throughout the relationship, the client and therapist must work on *interpersonal* issues associated with relationship development and social control. A successful therapy relationship requires mutual trust and an avoidance of impression management. When these interpersonal conditions exist, the client feels safe to divulge personal information in a manner that earns her or him the *intrapersonal* benefits associated with expression, clarification, and social validation.

Self-disclosure is part of a process of privacy regulation by which individuals control access to information about themselves. Though clients are expected to self-disclose in therapy, they may avoid divulging intimate information if they do not perceive that the situation is safe for disclosure. Therapists need to be sensitive about clients' misgivings in divulging intimate information. Though an unwillingness to self-disclose may derive in part from embarrassment or anxiety about their psychological problems, clients may also be concerned about limitations to confidentiality. Therapists are encouraged to pay more attention to their own role in maintaining confidentiality; though they support the principle of confidentiality, they may unintentionally divulge information about the client to coworkers and friends.

Therapist disclosure should be reviewed in the context of its function; that is, therapists should ask themselves, What are the possible functions of therapist disclosure in the client–therapist relationship? Certain kinds of therapist disclosure may assist in building a close therapy relationship and in providing social feedback to the client. Systematic research based on actual therapy sessions might examine (perhaps via diary-type studies) when the therapist is likely to divulge personal information and what effects it has on the client.

CHAPTER 8

Social Support in the Therapy Relationship

"If you have one stick, you can easily break it; if you have a bundle of sticks, they are very hard to break." This is a loose translation of part of a sermon heard recently concerning the sense of community that binds a church congregation together and that strengthens the individual and group efforts that are expended. The implications of the sense of community are consistent with B. Gottlieb's (1983a) discussion in the *American Psychologist* of the past and future of the study of social support. Gottlieb points out that in many ways the historical "base" for the study of social support is in community psychology, which blossomed along with the community mental health movement (itself given great impetus by President Kennedy in the early 1960s). The word *community* was used quite intentionally for areas of research (community psychology) and practice (community mental health) that involved nonprofessional mental health workers in a given geographic area who offered various kinds of aid and support (as opposed to traditional, individually oriented psychotherapy) and who reached "across" rather than "down" to those in need of help.

Moreover, research associated with the community movement paid attention to prevention, an issue all too often ignored by the traditional medical and psychological communities. It was within this atmosphere of indigenous caregiving that interest in the study of social support burgeoned, according to Gottlieb. There was a surfacing of "community psychology's interest in the qualities of social environments that help people to develop resources and to cope effectively, an interest that persists in contemporary research on the supportive functions of social networks" (1983a, p. 280).

Community mental health was part of a larger reformist spirit of the time, and in some measure it was a reaction against traditional approaches to mental health care. Perhaps because of its origins, the study of social support has almost completely taken place outside of the conventional psychotherapy context. The literature on social support is wide-ranging, but much of it has involved the definition and measurement of social support as well as its potential as a buffer against stressful life events, which may be indirectly (or even directly) linked to disease processes. Still other research has documented negative effects of social support. Although the form for assessing and exploring an individual's sources of social support has occasionally been the therapy situation, it seems evident that the therapy relationship is itself a mechanism for delivering social support, both to the client and to the therapist.

Essential commonalities appear between social support and psychotherapy. It is the purpose of the present chapter to clarify these commonalities. To lay the groundwork, we will summarize some of the current research on social support. Since this book is about the personal relationship between client and therapist, the literature on social support in personal relationships can help make sense of how social support is enacted and may be perceived in the therapy relationship.

Research in Social Support

Definitions of Support

It is easier to define social support operationally (what it does) than descriptively (what it is). *Webster's Seventh New Collegiate Dictionary* (1963) offers such synonyms for support as *uphold, advocate, back,* and *champion* (p. 884) but also notes that in giving definitions for these words, the word *support* "is least explicit about the nature of the assistance given."

Cobb (1976) described three components of social support as (1) knowledge that one is loved and cared for, (2) knowledge that one is esteemed and valued, and (3) knowledge that one is part of a larger group or social network. This perspective on support emphasizes affective ties between people and the individual's perceptions of being supported. Thus, feeling part of a social network may be as important as (or more important than) what the network actually *does* for the individual.

As Pearson (1986) noted in a review of social support, definitions take into account both quantitative and qualitative aspects of support. Quantitative approaches focus on the individual's social network, including network size, network density (how many network members have ties to each other), the actual availability of persons in the network, and the individual's ability to make use of the resources that the network has to offer. Qualitative approaches, on the other hand, are more concerned with how the individual perceives and evaluates the available support in his or her network, essentially the "meanings that people give their relationships" (Pearson, p. 390). Wortman and Dunkel-Schetter (1987, pp. 70–71) proposed a taxonomy of social support that appears to include both qualitative and quantitative aspects. These characteristics of social support include the following:

1. Expression of positive emotion toward the individual ("I care about you")
2. Support of the individual's feelings and beliefs ("I understand [and/or agree with] your feelings")
3. Encouraging the individual to openly express feelings and beliefs (e.g., self-disclosure: "You can tell me how you feel; I'll listen")
4. Offering the individual advice or information ("Here is the name of a good physician")
5. Provision of material aid to the individual ("I have paid your doctor bill")
6. Aiding the individual with specific tasks ("I'll do your grocery shopping this week")
7. Helping the individual feel part of a mutually supportive group ("You are an important part of this family")

This taxonomy appears to include both qualitative and quantitative aspects of social support and underlines social support's multidimensional qualities.

Sources of Support

The sources of social support are potentially as vast as the number of persons in one's whole social world, although many "nodding acquaintances" are not in fact potential sources of support. We gain our support most typically from spouses or other romantic partners, parents and other relatives, children (in some cases), friends and neighbors, coworkers (including subordinates and superordinates), medical and psychological professionals, and self-help organizations (Wortman & Dunkel-Schetter, 1987). Social support does sometimes come from unexpected sources (e.g., a meaningful conversation with a stranger on an airplane). Social network analysis is an important aspect of the assessment of social support, since the larger one's social network, the more numerous the potential sources of support.

One of the fastest growing forums for the delivery of social support is the self-help/peer-support social support group. A survey of the contents of a recently published volume on social support (B. Gottlieb, 1988) gives a perspective on the far-reaching nature of these groups. The purposes of such groups include helping bereaved children with the grieving process, preventing postnatal depression, supporting low-income mothers, training leaders for other support groups, supporting children in divorced families, helping cancer patients, and aiding in both smoking cessation and weight reduction (B. Gottlieb, 1983b). The breadth of problems addressed by such groups is staggering; in many ways they are the quintessence of community mental health.

Measurement of Support

Issues concerning the measurement of social support have occupied a sizable share of the social support literature. As noted earlier, assessment of social support has focused on two approaches, the quantitative/structural (e.g., network size and density) and the qualitative/functional (e.g., quality of support, how it is perceived). Assessment of the structural properties of social support has yielded modest information. It appears that a dearth of meaningful social relationships is associated with a higher incidence of illness and mortality although the mechanisms by which social ties may affect health have not been clearly articulated (Wortman & Dunkel-Schetter, 1987). Some research has indicated that there may be a curvilinear relationship between network characteristics and effective social support such that small, dense, enmeshed networks may actually be associated with poorer health (e.g., Wortman & Dunkel-Schetter, 1987), as may large, poorly interconnected networks. Networks of moderate size and density may be closest to ideal.

Most of the empirical work on social support has focused on the qualitative/functional domain and has employed both specific and general social support measures. Wortman and Dunkel-Schetter (1987) noted that the perceived availability of support, the perceived adequacy of support and the extent to which the individual can mobilize desired support and avoid nondesired support, are all important components of an individual's overall support gestalt.

One example of research on the measurement of social support is the extensive research program on both the measurement and concomitants of social support that has been developed by the Sarasons and their colleagues. In 1983, they (I. Sarason, Levine, Basham, & Sarason) published their first major paper on development of the Social Support Questionnaire. This 27-item scale yields both a number score (number of support persons in the network) and a satisfaction score (satisfaction with available support).

Across a series of studies, the Sarasons and their colleagues (e.g., B. Sarason, Shearin, Pierce, & Sarason, 1987) employed the Social Support Questionnaire and a number of additional social support questionnaires to examine both the relations *among* the various measures and the relations *between* these measures and several personality instruments. The social support measures employed in these studies in addition to the Social Support Questionnaire give some idea of the variety of measures available: the Social Network List (Stokes, 1983); the Inventory of Socially Supportive Behaviors (Barrera, Sandler, & Ramsey, 1981); the Family Environment Scale (Moos & Moos, 1981); the Interpersonal Support Evaluation List (Cohen, Mermelstein, Kamarck, & Hoberman, 1985); the Perceived Social Support (Friends and Family) scale (Procidano & Heller, 1983); and the Interview Schedule for Social Interaction (Henderson, Duncan-Jones, Byrne, & Scott, 1980). These measures include lists of network support persons, yes/no scales, Likert scales, and a structured interview. Research results indicate that measures of received support and of structural characteristics of the social network do not correlate with each other, but both correlate with measures of perceived available social support (B. Sarason et al., 1987). In turn, several perceived-availability measures appear to assess a common factor, essentially "the feeling that one is valued and esteemed" (B. Sarason et al., 1987, p. 830). Thus, one's own inner feelings of being loved, valued, and respected constitute one of the central features of social support, a finding that has direct implications for psychotherapy.

Some research suggests that individuals who differ in terms of various demographic and personality characteristics may also differ in their perceived (and received) social support. For example, research suggests that there are gender differences in social support, with women reporting greater social support as well as greater satisfaction with that support (e.g., B. Sarason, Sarason, Hacker, & Basham, 1985). Women also appear to be more socially competent (I. Sarason, Sarason, & Shearin, 1986), a quality that has been linked to social support. Additional research results are congruent with the hypothesis that social support is a possible moderator of stress and negative life events, with low social support contributing to "vulnerability" (e.g., I. Sarason & Sarason, 1986; I. Sarason, Sarason, Potter, & Antoni, 1985). (For a thorough review, see Wortman & Dunkel-Schetter, 1987.)

There has been enough research on the definitions, sources, and measurement of social support to have established the topic as a primary interest across several disciplines (e.g., psychology, sociology). However, what in some ways is most intriguing about social support is the more theoretical question of why social support is sometimes helpful and why it is sometimes harmful.

The Positives and Negatives of Support

When Support Works

Considerable research has explored whether social support is directly related to health outcomes (i.e., Does high social support contribute to good health and low support to poor health?) or whether support may interact with various stressors (as noted earlier in the Sarasons' research). The "assets benefits hypothesis" (e.g., Fleming & Baum, 1986) proposes that social support is directly related to positive life benefits (e.g., better health, longer life), whether or not the person receiving the support is under particular stress. Alternatively, it may be that *not* having social support is stressful in and of itself. A favored perspective is the so-called "buffering hypothesis," which suggests that "social support mitigates the effects of stress but does not necessarily provide benefit in the absence of stress. Conversely, lack of support is not necessarily stressful, but lack of support in the face of other stressors is associated with poorer outcomes" (Fleming & Baum, 1986, p. 219). Linking stress directly to health, Wortman and Dunkel-

Schetter (1987) proposed that social support may influence health by affecting (1) an individual's immediate appraisal of and reaction to stress (e.g., seeking immediate medical help), (2) an individual's motivation to cope effectively with a stressor (e.g., compliance with medication and health regimens), and (3) an individual's affective reactions to the present and the future (e.g., feelings of self-efficacy for coping with the stress and measured optimism about the future). As these authors noted, however, influence could also occur in the opposite direction, with an individual's way of experiencing and coping with stress affecting the social support she or he can elicit.

Thus, it appears that social support may be effective in a number of ways although the central theme in the preceding discussion is that social support "works" insofar as it helps the individual *feel* better about the self and the situation and, in turn, *behave* more effectively in the world (two phenomena that are also part of the therapy process).

When Support Doesn't Work

The dark side to social support is described by Coyne, Wortman, and Lehman (1988), who noted that support can be negative for both the receiver and the giver. These writers view social support as an occasion of reciprocal influence, a feedback loop, and they acknowledge that miscommunication can occur at any point within the loop. Consider the example of a married couple in which the husband has a heart attack: Although the stressful event may be construed somewhat differently by the partners, their initial efforts to pull together to deal with the crisis may obscure their disparate perceptions of the event (e.g., she views his heart attack as a temporary crisis, he views it as something that may affect his life forever). Although the wife is initially unstinting in her caregiving, the ongoing strain of managing work and family (with the husband not only not providing any support but actually *taking* support) reduces her ability to cope. However, she feels guilty about her impatience and is afraid to share her negative feelings with anyone, especially her husband. He, on the other hand, grows increasingly frustrated with being in a dependent position but does not feel ready to resume his old roles. He may feel required to "improve" even though his recovery progresses very slowly, if at all. His wife feels overly responsible for his recovery and becomes angry when he does not behave (and improve) in the expected fashion. The husband feels increasingly under attack and responds either by masking the extent of the continuing problems or by exaggerating the problems to "get her off his back." The situation deteriorates, with the partners alternately pushing and withdrawing. Indeed, miscommunication has characterized this feedback loop.

The obvious failure in this example is not so much a failure of social support as it is a failure in communication *about* social support, as Coyne et al. (1988) pointed out. What needs to be negotiated and renegotiated are the types of social support, the duration of social support, and the extent to which support can be made reciprocal, albeit in ways that are different from those previously employed (e.g., husband may be able to prepare dinners at home for the family well before he is able to resume working outside the home; wife may "do" less for the husband but be more cheerful and emotionally supportive). Social support can be very positive, or it can be given in the wrong way at the wrong time by the wrong person, to the detriment of both giver and recipient. Each person is thus well advised to be clear about her or his expectations.

Still other research involving negative effects for social support has proposed what is called a "pressure cooker" effect. Hobfoll and London (1986) assessed Israeli women during the June 1982 Israel–Lebanon conflict, a high-stress situation, and found that social support was related to greater psychological distress. The researchers found that women with high social support and *high-density social networks* were exposed to more intense interaction, resulting in interpersonal and related stressors.

It seems apparent that social support is a complex phenomenon that can be examined from a number of different directions. Earlier we discussed the popularity of self-help/peer-support social support groups and the range of problems they address. To communicate the "felt experience" of social support, we describe the experience of one of the authors, who functioned as the leader of such a group.

Case Example: Breast Cancer Support Group

In 1980, one of the authors (S. S. H.) was asked to work with a nursing administrator in a large local community hospital to develop and lead a support/education group for female patients who had recently undergone surgical treatment for breast cancer. The group met monthly at the hospital, were not charged any fees, and were offered a mix of discussion group sessions (quasi-crisis therapy) and programs of interest to breast cancer patients (e.g., presentations on nutrition, chemotherapy, reconstructive surgery, radiation therapy, and breast prostheses). Most patients were referred to the group by their surgeon immediately after mastectomy, but some heard about it from their oncologist. There was occasional advertising of the group meetings in the community section of the local newspaper, and eventually women also heard about the group through word of mouth.

It took several months to get the group established and to decide on a workable format for meetings. It appeared that alternating meetings that centered around a therapeutic group discussion with meetings focused on a particular relevant topic (usually with a guest speaker) provided maximum participant satisfaction and attendance. This author continued to work as a facilitator with the group for several years, during which time the group was the source of many of the types of social support mentioned earlier. Of the seven types of support suggested by Wortman and Dunkel-Schetter (1987) and discussed earlier in this chapter, all but "provision of material aid to the individual" (#5) were offered by the support/education group on a fairly consistent basis.

Although participation in the group varied, depending on the program and the time of year, usually six to ten women attended (sometimes with husbands or significant others). Social support was an integral part of the group. Expressions of positive emotions toward other members (#1) and support of members' feelings and beliefs (#2) occurred at every meeting, although they were particularly in evidence either when a woman was new to the group or when one of the group members experienced a health crisis, such as a cancer recurrence.

Self-disclosure (#3) was both offered and invited (certainly by some women more than by others), although it was frequently more content-oriented (e.g., "Yes, I'm on six months of chemo") than feeling-oriented (e.g., "I'm afraid of dying"). The reluctance of group members to display strong emotional reactions in the group seemed reasonable, given that the group was intended to offer support and education, not psychotherapy. In essence, the group members tried to accept nonjudgmentally whatever the other members brought to the group.

Advice and information (#4) were offered by group members on specific issues. These included exercises to increase flexibility of the mastectomy arm and methods to handle nausea during chemotherapy. However, rarely was the advice pushed at anyone: members were respectful of each other's boundaries. As noted earlier, provision of material aid (#5) was not one of the group's social support functions, although if the definition of material aid is broadened to include loans of books on breast cancer or loan of a prosthesis to a member who wants to try out a new type without the considerable expense of purchasing it, then material aid was most certainly given. More often, members aided each other with specific tasks (#6), such as transportation to group meetings or accompaniment to chemotherapy appointments. Occasionally, members would become personal friends outside of the group and would arrange to care for each other's children or help each other out in specific ways.

"Helping the individual feel part of a mutually supportive group," dimension #7 in Wortman and Dunkel-Schetter's list of types of support, was probably the most important dimension for this particular group—and perhaps for many such groups. Although it is just one of several dimensions an individual social support provider can offer, it assumes a more important role when the provider is a *group*. Most of the supportive behaviors exercised by the group occurred during group meetings, though the deepest expressions of caring happened outside the group, when group members would visit another member who was hospitalized with a cancer recurrence. This happened about a half-dozen times during the author's involvement with the group, and the depth of caring involved in this act is only apparent when one knows how frightening the specter of recurrence is to most cancer patients. They may go to great lengths to avoid confronting the idea of a recurrence; to voluntarily visit another patient in that situation is a real act of social support—if not of love.

The raw power of a group is not unlike that of a family, which by its very nature inevitably deals with the greatest joy and the most profound pain. Two very different incidents perhaps best summarize the meaning of the mastectomy group to the author. The joy was most powerfully expressed by the face of a 64-year-old woman who had been part of the group from its inception and who had made the group a part of the process of her decision regarding breast reconstruction. A veteran of mastectomy as well as of several unrelated surgeries, Mary had shared with the group her fear of additional surgery versus her personal wish to feel physically "whole" again. After going ahead with reconstruction, she returned to the group and on this particular evening talked about the total experience. Although both her words and her body language indicated that she was pleased overall with what she had done, the extent of her positive feelings about herself were unmistakable as this basically rather shy woman and several of the other group members concluded the meeting with a trip to the restroom for a session of "show and tell."

On the other hand, pain was most tangible for the group in a meeting right before Christmas when one of the most exuberant group members, a young woman in her mid-30s, told the group that she had just found out that her cancer had recurred. That she was terribly frightened was evident to the eight or so of us there. Her ashen face and trembling voice were in stark contrast to her usual bouncing good humor and the steady stream of comments and anecdotes with which she dominated the group whenever she attended a meeting. The first time she stood up in a meeting and started talking, everyone knew Maria! Whether it was the story of her bout with virulent breast cancer that required treatment at a famous cancer hospital halfway across the country or her reassurance that when your hair falls out during chemotherapy it sometimes grows back curly or her continuing and vocal determination to live, Maria was a dominating figure and an unforgettable inspiration to everyone who knew her. And on that December day it was as though an icy wind had blown through the room as she spoke of her terrible fear of what lay ahead. It would be a lie to say that the group rallied around her magnificently—we didn't. We broke out of our stunned silence to ask her questions and try to offer her comfort, to let her know that we cared for her. But the enormity of her reality, a reality that could tomorrow become reality for any one of those present, overwhelmed everyone in the room. Various kinds of social support were offered to Maria at other times, but on that particular day the social support group behaved like any family group would: we grieved.

The Therapy Relationship

Although it is relatively easy to acknowledge the social support value of a group, the social support literature has less frequently addressed the phenomenon of support in the individual therapy relationship. B. Gottlieb (1983b) devoted considerable attention to social support in clinical practice. However, his perspective was that of therapist as assessor, and perhaps in some ways orchestrator, of a given client's social support system, rather than therapist as *provider* of social support. In his case the therapist's role was to help the client elicit and organize better social support.

Our focus, however, is on the therapist's role in *providing* social support. Throughout this volume, we have presented the therapy relationship as something that occurs reciprocally, develops over time, and is subject to the same influences of attraction, exchange, responsiveness, gender role, privacy, and satisfaction that constrain all personal relationships. We have maintained that although therapy sets different constraints on these variables than do other types of close relationships, the essential nature of the interpersonal process is similar across all intimate relationships.

We have also been careful to acknowledge that therapists with different therapy orientations will set the constraints on these variables differently. However, no therapy is conducted without some interpersonal contact. There may be more talking or less talking, more eye contact or less eye contact, but any time two human beings sit together in a room for several hours, interpersonal interactions of some type occur and a relationship is being formed. Thus, the image of the therapist as a social support figure for the client will vary, depending on the therapist's theoretical orientation. However, the presence of social support is a given; only the amount and perhaps the quality of social support will vary.

Types of Therapist Support

Wortman and Dunkel-Schetter's (1987) taxonomy of social support (detailed earlier in this chapter) is a useful framework for presenting the ways in which a therapist serves as a support figure for a client. Most of the acts of support recognized by Wortman and Dunkel-Schetter occur to a greater or lesser extent during psychotherapy and will be discussed in the following paragraphs in the order in which they were originally introduced earlier in this chapter.

The expression of positive emotion toward the client is likely to vary in directness depending on the therapist's theoretical stance. For instance, an affectively-oriented therapist dealing with a client low in self-esteem might tell the client directly, "I wish you could feel as good about yourself as I feel about you—your strength, your commitment to your own growth." An analytic therapist might merely acknowledge the client's feelings, but with eye contact and a comforting tone of voice. "Positive emotion" can mean a great many things, including verbal support, touching (e.g., holding a grieving client), or orienting to and supporting the client nonverbally by facing the client in an open sitting position, making eye contact, and nodding. Whereas enacting "positive emotion" as a form of social support occurs in therapy, it also differentiates therapy from other personal relationships: many of the expressive avenues open to partners, family, and friends are unavailable to a therapist, who must set much more stringent limits on her or his own behavior. Failure to set limits in this realm may inadvertently lead to unacceptable sexual involvement (see Chapter 4). However, this caution is not to indicate that the therapist should turn away from emotionally supporting the client. As we noted earlier in the volume (see Chapter 1), the "therapeutic bond" is a major component of psychotherapy (Orlinsky & Howard, 1986), and one important aspect of that bond is therapist affirmation of the client.

Support by the therapist of the client's feelings and beliefs is a central aspect of psychotherapy. Exploration of the client's feelings and beliefs is a primary function of therapy—one that can probably be agreed upon by nearly all professionals. However, as this exploration occurs, the degree to which the therapist supports, challenges, or interprets these feelings and beliefs may vary greatly, depending both on the therapist's orientation and on the nature of the particular feelings and beliefs in question. For instance, much of the task of cognitive therapy is to identify and alter *irrational* beliefs. Support for such beliefs would not constitute social support and might well be antitherapeutic. In addition, the approach to feelings may differ considerably from the approach to beliefs. In the former case, therapists will grant the client the right to experience his or her feelings; in some cases getting the client to *acknowledge* feelings (much less accept them) is a primary task of therapy. In many cases, it is not the therapist who devalues the feelings but the client. The very act of probing for the client's feelings can be experienced by the client as supportive and accepting (or invasive, in some cases). A critical point in this process is the acceptance by the therapist of the client's negative or unacceptable feelings; such acceptance is perhaps even more important than the therapist's support of the client's positive feelings. Of course, social support is not the same thing as psychotherapy. The two overlap to the extent that socially supportive behaviors occur between client and therapist as one part of therapy. The intrapsychic, interpersonal, and behavioral changes that occur during successful psychotherapy go well beyond social support.

Beliefs and values have an attitudinal component that feelings lack, and they are thus more subject to evaluation and shaping by the therapist. It is in this realm that the supervisor's admonition to the young, inexperienced therapist to "work out your own issues" is most relevant. The therapist's own attitudes toward everything from sexual practices to religion to racial and ethnic differences will inevitably affect how he or she responds to clients. If a client is in therapy to deal with vocational issues and expresses strong disdain for homosexuals, how should the therapist (a believer in gay rights) respond? Or should the therapist respond at all? If the belief is seemingly unrelated to the focus of therapy, should it be attended to? If it is not attended to, will it remain an "issue" for the therapist and interfere with the therapy relationship? Such questions reaffirm the complexity of therapy, in which the therapist is not necessarily free to confront the client on particular attitudes or beliefs that differ from his or her own but is also not free to avoid dealing with them in some way (e.g., in supervision). Perhaps the essence of the particular form of social support inherent in therapy is that the therapist needs in some way to manifest support for the total client (including feelings, beliefs, values) without either endorsing or criticizing any one particular thing. The themes that tie the therapeutic process together are more useful than are most of the specific events that occur.

Encouraging the individual to openly express feelings and beliefs is perhaps the most unambiguous aspect of social support for the practicing therapist. The open expression of beliefs, thoughts, and feelings by the client is essential if therapy is to progress at all. Although some professionals propose that therapist self-disclosure is not appropriate (e.g., Greenson, 1967), client disclosure and self-expression seems absolutely necessary (e.g., Stiles, 1987). In fact, substantial research has focused on ways to foster client disclosure during therapy (e.g., McCarthy, 1979). There are various steps that a therapist can take to encourage client disclosure, including asking direct questions and reflecting the client's previous statements, thereby inviting more disclosure. Nonverbal behaviors such as leaning forward, making eye contact, nodding, and in general fully attending to what the client is saying are also considered facilitative of client expression of feelings and beliefs.

Jourard (1964) believed that the most effective way for a therapist to foster client disclosure was disclosure by the therapist. For example, the therapist might share his or her reactions to an experience the client is relating or might disclose that he or she, too, has felt depressed at times. Jourard assumed that therapist disclosure would model appropriate behavior for the client, reduce the client's fear of being judged, and essentially invite the client to engage in the reciprocal behavior of self-disclosure (see Chapter 3 for a discussion of reciprocity and exchange in the therapy relationship). Jourard's ideas have been explored in an extensive literature on client and therapist self-disclosure, and although the findings regarding disclosure are somewhat mixed (see S. Hendrick, 1987, for a review), most researchers in the field would agree that some types of therapist disclosure at some therapeutic junctures facilitate both disclosure and therapeutic progress in some clients (e.g., McCarthy, 1979; see also Chapters 6 and 7, this volume).

A social support aspect that is included in Wortman and Dunkel-Schetter's (1987) taxonomy, but one that initially seems less relevant to therapist and client, is the provision of material aid to the individual. Therapists are not viewed as being in the business of providing goods to individual clients; rather, they provide services. However, they may also give tangible aid in some rather diverse ways. First, therapists typically carry some part of their client load at reduced fee (or no fee) as part of a *pro bono* service to the larger community. Reducing a client's fee may be seen as allowing him or her to keep money that would otherwise have been spent for therapy and is, in a sense, material aid. A therapist who is a social worker and case manager for a client or family may substantially facilitate the provision of aid to the clients. For instance, the social worker arranges for low-cost housing for the client. Another material provision that can be extremely helpful to clients is medication, prescribed by a therapist/psychiatrist. To someone who is severely depressed, a prescription for a tricyclic antidepressant is literally "material aid."

Another aspect of social support involves helping the individual with specific tasks (such as, in our example of a breast cancer support group, providing transportation to group meetings). As with the aspect of social support in the preceding example, therapist exercise of this type of support is often indirect. For instance, although a therapist does not typically take a client to apply for a job, he or she might work with the client at some length to prepare for job seeking by, for instance, practicing the filling out of forms or role-playing an initial job interview. Such interventions are common occurrences in many therapies. The therapist's role is conceptualized not as performing a task for a client or even helping the client accomplish the task but, rather, as giving the client the "tools" with which to complete the task on his or her own.

A less content-bound instance of aiding the client with a particular task occurs when a client's immediate need in therapy is to express some kind of feeling. Aid may take the form of questions, gentle probing, interpretation of the client's fear of "feeling," exploration of one of the client's recent dreams, or role play with the client. Whatever the therapist's approach, the client is being assisted with the specific "task" of experiencing feelings, accepting them, and beginning the process of resolving them.

Finally, another way of providing social support is by helping a person feel part of a mutually supportive group. This social support behavior would seem analogous to cohesiveness, altruism, and aspects of the other "curative factors" in group psychotherapy outlined by Yalom (1975). One of these curative factors, cohesiveness, is defined by Yalom as "the attractiveness of a group for its members" (p. 46) and is viewed as analogous to the "relationship" in individual psychotherapy. Much of group development and interaction is devoted to fostering feelings of mutual support in group members, since a basis of mutual trust is necessary if the therapeutic work of the group is to proceed. In addition, a positive experience in a therapy or social support group can help an individual resolve previously unsatisfactory group experiences. Indeed, Yalom noted that "group membership, acceptance, and approval are of the utmost importance in the development of the individual" (p. 48). It seems to us that this aspect of mutual social support can be applied to the therapy dyad as well as to the therapy group in the sense that the essence of the experience is to help the client feel that she or he is not *alone*. To imagine the ongoing experience of two people who sit in a room together over weeks, months, and even years, who experience the change of seasons together and develop a history of a relationship with each other, one visualizes an interpersonal picture, not a solitary one. The therapist who can operate within this picture, veering neither to the extreme of enmeshment nor to the extreme of disengagement, is likely to convey to the client a sense of social support as well as a true sense of "relationship."

Types of Client Support

Portraying a therapist as a provider of social support to a client seems reasonable, but what about the reverse—portraying the client as a provider of social support to a therapist? Our thesis throughout this volume has been that the therapist–client relationship is in many ways similar to other personal relationships experienced by both therapist and client and operates by many of the same interpersonal rules. One of those previously discussed rules is reciprocity. As S. Sarason (1985) matter-of-factly stated, "Let us not forget that the clinician seeks the patient's help no less than the patient seeks the clinician's help" (p. 156). What Sarason seems to mean by this is that the client helps the therapist to help the client (i.e., an interpersonal process through which two people are seeking to understand each other), rather than that the client helps the therapist with his or her own personal issues. The mechanisms by which clients support therapists are somewhat different from those by which therapists support clients, though the felt experience may be much the same.

Applying the same taxonomy of social support that we used to analyze types of support from the therapist (namely, Wortman and Dunkel-Schetter's 7-point list of the characteristics of social support), we propose that the client expresses positive emotion toward the therapist through both verbal and nonverbal means. Sometimes clients express general appreciation for the therapist's help whereas on other occasions a specific therapy intervention or suggestion is acknowledged. One possible interpretation of a client's consistent and timely presence for scheduled appointments is that it is in part an expression of positiveness toward the therapist. Such affirmations by a client toward a therapist undoubtedly provide part of what we described in Chapter 3 as a therapist's reward in therapy, namely, the feeling that he or she is doing "good work" in the therapeutic role.

Perhaps the way in which a client is most effective in supporting a therapist's feelings and beliefs is by making attitudinal and behavioral changes during the course of therapy and moving closer to the therapist's conception of what is "health" or "progress" for her or him. We are *not* stating that the client does (or should) become more like the therapist, though that often happens but that the client moves closer to the goals that have been agreed upon by client and therapist. It is possible that in therapy the client will adopt feelings and attitudes that are similar to those of the therapist, and this may be somewhat gratifying to the therapist, but this is much less central to the therapy process than the client's movement toward health. As we noted in Chapter 3, seeing a client improve is one of the fundamental rewards of being a therapist.

How does the client encourage the therapist to openly express feelings and beliefs (e.g., self-disclose)? Clients frequently ask therapists direct questions; sometimes they have a hidden agenda, sometimes they just want a straight answer. For instance, when a new client asks about the process of psychotherapy, he or she could be "testing" the therapist—or just asking for information. The issue of therapist disclosure has been somewhat controversial, as we noted earlier in this chapter (see also Chapters 6 and 7), and for the therapist who is firmly against disclosure, individual requests or encouragements for disclosure may simply provide useful vehicles for interpretations. For the therapist who believes in disclosure under particular conditions, however, responding either to a client's expressed (or unexpressed) need for information or confirmation may necessitate a well-timed and placed therapist disclosure. Ideally, the client's response will be even fuller disclosure (e.g., McCarthy, 1979, 1982) or perhaps an expression of relief that someone else has had a response or experience similar to his or her own—a relief that reflects an experience much like Yalom's (1975) construct of "universality" (i.e., finding out that one's problem is not unique). Although therapist disclosure is designed to help the client rather than the therapist, it may be a positive experience for both.

The offering of advice or information to the therapist is probably an infrequent occurrence in therapy, as is aiding the therapist with specific tasks. Although the therapy relationship is reciprocal in some ways, it is not necessarily reciprocal in kind or amount. To the extent that advice, information, and help with tasks are offered in therapy, it is usually the therapist who does the offering. The extent to which the client might assume the offering role will likely depend on the therapist's theoretical stance, although this is an area of considerable potential difficulty.

On the other hand, the offering of provisions of aid to an individual is very much a part of what a client does in therapy. In a sense, payment for a session is provision of aid to a therapist (and it is also a reward, as discussed in Chapter 3). (Although some might argue that payment is not "aid," but only an even exchange for psychotherapy, we could use the same logic to reply that therapy is not aid, but merely even exchange for payment.) Clients also provide therapists with gifts at various times. Although we know that gift giving may take on different meanings depending on the occasion, level of giving, therapist's orientation, and so on, it must be handled very carefully no matter when it occurs. For a particular client at a particular time, giving a gift to the therapist may provide necessary confirmation of his or her own ability to give as well as to receive and may thus represent an important milestone in the client's therapy. A similar phenomenon is that part of the recovery process in Alcoholics Anonymous that is devoted to helping other members, especially newer recovering alcoholics, with their recovery program.

The last social support construct identified by Wortman and Dunkel-Schetter, helping the individual feel part of a mutually supportive group, certainly operates in the direction of client to therapist. We all exist as part of the human community, and whether the therapist is working with a group, a family, a couple, or an individual, a sense of mutuality and shared experience is central to the participants' feeling that the time spent is worthwhile. Again, we are not talking about equal support in both directions but, rather, some measure of support and recognition of value on the part of the client toward the therapist. Such recognition may be given by the client directly (e.g., telling the therapist some of the valuable things that he or she has learned in therapy) or indirectly (e.g., referring another client to the therapist). Indeed, no therapist is an island.

As we discussed earlier in this chapter, there are times when social support doesn't "work." If the social support that is given does not correspond to the support that is needed, it may represent a failure of communication rather than a failure of support. If the therapist errs in determining the type of therapeutic response required in a given situation (e.g., offering support when confrontation is required), therapeutic progress may slow down. If a therapist gives a lot of social support but displays little of the other behaviors that are necessary for therapeutic movement, the client may become dependent on or enmeshed with the therapist, may cease making progress, or may terminate therapy. There are times when the process is somewhat self-correcting and the client lets the therapist know that he or she missed the mark (e.g., "No, I'm not feeling depressed right now; my allergies are acting up"). However, the primary responsibility for judging the appropriate levels of social support to be offered the client rests with the therapist. Although it is difficult to offer absolute judgments, social support is probably at appropriate levels when the client is comfortable with (but not dependent on) psychotherapy and when the therapist can clearly ascertain movement (e.g., behavioral change) by the client. The affective and behavioral data provided by the therapy process offer the therapist useful feedback.

Therapy Outcome

In trying to summarize the overall therapeutic value of social support, particularly the support of the client by the therapist, it is useful to consider Orlinsky and Howard's (1986, p. 371) answer to the question, What is therapeutic about psychotherapy? Their answer included the following core ingredients in effective psychotherapeutic work: (1) the therapeutic bond between client and therapist, (2) certain therapeutic interventions, (3) focusing interventions on the client's feelings, (4) preparation of the client for therapy and collaboration during therapy, and (5) (within limits) having more rather than less therapy. Of these five ingredients, all but the last could be viewed as having some connection with social support behaviors of the therapist.

The way in which social support naturally occurs within a therapy relationship can perhaps best be demonstrated through consideration of a therapy session. The following is a transcript of part of a therapy session, with therapist–client dialogue on the left and relevant annotations on the right.

Case Transcript

The client is a 30-year-old man who entered therapy because of a recent divorce from his wife of 8 years. He shares custody of his 5-year-old son with his ex-wife. The therapist, a 55-year-old woman, has an eclectic orientation but draws many interventions and strategies from the cognitive–behavioral perspective. This is the sixth session.

C: This has been a terrible week. I thought things would get easier, but even after almost a year [since the divorce], I still have times when I don't think I can cope.

T: I know that you've been talking recently about feeling better, so this week must have felt like a real setback.

Comment: Therapist supports the client's feelings and beliefs.

C: Yeah, it did. I ran into Fran [ex-wife] at the mall the other night. She was with her new boyfriend, and when I saw them I felt angry. I went out of my way to avoid them, but I think Fran saw me. Anyway, I tried to keep going with what I was doing—I was looking for some new jogging shoes 'cause I got real fired up when we were talking last .week about how I could start getting back into doing things that I used to enjoy before Fran and I started having problems . . . but I just couldn't concentrate on anything after I saw her—or rather, them—so I just went home. Then I got real down, thinking I would just never get over it, never forget about her, never do anything. . . . Everything just seemed like "never."

Comment: Client refers to therapist offering advice or information and aiding with a task, all done during previous session.

T: So you were doing something for you, shopping for new jogging shoes, and then you saw Fran and her boyfriend and that was kind of like a tornado, blowing everything else away. Can you tell me more about the anger? Were there any thoughts that went along with it?

Comment: Therapist supports client and urges him to self-disclose.

C: Well, first I like felt this rush . . . anger . . . then I thought, what is

she doing out here with that
jerk? She should be home with
Tommy [their son]. She's being a
lousy mother, just like she was a
lousy wife—but man, that just
isn't true, damn it! She is a good
mother, and in lots of ways she
was a good wife. It just didn't
work. But I can't just start con-
demning her for everything; that
doesn't make any sense, and it
really doesn't help anything.
That's what I was thinking
about on the way home from the
mall—that it wasn't really any-
body's fault that our marriage
broke up. And then I just felt so
"heavy"—weighted down, like I
couldn't move. I just sat on the
couch for an hour like a zombie,
not even watching TV. It was
like I couldn't move.

T: This sounds like what has happened before—and we've talked
about it—that you still have a lot
of feelings for Fran and a lot of
pain about the divorce. When
you know you're going to see
her, you kind of get ready for it,
and things usually go okay. But
when you aren't ready, your feelings flash and you get angry,
either at her or at yourself. Then
you get tied up in knots. You get
almost irrational in the anger,
"blaming" all over the place. But
you are so used to being reasonable—and in control—that you
edit yourself. Your mind tells
your emotions that they are not

Comment: Therapist sup-
ports client by communicating understanding.

reasonable or logical and that therefore they shouldn't exist. But that doesn't work. Your negative feelings—your anger—just go underground, and then you get depressed.

C: Yeah, I know that's what happened. As I was going home from the mall, I thought, damn, here we go again . . . but I did it anyway and ended up losing the whole evening and then feeling rotten for a couple of days afterward. God, when will it end?

T: I hear your frustration—and your impatience. Divorce is painful, and it hurts for a while. I wish you could just give yourself a break and let yourself feel unreasonable once in a while. You don't have to throw things or anything like that—(*client laughs, then both laugh*)—yes, I know, you're about as likely to throw something as Mr. Spock is to have an anxiety attack. That's what I mean—give it a break.

Comment: Therapist expresses support for and positive emotion toward client.

Comment: Therapist encourages client to express feelings.

C: I can't give it a break; that's why I'm here! Or at least it's really hard to give it a break and just let down for awhile.

T: I know. I'm not trying to come down on you; you do a good enough job of that yourself. We've talked about your resistance to getting out of control before, but we haven't talked

Comment: Therapist supports client by reframing previous suggestion to "give it a break."

about where it started. When you gave me your family history in our first session, we went over a lot of things very quickly. Could you tell me a little more about how it was growing up in your family? How did it *feel* to be a kid in your house?

Comment: Therapist encourages client to self-disclose.

Although we have presented just a brief section of a therapy session, it is apparent that occasions for social support by the therapist occur frequently in therapy, though they may be called many things besides social support. Client support of the therapist occurs just as surely but considerably less frequently. Two instances of client support of the therapist in the above session are (1) the client's trip to the mall, itself a follow-up to material talked about in a previous therapy session, and (2) the client's willingness to confront the therapist, when he says, "I can't give it a break; that's why I'm here!" For a client who is likely to be very hard on himself and very guarded, this shows considerable trust in the therapist and in the relationship, especially for so early in the process.

Conclusions

This chapter has attempted to draw links between the process of social support, as it has been researched by social and community psychologists and other professionals, and the psychotherapy relationship. Although we have presented some material on the definitions of and sources of social support, as well as its measurement, our primary concern has been to show how some of the basic types of social support are translated into what occurs between therapist and client during the therapy hour. It seems clear to us that social support is given by both therapist and client, though the reciprocal nature of the relationship is far from balanced. Therapists are the primary (though not the only) social support providers in psychotherapy.

It is important to note, despite the emphasis in this chapter on social support being enacted between the therapist and the client, that other people in the client's social network provide support to the client, just as the therapist's social network provides support to the therapist.

For instance, a client may talk to friends, coworkers, or family members about going to therapy, which may validate (or on occasion undermine) the therapy process. Therapists may talk to friends, spouses, and colleagues about clients and may receive social support for their professional work in general or for their work with specific clients. Such structural attributes as social network size, density, interconnectedness, and overlap are likely to influence one's social choices (e.g., Milardo, 1986): individuals from dense, interconnected networks may be less likely to form strong personal attachments with persons outside the network (e.g., a relationship with a therapist).

Although we have been concerned with generalizing from the social support literature to psychotherapy, reverse generalization is also important. In particular, some of the conditions placed on the provision of support during psychotherapy—that it take account of both the provider and the one being supported, that it be given at the right time and with respect for the boundaries of the persons involved, and that it be viewed as reciprocal in *nature* but not necessarily in *amount*—seem to us to apply equally well to social support provision in families, groups, and community agencies. Social support is in some measure "in the eye of the beholder": if the beholder (i.e., recipient) does not experience the offering as beneficial, then the possibility remains that it is not support. Support is more useful when it is appropriate than when it is unstinting, and the best way to make it appropriate is for the persons involved to communicate about it. Communicating about social support and tailoring the support to fit the existing need seem to be two aspects of the therapy relationship that have positive implications for the wider network of personal relationships.

CHAPTER 9

Concluding Remarks

Major Themes

When the therapy relationship is viewed as a personal relationship, certain themes emerge. First, a source of tension or confusion in the therapy relationship is revealed. Because the therapy relationship is neither completely like other personal relationships nor like other professional relationships, clients and therapists must work to discover the possibilities and the limitations of the relationship. On the one hand, clients pay a fee and are expected to meet with the therapist, talk only in a particular place and at a particular time, and only for 45 to 50 minutes. This structuring of the relationship is characteristic of other professional relationships. Indeed, the regularity of sessions and their time limits are more structured than would be true in many professional relationships. For example, one sees a physician for briefer visits on average but with the expectation that she or he will spend as much time as needed during an appointment to address a specific medical problem. In therapy the number of visits are generally calculated to fit the client's needs but any particular session is expected to end on time.

On the other hand, within the session the client shares personal and intimate information with the therapist, expresses deeply felt emotions, and usually comes to believe that the therapist cares for her or him. The client is also likely to express positive feelings for the therapist. As in personal relationships, a high degree of mutual trust, respect, and affection may develop between client and therapist. Negative feelings such as jealousy, envy, or disappointment may arise, but these are also characteristic of close relationships. The need to maintain both a personal and professional stance in the relationship can be problematic for client and therapist. For clients there may be unresolved disappointment that the therapist cannot have a genuinely personal (i.e., unrestrained) relationship with them. On the other hand, therapists may have trouble maintaining the professional side of the relationship and may befriend clients, have sexual relationships with them, or use the therapy relationship for their own gratification.

By examining the therapy relationship through the many lenses provided by theory and research on personal relationships, the preceding chapters illuminate the various ways in which the therapy relationship operates like other personal relationships—and the ways in which it does not. By being aware of the differences between ordinary personal relationships and the therapy relationship, therapists can avoid the "seductions" into unprofessional behavior for themselves and for their clients.

A second theme that emerges from these chapters is relationship development (see Chapter 5) and the ways in which the therapy relationship varies over time. While time is a factor, implicitly or explicitly, in every facet of therapy, it has special significance for the concept of "investments" in a relationship, which accumulate over the course of its development (see Chapter 3). The development of the personal relationship in therapy is especially salient when one compares the sessions that define its temporal boundaries: the tension between personal and professional aspects of the therapy relationship is probably most intense at the beginning of therapy, when the roles of client and therapist are being established, and at the end, when the client and therapist, who have developed a close relationship, are saying goodbye and may never talk together again.

A third emphasis in the book is the impact of the therapy relationship on the therapist. Often therapy is presented as something that therapists *do* and clients *have done to* them. When the focus is on the therapy relationship, especially when it is viewed as a personal relationship, it is clear that *both* client and therapist contribute to the relationship and *both* client and therapist are affected by it. There are rewards and costs in the therapy relationship for both client and therapist (see Chapter 3), variables that lead to attraction for both client and therapist (see Chapter 4), and ways of being responsive for both client and therapist (see Chapter 6).

Implications for Clinical Practice and Research

This volume raises various issues for the practice of psychotherapy: the need to address in therapy the clients' and the therapists' assumptions about the therapy relationship; the impact of early versus later impressions and expectancies on mutual liking and trust; clients' concerns about confidentiality and embarrassment over divulging personal information that they may have shared with few (if any) other persons. The book doesn't present a particular set of therapeutic interventions that naturally follow from our approach but encourages therapists and clients to openly acknowledge personal issues in their relationship.

What about the implications of a personal relationship for research on therapy? The major concepts discussed in this book, including social exchange, interpersonal attraction, relationship development over time, responsiveness, privacy, roles and social support, suggest directions for research on the social process in psychotherapy and even therapeutic outcomes. It may be possible, for instance, to devise empirical scales measuring major social exchange constructs such as rewards, costs, comparison level, comparison level for alternatives, and investments and determine their impact on client and therapist satisfaction and commitment as well as on personal growth (see Chapter 3). Given that measures of social attraction and social exchange early in a relationship differentiate relationships that later will be successful or unsuccessful, it would be worthwhile examining further whether factors predicting eventual success in therapy can be determined at a relatively early stage in the therapy process. It is also possible that therapist factors with high predictive value are ones that therapists could learn to use in establishing better therapy relationships with clients. On the other hand, given the "gradual view" that personal relationships develop slowly over time (the approach represented by social penetration theory, described in Chapter 5), perhaps research over different stages of therapy could indicate which social exchange and attraction variables are important at particular points in time.

Despite the apparent asymmetry of the therapy relationship, (e.g., the client pays for therapy, the client is expected to self-disclose), the therapist's "responsiveness" to the client contributes significantly to the progress of therapy (see Chapter 6). Responsiveness may occur in the expressions of concern that are displayed verbally and nonverbally by the therapist. Empirical studies would be worthwhile on the ways in which therapists convey concern, attentiveness, and interest in their clients (see Chapter 6).

Finally, the relevance for research on the therapy relationship should not be overlooked by personal relationship researchers. Though relationship researchers have generally focused on symmetrical or mutual relationships (such as friendships and love relationships), therapy provides an opportunity to study how personal relationships develop when there is unequal involvement in the relationship (which is also the case in the personal relationships that emerge between parents and their children as well as between employers and employees). The study of the therapy relationship as a personal relationship can provide fresh insights for the student of personal relationships as well as for the clinician.

References

Adams, J. S. (1965). Inequity in social exchange. In L. Berkowitz (Ed.), *Advances in experimental social psychology* (Vol. 2, pp. 267–299). New York: Academic Press.

Ainsworth, M. D. S. (1982). Attachment: Retrospect and prospect. In C. M. Parkes & J. Stevenson-Hinde (Eds.), *The place of attachment in human behavior* (pp. 3–30). New York: Basic Books.

Ainsworth, M. D. S., Blehar, M. C., Waters, E., & Wall, S. (1978). *Patterns of attachment: A psychological study of the strange situation.* Hillsdale, NJ: Erlbaum.

Alexander, L. B., & Luborsky, L. (1986). The Penn Helping Alliance Scales. In L. S. Greenberg & W. M. Pinsof (Eds.), *The psychotherapeutic process: A research handbook* (pp. 325–366). New York: Guilford Press.

Altman, I. (1973). Reciprocity of interpersonal exchange. *Journal for the Theory of Social Behavior, 3*, 249–261.

Altman, I. (1975). *The environment and social behavior.* Monterey, CA: Brooks/Cole.

Altman, I., & Taylor, D. A. (1973). *Social penetration: The development of interpersonal relationships.* New York: Holt, Rinehart & Winston.

Altman, I., Vinsel, A., & Brown, B. H. (1981). Dialectic conceptions in social psychology: An application to social penetration and privacy regulation. In L. Berkowitz (Ed.), *Advances in experimental social psychology* (Vol. 14, pp. 107–160). New York: Academic Press.

American Psychological Association. (1981). Ethical principles of psychologists. *American Psychologist, 36*, 633–651.

American Psychological Association. (1987). General guidelines for providers of psychological services. *American Psychologist, 42*, 712–723.

Anchor, K. N., & Sandler, H. M. (1976). Psychotherapy sabotage revisited: The better half of individual psychotherapy. *Journal of Clinical Psychology, 32*, 146–148.

Anderson, B., & Anderson, W. (1985). Client perceptions of counselors using positive and negative self-involving statements. *Journal of Counseling Psychology, 32*, 462–465.

Archer, R. L., Hormuth, S. E., & Berg, J. H. (1982). Avoidance of self-disclosure: An experiment under conditions of self-awareness. *Personality and Social Psychology Bulletin, 8*, 122–128.

Argyle, M., & Dean, J. (1965). Eye-contact, distance and affiliation. *Sociometry, 28*, 289–304.

Aries, E. J., & Johnson, F. L. (1983). Close friendship in adulthood: Conversational content between same-sex friends. *Sex Roles, 9*, 1183–1196.

Atkinson, D. R., Furlong, M. J., & Poston, W. C. (1986). Afro-American preferences for counselor characteristics. *Journal of Counseling Psychology, 33*, 326–330.

Atkinson, D. R., Poston, W. C., Furlong, M. J., & Mercado, P. (1989). Ethnic group preferences for counselor characteristics. *Journal of Counseling Psychology, 36*, 68–72.

Axsom, D., & Cooper, J. (1985). Cognitive dissonance and psychotherapy: The role of effort justification in inducing weight loss. *Journal of Experimental Social Psychology, 21*, 149–160.

Bailey, W., Hendrick, C., & Hendrick, S. S. (1987). Relation of sex and gender role to love, sexual attitudes, and self-esteem. *Sex Roles, 16*, 637–648.

Baird, K. A., & Rupert, P. A. (1987). Clinical management of confidentiality: A survey of psychologists in seven states. *Professional Psychology: Research and Practice, 18*, 347–352.

Barrera, M. J., Sandler, I. N., & Ramsey, T. B. (1981). Preliminary development of a scale of social support: Studies on college students. *American Journal of Community Psychology, 9*, 435–447.

Barrett-Lennard, G. T. (1986). The Relationship Inventory now: Issues and advances in theory, method, and use. In L. S. Greenberg & W. M. Pinsof (Eds.), *The psychotherapeutic process: A research handbook* (pp. 439–476). New York: Guilford Press.

Basch, M. F. (1980). *Doing psychotherapy*. New York: Basic Books.

Bayles, M. D. (1981). *Professional ethics*. Belmont, CA: Wadsworth.

Beck, A. T., Rush, A. J., Shaw, B. F., & Emery, G. (1979). *Cognitive therapy of depression*. New York: Guilford Press.

Bem, D. (1972). Self-perception theory. In L. Berkowitz (Ed.), *Advances in experimental social psychology* (Vol. 6, pp. 1–62). New York: Academic Press.

Bem, S. L. (1974). The measurement of psychological androgyny. *Journal of Consulting and Clinical Psychology, 42*, 155–162.

Benbenishity, R. (1988). Gaps between expectations and perceived reality of therapists and clients. *Journal of Clinical Psychology, 43*, 231–236.

Berg, J. H. (1984). The development of friendship between roommates. *Journal of Personality and Social Psychology, 46*, 346–356.

Berg, J. H. (1987). Responsiveness and self-disclosure. In V. J. Derlega & J. H. Berg (Eds.), *Self-disclosure: Theory, research, and therapy* (pp. 101–130). New York: Plenum Press.

Berg, J. H., & Archer, R. L. (1980). Disclosure or concern: A second look at liking for the norm-breaker. *Journal of Personality , 48*, 245–257.

Berg, J. H., & Archer, R. L. (1982). Responses to self-disclosure and interaction goals. *Journal of Experimental Social Psychology, 18,* 501-512.

Berg, J. H., & Archer, R. L. (1983). The disclosure-liking relationship: Effects of self-perception, order of disclosure, and topical similarity. *Human Communication Research, 10,* 269-281.

Berg, J. H., & Clark, M. S. (1986). Differences in social exchange between intimate and other relationships: Gradually evolving or quickly apparent? In V. J. Derlega & B. A. Winstead (Eds.), *Friendship and social interaction* (pp. 101-128). New York: Springer-Verlag.

Berg, J. H., & McQuinn, R. D. (1986). Attraction and exchange in continuing and noncontinuing dating relationships. *Journal of Personality and Social Psychology, 50,* 942-952.

Berg, J. H., & McQuinn, R. D. (1989). Loneliness and aspects of the social support network. *Journal of Social and Personal Relationships, 6,* 359-372.

Berg, J. H., & Peplau, L. A. (1982). Loneliness: The effects of self-disclosure and androgyny. *Personality and Social Psychology Bulletin, 8,* 624-630.

Berg, J. H., & Wright-Buckley, C. (1988). Effects of racial similarity and interviewer intimacy in a peer counseling analogue. *Journal of Counseling Psychology, 35,* 377-384.

Bernstein, B. L., Hofmann, N. B., & Wade, P. (1987). Preferences for counselor gender: Students' sex role, other characteristics, and type of problem. *Journal of Counseling Psychology, 34,* 20-26.

Berscheid, E., & Peplau, L. A. (1983). The emerging science of relationships. In H. H. Kelley, E. Berscheid, A. Christensen, H. H. Harvey, T. L. Huston, G. Levinger, E. McClintock, L. A. Peplau, & D. R. Peterson, *Close relationships* (pp. 1-19). New York: W. H. Freeman.

Berscheid, E., & Walster, E. (1974a). A little bit about love. In T. L. Huston (Ed.), *Foundations of interpersonal attraction* (pp. 355-381). New York: Academic Press.

Berscheid, E., & Walster, E. (1974b). Physical attractiveness. In L. Berkowitz (Ed.), *Advances in experimental social psychology* (Vol. 7, pp. 157-215). New York: Academic Press.

Blier, M. J., Atkinson, D. R., & Geer, C. A. (1987). Effect of client gender and counselor gender and sex roles on willingness to see the counselor. *Journal of Counseling Psychology, 34,* 27-30.

Bordin, D. (1979). The generalizability of the psychoanalytic concept of the working alliance. *Psychotherapy: Theory, Research, and Practice, 16,* 252-260.

Bouhoutsos, J., Holroyd, J., Lerman, H., Forer, B., & Greenberg, M. (1983). Sexual intimacy between psychotherapists and patients. *Professional Psychology: Research and Practice, 14,* 185-196.

Bowen, M. (1978). *Family therapy in clinical practice.* New York: Jason Aronson.

Bowlby, J. (1969). *Attachment and loss: Vol. 1. Attachment.* New York: Basic Books.

Braiker, H. B., & Kelley, H. H. (1979). Conflict in the development of close relationships. In R. L. Burgess & T. L. Huston (Eds.), *Social exchange in developing relationships* (pp. 135–168). New York: Academic Press.

Brehm, S. S. (1985). *Intimate relationships.* New York: Random House.

Breuer, J., & Freud, S. (1966). *Studies on hysteria.* New York: Avon. (Original work published 1895)

Brigham, K. S., & Brigham, J. C. (1985). The influence of psychotherapy fee on observers' evaluations of therapists and clients. *Journal of Social and Clinical Psychology, 3,* 224–231.

Broverman, I. K., Broverman, D. M., Clarkson, F. S., Rosenkrantz, P. S., & Vogel, S. R. (1970). Sex-role stereotypes and clinical judgments of mental health. *Journal of Consulting and Clinical Psychology, 34,* 1–7.

Bundza, K. A., & Simonson, M. R. (1973). Therapist self-disclosure: Its effect on impressions of therapist and willingness to disclose. *Psychotherapy: Theory, Research, and Practice, 10,* 215–217.

Buss, D. M., & Barnes, M. (1986). Preferences in human mate selection. *Journal of Personality and Social Psychology, 50,* 559–570.

Byrne, D. (1969). Attitudes and attraction. In L. Berkowitz (Ed.), *Advances in experimental social psychology* (Vol. 4, pp. 35–89). New York: Academic Press.

Byrne, D. (1971). *The attraction paradigm.* New York: Academic Press.

Byrne, D., Clore, G. L., & Smeaton, G. (1986). The attraction hypothesis: Do similar attitudes affect anything? *Journal of Personality and Social Psychology, 51,* 1167–1170.

Carkhuff, K. R., & Pierce, R. (1967). The differential effects of counselor race and social class upon patient depth of self-exploration in an initial clinical interview. *Journal of Consulting Psychology, 31,* 632–634.

Carr, J. E. (1970). Differentiation in similarity of patient and therapist and the outcome of psychotherapy. *Journal of Abnormal Psychology, 76,* 361–369.

Cash, T. F., & Derlega, V. J. (1978). The matching hypothesis: Physical attractiveness among same-sexed friends. *Personality and Social Psychology Bulletin, 4,* 240–243.

Cattell, R. B., & Eber, S. W. (1966). *The Sixteen Personality Factor Questionnaire* (3rd ed.). Champaign, IL: Institute for Personality and Ability Testing.

Chaikin, A. L., & Derlega, V. J. (1974). *Self-disclosure.* Morristown, NJ: General Learning Press.

Chelune, G. J., Sultan, F. E., Vosk, B. N., Ogden, J. K., & Waring, E. M. (1984). Self-disclosure patterns in clinical and nonclinical couples. *Journal of Clinical Psychology, 40,* 213–215.

Clark, M. S. (1984). Record keeping in two types of relationships. *Journal of Personality and Social Psychology, 47,* 549–557.

Clark, M. S., & Mills, J. (1979). Interpersonal attraction in exchange and communal relationships. *Journal of Personality and Social Psychology, 37,* 12–24.

Clark, M. S., Mills, J., & Powell, M. C. (1986). Keeping track of needs in communal and exchange relationships. *Journal of Personality and Social Psychology, 51*, 333–338.

Clark, M. S., Ouellette, R., Powell, M. C., & Milberg, S. (1987). Recipient's mood, relationship type, and helping. *Journal of Personality and Social Psychology, 53*, 94–103.

Clark, M. S., & Reis, H. T. (1988). Interpersonal processes in close relationships. *Annual Review of Psychology, 39*, 609–672.

Cleaver, G. (1987). Marriage enrichment by means of a structured communication programme. *Family Relations: Journal of Applied Family and Child Studies, 36*, 49–54.

Cobb, S. (1976). Social support as a moderator of life stress. *Psychosomatic Medicine, 38*, 300–314.

Cohen, S., Mermelstein, R., Kamarck, T., & Hoberman, H. N. (1985). Measuring the functional components of social support. In I. Sarason & B. Sarason (Eds.), *Social support: Theory, research and applications* (pp. 73–94). Dordrecht, The Netherlands: Martinus Nijhoff.

Coie, J. D., Pennington, B. F., & Buckley, H. H. (1974). Effects of situational stress and sex roles on the attribution of psychological disorder. *Journal of Consulting and Clinical Psychology, 42*, 559–568.

Condon, J. W., & Crano, W. D. (1988). Inferred evaluation and the relation between attitude similarity and interpersonal attraction. *Journal of Personality and Social Psychology, 54*, 789–797.

Cooper, J., & Axsom, D. (1982). Effort justification in psychotherapy. In G. Weary & H. Mirels (Eds.), *Integrations of clinical and social psychology* (pp. 214–230). London: Oxford University Press.

Coyne, J. C., Wortman, C. B., & Lehman, D. R. (1988). The other side of support: Emotional overinvolvement and miscarried helping. In B. H. Gottlieb (Ed.), *Marshaling social support: Formats, processes, and effects* (pp. 305–330). Newbury Park, CA: Sage Publications.

Cross, D. G., Sheehan, P. W., & Khan, J. A. (1982). Short- and long-term follow-up of clients receiving insight-oriented therapy and behavior therapy. *Journal of Consulting and Clinical Psychology, 50*, 103–112.

Danish, S. J., D'Augelli, A. R., & Brock, G. W. (1976). An evaluation of helping skills training: Effects on helpers' verbal responses. *Journal of Counseling Psychology, 23*, 259–266.

Davidson, B., Balswick, J., & Halverson, C. (1983). Affective self-disclosure and marital adjustment: A test of equity theory. *Journal of Marriage and the Family, 45*, 93–102.

Davis, D. (1982). Determinants of responsiveness in dyadic interactions. In W. Ickes & E. G. Knowles (Eds.), *Personality, roles, and social behavior* (pp. 85–140). New York: Springer-Verlag.

Davis, D., & Holtgraves, T. (1984). Perceptions of unresponsive others: Attributions, attraction, understandability, memory of their utterances. *Journal of Experimental Social Psychology, 20*, 383–408.

Davis, D., & Perkowitz, W. T. (1979). Consequences of responsiveness in dyadic interactions: Effects of probability of response and proportion of content related responses. *Journal of Personality and Social Psychology, 37*, 534–550.

Davis, J. D. (1976). Self-disclosure in an acquaintance exercise: Responsibility for level of intimacy. *Journal of Personality and Social Psychology, 33,* 787–792.

Davis, J. D. (1978). When boy meets girl: Sex roles and the negotiation of intimacy in an acquaintance exercise. *Journal of Personality and Social Psychology, 36,* 684–692.

Davis, K. E., & Todd, M. J. (1985). Assessing friendship: Prototypes, paradigm cases, and relationship description. In S. W. Duck & D. Perlman (Eds.), *Understanding personal relationships: An interdisciplinary approach* (pp. 17–38). London: Sage Publications

Deardorff, W. W., Cross, H. J., & Hupprich, W. R. (1984). Malpractice liability in psychotherapy: Client and practitioner perspectives. *Professional Psychology: Research and Practice, 15,* 590–600.

Denton, L. (1987, June). Child abuse reporting laws: Are they a barrier to helping troubled families? *The APA Monitor,* pp. 1, 22, 23.

Derlega, V. J., & Chaikin, A. L. (1975). *Sharing intimacy: What we reveal to others and why.* Englewood Cliffs, NJ: Prentice-Hall.

Derlega, V. J., & Chaikin, A. L. (1977). Privacy and self-disclosure in social relationships. *Journal of Social Issues, 33*(3), 102–115.

Derlega, V. J., & Grzelak, J. (1979). Appropriateness of self-disclosure. In G. J. Chelune (Ed.), *Self-disclosure* (pp. 151–176). San Francisco: Jossey-Bass.

Derlega, V. J., Lewis, R. J., Harrison, S., Winstead, B. A., & Costanza, R. (1986). Gender differences in the initiation and attribution of tactile intimacy. *Journal of Nonverbal Behavior, 13,* 83–96.

Derlega, V. J., Lovell, R., & Chaikin, A. L. (1976). Effects of therapist disclosure and its perceived appropriateness on client self-disclosure. *Journal of Consulting and Clinical Psychology, 44,* 866.

Derlega, V. J., & Margulis, S. T. (1982). Why loneliness occurs: The interrelationship of social-psychological and privacy concepts. In L. A. Peplau & D. Perlman (Eds.), *Loneliness: A sourcebook of current theory, research and therapy* (pp. 152–165). New York: Wiley-Interscience.

Derlega, V. J., Margulis, S. T., & Winstead, B. A. (1987). A social-psychological analysis of self-disclosure in psychotherapy. *Journal of Social and Clinical Psychology, 5,* 205–215.

Derlega, V. J., Wilson, M., & Chaikin, A. L. (1976). Friendship and disclosure reciprocity. *Journal of Personality and Social Psychology, 34,* 578–582.

Derlega, V. J., Winstead, B. A., Wong, P. T. P., & Greenspan, M. (1987). Self-disclosure and relationship development: An attributional analysis. In M. E. Roloff & G. R. Miller (Eds.), *Interpersonal processes: New directions in communication research* (pp. 172–187). Newbury Park, CA: Sage Publications.

Derlega, V. J., Winstead, B. A., Wong, P. T. P., & Hunter, S. (1985). Gender effects in an initial encounter: A case where men exceed women in disclosure. *Journal of Social and Personal Relationships, 2,* 25–44.

Deutsch, C. J. (1984). Self-reported sources of stress among psychotherapists. *Professional Psychology: Research and Practice, 6,* 833–845.

DeWald, P. A. (1969). *Psychotherapy: A dynamic approach* (2nd ed.). New York: Basic Books.

Dies, R. R. (1973). Group therapist self-disclosure: An evaluation by clients. *Journal of Counseling Psychology, 20*, 344-348.

Dies, R. R., & Cohen, L. (1976). Content considerations in group therapist self-disclosure. *International Journal of Group Psychotherapy, 26*, 71-88.

Dinkmeyer, D. C., Pew, W. L., & Dinkmeyer, D. C., Jr. (1979). *Adlerian counseling and psychotherapy.* Monterey, CA: Brooks/Cole.

Dion, K., Berscheid, E., & Walster, E. (1972). What is beautiful is good. *Journal of Personality and Social Psychology, 24*, 290-295.

Doster, J. A., & Brooks, S. J. (1974). Interviewer disclosure modeling, information revealed, and interviewee verbal behavior. *Journal of Consulting and Clinical Psychology, 42*, 420-426.

Doster, J. A., & Nesbitt, J. G. (1979). Psychotherapy and self-disclosure. In G. J. Chelune (Ed.), *Self-disclosure* (pp. 177-224). San Francisco: Jossey-Bass.

Duck, S. W., & Gilmour, R. (Eds.). (1981). *Personal relationships 1: Studying personal relationships.* London: Academic Press.

Duck, S. W., & Sants, H. (1983). On the origin of the specious: Are personal relationships really interpersonal states? *Journal of Social and Clinical Psychology, 1*, 27-41.

Duval, S., & Wicklund, R. A. (1972). *A theory of objective self-awareness.* New York: Academic Press.

Ebbesen, E. B., Kjos, G. L., & Konecni, V. J. (1976). Spatial ecology: Its effects on the choice of friends and enemies. *Journal of Experimental Social Psychology, 12*, 505-518.

Eidelson, R. J. (1980). Interpersonal satisfaction and level of involvement: A curvilinear relationship. *Journal of Personality and Social Psychology, 39*, 460-470.

Ellis, A. (1984). Rational-emotive therapy. In R. J. Corsini (Ed.), *Current psychotherapies* (3rd ed., pp. 196-238). Itasca, IL: Peacock.

Ellsworth, P. C., Carlsmith, J. M., & Henson, A. (1972). The stare as a stimulus to flight in human subjects. *Journal of Personality and Social Psychology, 21*, 302-311.

Ellsworth, P. C., & Ross, L. (1975). Intimacy in response to direct gaze. *Journal of Experimental Social Psychology, 11*, 592-613.

Emmelkamp, P. M., Van Linden Van den Heuvell, C., Ruphan, M., & Sanderman, R. (1988). Cognitive and behavioral interventions: A comparative evaluation with clinically distressed couples. *Journal of Family Psychology, 1*, 365-377.

Falbo, T., & Peplau, L. A. (1980). Power strategies in intimate relationships. *Journal of Personality and Social Psychology, 38*, 618-628.

Fehr, B. (1988). Prototype analysis of the concepts of love and commitment. *Journal of Personality and Social Psychology, 545*, 557-579.

Fernbach, B., Winstead, B. A., & Derlega, V. J. (1989). Sex differences in diagnoses and treatment recommendations for antisocial personality and somatization disorders. *Journal of Social and Clinical Psychology, 8,* 238–255.

Festinger, L. (1954). A theory of social comparison processes. *Human Relations, 7,* 117–140.

Festinger, L. (1957). *A theory of cognitive dissonance.* Stanford: Stanford University Press.

Finney, J. C. (1975). Therapist and patient after hours. *American Journal of Psychotherapy, 29,* 593–602.

Fishbein, M. J., & Laird, J. D. (1979). Concealment and disclosure: Some effects of information control on the person who controls. *Journal of Experimental Social Psychology, 15,* 114–121.

Fisher, K. (1985, October). Court protects talk within therapy session. *The APA Monitor,* p. 32.

Fleming, R., & Baum, A. (1986). Social support and stress: The buffering effects of friendship. In V. J. Derlega & B. A. Winstead (Eds.), *Friendship and social interaction* (pp. 207–226). New York: Springer-Verlag.

Ford, M. F., & Widiger, T. A. (1987, August). *Sex bias in diagnosis of antisocial and histrionic personality disorders.* Paper presented at the 95th Annual Convention of the American Psychological Association, New York, NY.

Framo, J. L. (1982). *Explorations in marital and family therapy.* New York: Springer.

Franzoi, S. L., & Davis, M. H. (1985). Adolescent self-disclosure and loneliness: Private self-consciousness and parental influences. *Journal of Personality and Social Psychology, 48,* 768–780.

French, J. R., & Raven, B. (1959). The basis of social power. In D. Cartwright (Ed.), *Studies in social power* (pp. 150–167). Ann Arbor: University of Michigan Press.

Freud, S. (1937). Analysis terminable and interminable. *Standard Edition, 23,* 209–253.

Freud, S. (1954). *The origins of psychoanalysis.* New York: Basic Books. (Original work published 1904)

Freud, S. (1956). Recommendations for physicians on the psychoanalytic method of treatment. In E. Jones (Ed.), *Collected papers* (Vol. 2, pp. 323–333). London: Hogarth Press. (Original work published 1912)

Fromm-Reichmann, F. (1950). *Principles of intensive psychotherapy.* Chicago: University of Chicago Press.

Gelso, C. J., & Carter, J. A. (1985). The relationship in counseling and psychotherapy: Components, consequences, and theoretical antecedents. *The Counseling Psychologist, 13,* 155–243.

Gilbert, L. A. (1980). Feminist therapy. In A. M. Brodsky & R. T. Hare-Mustin (Eds.), *Women and psychotherapy: An assessment of research and practice* (pp. 245–265). New York: Guilford Press.

Gilbert, L. A. (1987). Female and male emotional dependency and its implications for the therapist–client relationship. *Professional Psychology: Research and Practice, 18,* 555–561.

Gladis, S. D. (1985). Notes are not enough. *Training and Development Journal, 39,* 35–38.

Glander, M. H., Locke, D. C., & Leonard, R. (1987). The Marital Satisfaction Inventory: Evaluating the Couple Communication Program. *American Mental Health Counselors Association Journal, 9,* 84–91.

Glover, E. (1955). *The technique of psycho-analysis.* New York: International Universities Press.

Goffman, E. (1971). *Relations in public.* New York: Harper & Row.

Goldfried, M. R., & Davison, G. C. (1976). *Clinical behavior therapy.* New York: Holt, Rinehart & Winston.

Gomes-Schwartz, B. (1978). Effective ingredients in psychotherapy: Prediction of outcome from process variables. *Journal of Consulting and Clinical Psychology, 46,* 1023–1035.

Gorkin, M. (1987). *The uses of countertransference.* Northvale, NJ: Jason Aronson.

Gottlieb, B. H. (1983a). Social support as a focus for integrative research in psychology. *American Psychologist, 38,* 278–287.

Gottlieb, B. H. (1983b). *Social support strategies: Guidelines for mental health practice.* Beverly Hills: Sage Publications.

Gottlieb, B. H. (Ed.). (1988). *Marshaling social support: Formats, processes, and effects.* Newbury Park, CA: Sage Publications.

Gottlieb, B. H. (in press). Stress and support processes in close relationships. In J. Eckenrode (Ed.), *The social context of coping.* New York: Plenum Press.

Gottlieb, F. (1986). Continuity and change. In H. C. Fishman & B. L. Rosman (Eds.). *Evolving models for family change: A volume in honor of Salvador Minuchin* (pp. 263–277). New York: Guilford Press.

Graff, R. W. (1970). The relationship of counselor self-disclosure to counselor effectiveness. *The Journal of Experimental Education, 38,* 19–22.

Greenson, R. (1967). *The technique and practice of psychoanalysis.* New York: International Universities Press.

Gurman, A. S. (1977). The patient's perception of the therapeutic relationship. In A. S. Gurman & A. Razin (Eds.), *Effective psychotherapy: A handbook of research* (pp. 503–543). New York: Pergamon Press.

Gutek, B. A., Nakamura, C. Y., Gahart, M., Handschumacher, I., & Russell, D. (1980). Sexuality and the workplace. *Basic and Applied Social Psychology, 1,* 255–265.

Guy, J. D., & Liaboe, G. P. (1986). The impact of conducting psychotherapy on psychotherapists' interpersonal functioning. *Professional Psychology: Research and Practice, 17,* 111–114.

Hadley, S. W., & Strupp, H. H. (1976). Contemporary views on negative effects: An integrated account. *Archives of General Psychiatry, 33,* 1291–1302.

Hall, E. (1966). *The hidden dimension.* New York: Doubleday.

Halverson, C. F., & Shore, R. E. (1969). Self-disclosure and interpersonal functioning. *Journal of Consulting and Clinical Psychology, 33,* 213–217.

Hatfield, E., & Sprecher, S. (1986). Measuring passionate love in intimate relations. *Journal of Adolescence, 9,* 383–410.

Hays, R. B. (1984). The development and maintenance of friendship. *Journal of Social and Personal Relationships, 1,* 75–98.

Hays, R. B. (1985). A longitudinal study of friendship development. *Journal of Personality and Social Psychology, 48,* 909–924.

Hazan, C., & Shaver, P. (1987). Romantic love conceptualized as an attachment process. *Journal of Personality and Social Psychology, 52,* 511–524.

Heider, F. (1958). *The psychology of interpersonal relations.* New York: Wiley.

Henderson, S., Duncan-Jones, P., Byrne, D. G., & Scott, R. (1980). Measuring social relationships: The interview schedule for social interactions. *Psychological Medicine, 10,* 723–734.

Hendrick, C. (1983). Clinical social psychology: A birthright reclaimed. *Journal of Social and Clinical Psychology, 1,* 66–87.

Hendrick, C., & Hendrick, S. (1983). *Liking, loving, & relating.* Monterey, Ca: Brooks/Cole.

Hendrick, C., & Hendrick, S. S. (1986). A theory and method of love. *Journal of Personality and Social Psychology, 50,* 392–402.

Hendrick, C., & Hendrick, S. S. (1990). A relationship-specific version of the Love Attitudes Scale. *Journal of Social Behavior and Personality, 5,* 239–254.

Hendrick, S. S. (1981). Self-disclosure and marital satisfaction. *Journal of Personal and Social Psychology, 40,* 1150–1159.

Hendrick, S. S. (1983). Ecumenical (social and clinical and X, Y, Z . . .) psychology. *Journal of Social and Clinical Psychology, 1,* 79–87.

Hendrick, S. S. (1987). Counseling and self-disclosure. In V. J. Derlega & J. M. Berg (Eds.), *Self-disclosure: Theory, research, and therapy* (pp. 303–327). New York: Plenum Press.

Hendrick, S. S. (1988). Counselor self-disclosure. *Journal of Counseling and Development, 66,* 419–424.

Hendrick, S. S., & Hendrick, C. (1987). Love and sexual attitudes, self-disclosure, and sensation seeking. *Journal of Social and Personal Relationships, 4,* 281–297.

Hendrick, S. S., Hendrick, C., & Adler, N. L. (1988). Romantic relationships: Love, satisfaction, and staying together. *Journal of Personality and Social Psychology, 54,* 980–988.

Henley, N. (1977). *Body politics.* Englewood Cliffs, NJ: Prentice-Hall.

Hill, C. E., Tanney, M. F., Leonard, M. M., & Reiss, J. A. (1977). Counselor reactions to female clients: Type of problem, age of client, and sex of counselor. *Journal of Counseling Psychology, 24,* 60–65.

Hill, T., & Lewicki, P. (1991). Personality and the unconscious. In V. J. Derlega, B. A. Winstead, & W. H. Jones (Eds.), *Personality: Contemporary theory and research* (pp. 207–229). Chicago: Nelson-Hall.

Ho, M. K. (1987). *Family therapy with ethnic minorities.* Newbury Park, CA: Sage Publications.

Hobfoll, S. E., & London, P. (1986). The relationship of self-concept and social support to emotional distress among women during war. *Journal of Social and Clinical Psychology, 4,* 189–203.

Hoffman, M. A., & Spencer, G. P. (1977). Effect of interviewer self-disclosure and interviewer–subject sex pairing on perceived and actual subject behavior. *Journal of Counseling Psychology, 24,* 383–390.

Hoffman-Graff, M. A. (1977). Interviewer use of positive and negative self-disclosure and interviewer–subject sex pairing. *Journal of Counseling Psychology, 24*, 184–190.

Holland, A. L., Atkinson, D. R., & Johnson, M. E. (1987). Effects of sexual attitude and sex similarity on perceptions of the counselor. *Journal of Counseling Psychology, 34*, 322–325.

Holroyd, J. C., & Brodsky, A. M. (1977). Psychologists' attitudes and practices regarding erotic and nonerotic physical contact with patients. *American Psychologist, 32*, 843–849.

Homans, G. C. (1961). *Social behavior: Its elementary forms.* New York: Harcourt, Brace, Jovanovich.

Horn-George, J. B., & Anchor, K. N. (1982). Perceptions of the psychotherapy relationship in long- versus short-term therapy. *Professional Psychology, 13*, 483–491.

Horvath, A. O., & Greenberg, L. S. (1986). The development of the Working Alliance Inventory. In L. S. Greenberg & W. M. Pinsof (Eds.), *The psychotherapeutic process: A research handbook* (pp. 529–556). New York: Guilford Press.

Horwitz, L. (1974). *Clinical prediction in psychotherapy.* New York: Jason Aronson.

Hunt, D. D., Carr, H. E., Dagadakis, C. S., & Walker, E. A. (1985). Cognitive match as a predictor of psychotherapy outcome. *Psychotherapy: Theory, Research, and Practice, 22*, 718–721.

Huston, T. L., & Levinger, G. (1978). Interpersonal attraction and relationships. *Annual Review of Psychology, 29*, 115–156.

Jamieson, D. W., Lydon, J. E., & Zanna, M. P. (1987). Attitude and activity preference similarity: Differential bases of interpersonal attraction for low and high self-monitors. *Journal of Personality and Social Psychology, 53*, 1052–1060.

Jellison, J. M., & Oliver, D. F. (1983). Attitude similarity and attraction: An impression management approach. *Personality and Social Psychology Bulletin, 9*, 111–115.

Johnson, F. L., & Aries, E. J. (1983). Conversational patterns among same-sex pairs of late-adolescent close friends. *Journal of Genetic Psychology, 142*, 225–238.

Johnson, M. P., & Leslie, L. (1982). Couple involvement and network structure: A test of the dyadic withdrawal hypothesis. *Social Psychology Quarterly, 45*, 34–43.

Jones, W. H., Freemon, J. E., & Goswick, R. A. (1981). The persistence of loneliness: Self and other determinants. *Journal of Personality, 49*, 27–48.

Jones, W. H., Hobbs, S. A., & Hockenbury, D. (1982). Loneliness and social skills deficits. *Journal of Personality and Social Psychology, 42*, 682–689.

Jourard, S. M. (1964). *The transparent self.* Princeton, NJ: Van Nostrand Reinhold.

Jourard, S. M. (1971). *The transparent self* (2nd ed.). New York: D. Van Nostrand.

Jourard, S. M., & Friedman, R. (1970). Experimenter–subject distance and self-disclosure. *Journal of Personality and Social Psychology, 15,* 278–282.

Kaslow, F., Cooper, B., & Linsenberg, M. (1979). Family therapist authenticity as a key factor in outcome. *International Journal of Family Therapy, 1,* 184–199.

Kaul, T. J., & Bednar, R. L. (1986). Experiential group research: Results, questions, and suggestions. In S. L. Garfield & A. E. Bergin (Eds.), *Handbook of psychotherapy and behavior change* (3rd ed., pp. 671–714). New York: Wiley.

Kelley, H. H. (1979). *Close relationships: Their structures and processes.* Hillsdale, NJ: Erlbaum.

Kelley, H. H. (1983). Love and commitment. In H. H. Kelley, E. Berscheid, A. Christensen, J. H. Harvey, T. L. Huston, G. Levinger, E. McClintock, L. A. Peplau, & D. R. Peterson, *Close relationships* (pp. 265–314). New York: W. H. Freeman.

Kelley, H. H., Berscheid, E., Christensen, A., Harvey, J. H., Huston, T. L., Levinger, G., McClintock, E., Peplau, L. A., & Peterson, D. R. (1983). *Close relationships.* New York: W. H. Freeman.

Kelley, H. H., Cunningham, J. D., Grisham, J. A., Lefebvre, L. M., Sink, C. R., & Yablon, G. (1978). Sex differences in comments made during conflict within close heterosexual pairs. *Sex Roles, 4,* 473–491.

Kelley, H. H., & Thibaut, J. W. (1978). *Interpersonal relations: A theory of interdependence.* New York: Wiley-Interscience.

Kelly, G. A. (1955). *A theory of personality: The psychology of personal constructs.* New York: Norton.

Kelvin, P. (1977). Predictability, power and vulnerability in interpersonal attraction. In S. Duck (Ed.), *Theory and practice in interpersonal attraction* (pp. 355–378). New York: Academic Press.

Kerckhoff, A. C., & Davis, K. E. (1962). Value consensus and need complementarity in mate selection. *American Sociological Review, 27,* 295–303.

Kernberg, O. (1984). *Severe personality disorders.* New Haven: Yale University Press.

Kiesler, D. J. (1979). An interpersonal communication analysis of relationship in psychotherapy. *Psychiatry, 42,* 299–311.

Kirsch, I., Tennen, H., Wickless, C., Saccone, A. J., & Cody, S. (1983). The role of expectations in fear reduction. *Behavior Therapy, 14,* 520–533.

Lambert, M. J., Shapiro, D. A., & Bergin, A. E. (1986). The effectiveness of psychotherapy. In S. L. Garfield & A. E. Bergin (Eds.). *Handbook of psychotherapy and behavior change* (3rd ed., pp. 157–211). New York: Wiley.

Landy, D., & Sigall, H. (1974). Beauty is talent: Task evaluation as a function of the performer's physical attractiveness. *Journal of Personality and Social Psychology, 29,* 299–304.

Langer, E. J. (1978). Rethinking the role of thought in social interaction. In J. H. Harvey, W. Ickes, & R. F. Kidd (Eds), *New directions in attribution research* (Vol. 2, pp. 35–58). Hillsdale, NJ: Erlbaum.

Langs, R. (1979). *The therapeutic environment.* New York: Jason Aronson.

Lansford, E. (1986). Weakenings and repairs of the working alliance in short-term psychotherapy. *Professional Psychology: Research and Practice, 17,* 364–366.

Laws, J. L. (1971). A feminist review of the marital adjustment literature: The rape of the Locke. *Journal of Marriage and the Family, 33,* 483–516.

Leary, M. R., & Miller, R. S. (1986). *Social psychology and dysfunctional behavior.* New York: Springer-Verlag.

Lee, J. A. (1973). *The colors of love: An exploration of the ways of loving.* Don Mills, Ontario: New Press.

Lerner, M. J. (1977). The justice motive in social behavior: Some hypotheses as to its origins and forms. *Journal of Personality, 45,* 1–52.

Lerner, M. J. (1982). The justice motive in human relations and the economic model of man: A radical analysis of facts and fictions. In V. J. Derlega & J. Grzelak (Eds.), *Cooperation and helping behavior: Theories and research* (pp. 249–278). New York: Academic Press.

Leventhal, G. S. (1976). Fairness in social relationships. In J. Thibaut, J. J. Spence, & R. C. Carson (Eds.), *Contemporary topics in social psychology* (pp. 212–238). Morristown, NJ: General Learning Press.

Levinger, G. (1980). Toward the analysis of close relationships. *Journal of Experimental Social Psychology, 16,* 510–544.

Levinger, G., & Senn, D. J. (1967). Disclosure of feeling in marriage. *Merrill-Palmer Quarterly of Behavior and Development, 13,* 237–249.

Levinger, G., & Snoek, D. J. (1972). *Attraction in relationship: A new look at interpersonal attraction.* Morristown, NJ: General Learning Press.

London, P. (1986). *The modes and morals of psychotherapy* (2nd ed.). Washington, DC: Hemisphere.

Lott, A. J., & Lott, B. E. (1974). The role of reward in the formation of positive interpersonal attitudes. In T. L. Huston (Ed.), *Foundations of interpersonal attraction* (pp. 171–192). New York: Academic Press.

Luborsky, L. A., McLellan, T., Woody, G. E., O'Brien, C. P., & Auerbach, A. (1985). Therapist success and its determinants. *Archives of General Psychiatry, 42,* 602–611.

Maddux, J. E., Stoltenberg, C. D., Rosenwein, R., & Leary, M. R. (1987). Social processes in clinical and counseling psychology: Introduction and orienting assumptions. In J. E. Maddux, C. D. Stoltenberg, & R. Rosenwein (Eds.), *Social processes in clinical and counseling psychology* (pp. 1–13). New York: Springer-Verlag.

Mahrer, A. R. (1967). *The goals of psychotherapy.* New York: Appleton-Century-Crofts.

Malan, D. H. (1976). *The frontier of brief psychotherapy: An example of the convergence of research and clinical practice.* New York: Plenum Press.

Malan, D. H. (1979). *Individual psychotherapy and the science of psychodynamics.* London: Butterworths.

Maltsberger, J. T., & Buie, D. H. (1974). Countertransference hate in the treatment of suicidal patients. *Archives of General Psychiatry, 30,* 625–633.

Marecek, J., & Johnson, M. (1980). Gender and the process of therapy: In A. M.

Brodsky & R. T. Hare-Mustin (Eds.), *Women and psychotherapy: An assessment of research and practice* (pp. 67–93). New York: Guilford Press.

Margulis, S. T. (1979). *Privacy as information management: A social psychological and environmental framework* (NBSIR 79-1793). Washington, DC: National Bureau of Standards.

Margulis, S. T., Derlega, V. J., & Winstead, B. A. (1984). Implications of social psychological concepts for a theory of loneliness. In V. J. Derlega (Ed.), *Communication, intimacy, and close relationships* (pp. 133–160). Orlando, FL: Academic Press.

Marmar, C. R., Horowitz, M. J., Weiss, D. S., & Marziali, E. (1986). The development of the Therapeutic Alliance Rating System. In L. S. Greenberg & W. M. Pinsof (Eds.), *The psychotherapeutic process: A research handbook* (pp. 367–390). New York: Guilford Press.

Mayo, P. R. (1968). Self-disclosure and neurosis. *British Journal of Social and Clinical Psychology, 7,* 140–148.

McCarthy, P. R. (1979). Differential effects of self-disclosing versus self-involving counselor statements across counselor–client gender pairings. *Journal of Counseling Psychology, 26,* 538–541.

McCarthy, P. R. (1982). Differential effects of counselor self-referent responses and counselor status. *Journal of Counseling Psychology, 29,* 125–131.

McCarthy, P. R., & Betz, N. E. (1978). Differential effects of self-disclosing versus self-involving counselor statements. *Journal of Counseling Psychology, 25,* 251–256.

McLaughlin, M. L., Cody, M. J., & Rosenstein, N. E. (1983). Account sequences in communication between strangers. *Communication Monographs, 50,* 102–128.

Mehrabian, A. (1972). *Nonverbal communication.* Chicago: Aldine-Atherton.

Menninger, K. (1958). *Theory of psychoanalytic technique.* New York: Basic Books.

Milardo, R. M. (1986). Personal choice and social constraint in close relationships: Applications of network analysis. In V. J. Derlega & B. A. Winstead (Eds.), *Friendship and social interaction* (pp. 145–166). New York: Springer-Verlag.

Miller, D. J., & Thelen, M. H. (1986). Knowledge and beliefs about confidentiality in psychotherapy. *Professional Psychology: Research and Practice, 17,* 15–19.

Miller, L. C., & Berg, J. H. (1984). Selectivity and urgency in interpersonal exchange. In V. J. Derlega (Ed.), *Communication, intimacy, and close relationships* (pp. 161–205). Orlando, FL: Academic Press.

Miller, L. C., Berg, J. H., & Archer, R. L. (1983). Openers: Individuals who elicit intimate self-disclosure. *Journal of Personality and Social Psychology, 44,* 1234–1244.

Miller, L. C., Berg, J. H., & Rugs, D. (1984, August). *Selectivity in exchange: When you give me what I need.* Paper presented at the 93rd Annual Convention of the American Psychological Association, Toronto, Canada.

Miller, L. C., & Read, S. J. (1989). Inter-personalism: Toward a goal-based theory of persons in relationships. In L. Pervin (Ed.), *Goal concepts in personality and social psychology* (pp. 413–472). Hillsdale, NJ: Erlbaum.

Miller, S. M., & Kirsch, N. (1987). Sex differences in cognitive coping with stress. In R. C. Barnett, L. Bienner, & C. K. Baruch (Eds.), *Gender and stress* (pp. 278–307). New York: Free Press.

Mills, J., & Clark, M. S. (1982). Exchange and communal relationships. In L. Wheeler (Ed.), *Review of personality and social psychology* (Vol. 3, pp. 121–144). Beverly Hills: Sage Publications.

Moos, R. H., & Moos, B. S. (1981). *Family Environment Scale.* Palo Alto, CA: Consulting Psychologists Press.

Morris, R. J., & Suckerman, K. R. (1974). Therapist warmth as a factor in automated systematic desensitization. *Journal of Consulting and Clinical Psychology, 42,* 244–250.

Morton, J. L. (1978). Intimacy and reciprocity of exchange: A comparison of spouses and strangers. *Journal of Personality and Social Psychology, 36,* 72–81.

Mowrer, O. H. (1968). Loss and recovery of community: A guide to the theory and practice of integrity theory. In G. Gazda (Ed.), *Innovation in group psychotherapy* (pp. 130–189). Springfield, IL: Charles C. Thomas.

Murphy, K. C., & Strong, S. R. (1972). Some effects of similarity self-disclosure. *Journal of Counseling Psychology, 19,* 121–124.

Murstein, B. I. (1970). Stimulus–value–role: A theory of marital choice. *Journal of Marriage and the Family, 32,* 465–481.

Murstein, B. I. (1972). Physical attraction and marital choice. *Journal of Personality and Social Psychology, 22,* 8–12.

Murstein, B. I., & Christy, P. (1976). Physical attractiveness and marriage adjustment in middle-aged couples. *Journal of Personality and Social Psychology, 34,* 537–542.

Neimeyer, R. A., & Mitchell, K. A. (1988). Similarity and attraction: A longitudinal study. *Journal of Social and Personal Relationships, 5,* 131–148.

Newcomb, T. M. (1961). *The acquaintance process.* New York: Holt, Rinehart & Winston.

Nguyen, T., Heslin, R., & Nguyen, M. (1975). The meanings of touch: Sex differences. *Journal of Communication, 25,* 92–105.

Noller, P. (1981). Gender and marital adjustment level differences in decoding messages from spouses and strangers. *Journal of Personality and Social Psychology, 41,* 272–278.

O'Malley, S. S., Suh, C. S., & Strupp, H. H. (1983). The Vanderbilt Psychotherapy Process Scale: A report on the scale development and a process-outcome study. *Journal of Consulting and Clinical Psychology, 51,* 581–586.

Orlinsky, D. E., & Howard, K. I. (1978). The relation of process to outcome in psychotherapy. In S. L. Garfield & A. E. Bergin, (Eds.), *Handbook of psychotherapy and behavior change* (2nd ed., pp. 283–329). New York: Wiley.

Orlinsky, D. E., & Howard, K. I. (1980). Gender and psychotherapeutic outcome. In A. M. Brodsky & R. T. Hare-Mustin (Eds.), *Women and psycho-*

therapy: An assessment of research and practice (pp. 3-34). New York: Guilford Press.

Orlinsky, D. E., & Howard, K. I. (1986). Process and outcome in psychotherapy. In S. L. Garfield & A. E. Bergin (Eds.), *Handbook of psychotherapy and behavior change* (3rd ed., pp. 311-381). New York: Wiley.

Palisi, B. J., & Ransford, H. E. (1987). Friendship as a voluntary relationship: Evidence from national surveys. *Journal of Social and Personal Relationships, 4*, 243-259.

Paradise, L. V., Conway, B. S., & Zweig, J. (1986). Effects of expert and referent influence, physical attractiveness, and gender on perceptions of counselor attributes. *Journal of Counseling Psychology, 33*, 16-22.

Patterson, C. H. (1985). *The therapeutic relationship: Foundations for an eclectic psychotherapy.* Monterey, CA.: Brooks/Cole.

Patterson, M. L. (1976). An arousal model of interpersonal intimacy. *Psychological Review, 83*, 235-245.

Patterson, M. L. (1982). A sequential functional model of non-verbal exchange. *Psychological Review, 89*, 231-249.

Pearson, J. E. (1986). The definition and measurement of social support. *Journal of Counseling and Development, 64*, 390-395.

Pennebaker, J. W. (1985). Traumatic experience and psychosomatic disease: Exploring the roles of behavioral inhibition, obsession, and confiding. *Canadian Psychologist, 26*, 82-95.

Pennebaker, J. W., & Beall, S. (1986). Cognitive, emotional, and physiological components of confiding: Behavioral inhibition and disease. *Journal of Abnormal Psychology, 95*, 274-281.

Pennebaker, J. W., & Hoover, C. W. (1986). Inhibition and cognition: Toward an understanding of trauma and disease. In R. J. Davidson, G. E. Schwartz, & D. Shapiro (Eds.), *Consciousness and self-regulation* (Vol. 4, pp. 107-136). New York: Plenum Press.

Pennebaker, J. W., & O'Heeron, R. C. (1984). Confiding in others and illness rates among spouses of suicide and accident death victims. *Journal of Abnormal Psychology, 93*, 473-476.

Peplau, L. A. (1983). Roles and gender. In H. H. Kelley, E. Berscheid, A. Christensen, J. H. Harvey, T. L. Huston, G. Levinger, E. McClintock, L. A. Peplau, & D. R. Peterson, *Close relationships* (pp. 220-264). New York: W. H. Freeman.

Peplau, L. A., & Gordon, S. L. (1985). Women and men in love: Gender differences in close heterosexual relationships. In V. E. O'Leary, R. K. Unger, & B. S. Wallston (Eds.), *Women, gender, and social psychology* (pp. 257-291). Hillsdale, NJ: Erlbaum.

Perlman, D., & Fehr, B. (1986). Theories of friendship: The analysis of interpersonal attraction. In V. J. Derlega & B. A. Winstead (Eds.), *Friendship and social interaction* (pp. 9-40). New York: Springer-Verlag.

Petro, C. S., & Putman, B. A. (1979). Sex-role stereotypes: Issues of attitudinal changes. *Sex Roles, 5*, 29-39.

Piner, K. E., & Berg, J. H. (1987, August). *The effect of availability on verbal and non-verbal interaction styles.* Paper presented at the 95th Annual Convention of the American Psychological Association, New York, NY.

Piner, K. E., Berg, J. H., & Miller, L. C. (1986, April). *The influence of timing on responsiveness.* Paper presented at the 32nd Annual Meeting of the Southeastern Psychological Association, Orlando, FL.

Pope, K. S., Keith-Spiegel, P., & Tabachnick, B. G. (1986). Sexual attraction to clients: The human therapist and the (sometimes) inhuman training system. *American Psychologist, 41,* 147–158.

Pope, K. S., Tabachnick, B. G., & Keith-Spiegel, P. (1987). Ethics of practice: The beliefs and behaviors of psychologists as therapists. *American Psychologist, 42,* 993–1006.

Powers, E. A., & Bultena, G. L. (1976). Sex differences in intimate friendships in old age. *Journal of Marriage and the Family, 38,* 739–747.

Prager, K. J. (1986). Intimacy status: Its relationship to locus of control, self-disclosure, and anxiety in adults. *Personality and Social Psychology Bulletin, 12,* 91–109.

Procidano, M. E., & Heller, K. (1983). Measures of perceived social support from friends and from family: Three validation studies. *American Journal of Community Psychology, 11,* 1–24.

Purvis, J. A., Dabbs, I., & Hopper, C. (1984). The "Opener": Skilled user of facial expression and speech pattern. *Personality and Social Psychology Bulletin, 10,* 60–66.

Rands, M., & Levinger, G. (1979). Implicit theories of relationship: An intergenerational study. *Journal of Personality and Social Psychology, 37,* 645–661.

Reich, A. (1951). On countertransference. *International Journal of Psycho-Analysis, 32,* 25–31.

Reich, A. (1960). Further remarks on countertransference. *International Journal of Psycho-Analysis, 41,* 389–395.

Reisman, J. M. (1986). Psychotherapy as a professional relationship. *Professional Psychology: Research and Practice, 17,* 565–569.

Remer, P., Roffey, B. H., & Buckholtz, A. (1983). Differential effects of positive versus negative self-involving counselor responses. *Journal of Counseling Psychology, 30,* 121–125.

Render, H., & Weiss, O. (1959). *Nurse–patient relationships in psychiatry.* New York: McGraw-Hill.

Reynolds, C. L., & Fischer, C. H. (1983). Personal versus professional evaluations of self-disclosing and self-involving counselors. *Journal of Counseling Psychology, 30,* 451–454.

Rodolfa, E. R., Kraft, W. A., & Reilley, R. R. (1988). Stressors of professionals and trainees at APA-approved counseling and VA medical center internship sites. *Professional Psychology: Research and Practice, 19,* 43–49.

Rogers, C. R. (1951). *Client-centered therapy.* Boston: Houghton Mifflin.

Roger, C. R. (1957). The necessary and sufficient conditions of therapeutic personality change. *Journal of Consulting Psychology, 21,* 95–103.

Rosenbaum, M. E. (1986a). Comment on a proposed two-stage theory of relationship formation: First, repulsion; then, attraction. *Journal of Personality and Social Psychology, 51,* 1171–1172.

Rosenbaum, M. E. (1986b). The repulsion hypothesis: On the nondevelopment of relationships. *Journal of Personality and Social Psychology, 51,* 1156–1166.

Rosenfeld, L. B. (1979). Self-disclosure avoidance: Why I am afraid to tell you who I am. *Communication Monographs, 46,* 63–74.

Rubanowitz, D. E. (1987). Public attitudes toward psychotherapist–client confidentiality. *Professional Psychology: Research and Practice, 18,* 613–618.

Rudy, J. P., McLemore, C. W., & Gorsuch, R. L. (1985). Interpersonal behavior and therapeutic progress: Therapists and clients rate themselves and each other. *Psychiatry, 48,* 264–281.

Rusbult, C. E. (1980a). Commitment and satisfaction in romantic associations: A test of the investment model. *Journal of Experimental Social Psychology, 16,* 172–186.

Rusbult, C. E. (1980b). Satisfaction and commitment in relationships. *Representative Research in Social Psychology, 11,* 96–105.

Rusbult, C. E. (1983). A longitudinal test of the investment model: The development (and deterioration) of satisfaction and commitment in heterosexual involvements. *Journal of Personality and Social Psychology, 45,* 101–117.

Rusbult, C. E. (1987). Responses to dissatisfaction in close relationships: The exit–voice–loyalty–neglect model. In D. Perlman & S. Duck (Eds.), *Intimate relationships: Development, dynamics, and deterioration* (pp. 209–237). Newbury Park, CA: Sage Publications.

Rusbult, C. E., Johnson, D. J., & Morrow, G. D. (1986). Predicting satisfaction and commitment in adult romantic involvements: An assessment of the generalizability of the investment model. *Social Psychology Quarterly, 49,* 81–89.

Rusbult, C. E., Zembrodt, I. M., & Gunn, L. K. (1982). Exit, voice, loyalty and neglect: Responses to dissatisfaction in romantic involvements. *Journal of Personality and Social Psychology, 43,* 1230–1242.

Sachs, J. S. (1983). Negative factors in brief psychotherapy: An empirical assessment. *Journal of Consulting and Clinical Psychology, 51,* 557–564.

Saltzman, C., Luetgert, M. J., Roth, C. H., Creaser, J., & Howard, L. (1976). Formation of a therapeutic relationship: Experiences during the initial phase of psychotherapy as predictors of treatment duration and outcome. *Journal of Consulting and Clinical Psychology, 44,* 546–555.

Sarason, B. R., Sarason, I. G., Hacker, T. A., & Basham, R. B. (1985). Concomitants of social support: Social skills, physical attractiveness, and gender. *Journal of Personality and Social Psychology, 49,* 469–480.

Sarason, B. R., Shearin, E. N., Pierce, G. R., & Sarason, I. G. (1987). Interrelations of social support measures: Theoretical and practical implications. *Journal of Personality and Social Psychology, 52,* 813–832.

Sarason, I. G., Levine, H. M., Basham, R. B., & Sarason, B. R. (1983). Assessing social support: The Social Support Questionnaire. *Journal of Personality and Social Psychology, 44,* 127–139.

Sarason, I. G., & Sarason, B. R. (1986). Experimentally provided social support. *Journal of Personality and Social Psychology, 50,* 1222–1225.

Sarason, I. G., Sarason, B. R., Potter, E. H., & Antoni, M. H. (1985). Life events, social support, and illness. *Psychosomatic Medicine, 47,* 156–163.

Sarason, I. G., Sarason, B. R., & Shearin, E. N. (1986). Social support as an individual difference variable: Its stability, origins, and relational aspects. *Journal of Personality and Social Psychology, 50,* 845–855.

Sarason, I. G., Sarason, B. R., Shearin, E. N., & Pierce, G. R. (1987). A brief measure of social support: Practical and theoretical implications. *Journal of Social and Personal Relationships, 4,* 497–510.

Sarason, S. B. (1985). *Caring and compassion in clinical practice.* San Francisco: Jossey-Bass.

Schachter, S. (1964). The interaction of cognitive and physiological determinants of emotional state. In L. Berkowtiz (Ed.), *Advances in experimental social psychology* (Vol. 1, pp. 49–80). New York: Academic Press.

Schachter, S., & Singer, J. E. (1962). Cognitive, social and physiological determinants of emotional state. *Psychological Review, 69,* 379–399.

Scheflen, A. E. (1965). Quasi-courtship behavior in psychotherapy. *Psychiatry, 28,* 245–257.

Schofield, W. (1964). *Psychotherapy: The purchase of friendship.* Englewood Cliffs, NJ: Prentice-Hall.

Searles, H. F. (1979). *Countertransference and related subjects—Selected papers.* New York: International Universities Press.

Segal, M. W. (1974). Alphabet and attraction: An unobtrusive measure of the effect of propinquity in a field setting. *Journal of Personality and Social Psychology, 30,* 654–657.

Shapiro, D. A. (1981). Comparative credibility of treatment rationales: Three tests of expectancy theory. *British Journal of Clinical Psychology, 20,* 111–122.

Sharabany, R., Gershoni, R., & Hofman, J. E. (1981). Girlfriend, boyfriend: Age and sex difference in intimate friendship. *Developmental Psychology, 17,* 800–808.

Shaver, P., Hazan, C., & Bradshaw, D. (1988). Love as attachment: The integration of three behavioral systems. In R. J. Sternberg & M. Barnes (Eds.), *The psychology of love* (pp. 69–99). New Haven, CT: Yale University Press.

Shimkunas, A. M. (1972). Demand for intimate self-disclosure and pathological verbalizations in schizophrenia. *Journal of Abnormal Psychology, 80,* 197–205.

Simmel, G. (1950). *The sociology of Georg Simmel* (K. H. Wolff, trans.). New York: The Free Press.

Simonson, N. R., & Bahr, S. (1974). Self-disclosure by the professional and paraprofessional therapist. *Journal of Consulting and Clinical Psychology, 42,* 359–363.

Smith, M. L. (1980). Sex bias in counseling and psychotherapy. *Psychological Bulletin, 87,* 392–407.

Snyder, M. (1984). When belief causes reality. In L. Berkowitz (Ed.), *Advances in experimental social psychology* (Vol. 19, pp. 247–305). New York: Academic Press.

Snyder, M., Berscheid, E., & Glick, P. (1985). Focusing on the exterior and the interior: Two investigations of the initiation of personal relationships. *Journal of Personality and Social Psychology, 48,* 1427–1439.

Snyder, M., & Swann, W. B. (1978). Hypothesis testing processes in social interaction. *Journal of Personality and Social Psychology, 36,* 1202–1212.

Snyder, M., Tanke, E. D., & Berscheid, E. (1977). Social perception and interpersonal behavior: On the self-fulfilling nature of social stereotypes. *Journal of Personality and Social Psychology, 35,* 656–666.

Solano, G. H., Batten, P. G., & Parish, E. A. (1982). Loneliness and patterns of self-disclosure. *Journal of Personality and Social Psychology, 43,* 524–531.

Sollie, D. L., & Scott, J. P. (1983). Teaching communication skills: A comparison of videotape feedback methods. *Family Relations: Journal of Applied Family and Child Studies, 32,* 503–511.

Stiles, W. B. (1978). Verbal response modes and dimensions of interpersonal rolls: A method of discourse analysis. *Journal of Personality and Social Psychology, 36,* 693–703.

Stiles, W. B. (1987). "I have to talk to somebody": A fever model of disclosure. In V. J. Derlega & J. H. Berg (Eds.), *Self-disclosure: Theory, research, and therapy* (pp. 257–282). New York: Plenum Press.

Stokes, J. P. (1983). Predicting satisfaction with social support from social network structure. *American Journal of Community Psychology, 11,* 141–152.

Stone, L. (1961). *The psychoanalytic situation.* New York: International Universities Press.

Stouffer, S. A., Suchman, A. A., DeVinney, L. C., Star, S. A., & Williams, R. M. (1949). *The American soldier: Vol. 1. Adjustment during army life.* Princeton: Princeton University Press.

Stricker, G. (1977). Implications of research for psychotherapeutic treatment of women. *American Psychologist, 32,* 14–22.

Strong, S. R., & Claiborn, C. D. (1982). *Change through interaction: Social psychological processes of counseling and psychotherapy.* New York: Wiley-Interscience.

Strupp, H. H. (1973). On the basic ingredients of psychotherapy. *Journal of Consulting and Clinical Psychology, 41,* 1–8.

Strupp, H. H., & Binder, J. L. (1984). *Psychotherapy in a new key: A guide to time-limited dynamic psychotherapy.* New York: Basic Books.

Strupp, H. H., Fox, R. E., & Lessler, K. (1969). *Patients view their psychotherapy.* Baltimore: Johns Hopkins University Press.

Stryker, S., & Statham, A. (1985). Symbolic interaction and role theory. In G. Lindzey & E. Aronson (Eds.), *Handbook of social psychology* (Vol. 1, 3rd ed., pp. 311–378). New York: Random House.

Sue, S. (1988). Psychotherapeutic services for ethnic minorities. *American Psychologist, 43,* 301–308.

Suh, C. S., Strupp, H. H., & O'Malley, S. S. (1986). The Vanderbilt Process

Measures: The Psychotherapy Process Scale (VPPS) and the Negative Indicators Scale (VNIS). In L. S. Greenberg & W. M. Pinsof (Eds.), *The psychotherapeutic process: A research handbook* (pp. 285–323). New York: Guilford Press.

Sullivan, H. S. (1953). *The interpersonal theory of psychiatry*. New York: Norton.

Sullivan, H. S. (1954). *The psychiatric interview*. New York: Norton.

Swann, W. B., & Read, S. H. (1981). Self-verification processes: How we sustain our self-conceptions. *Journal of Experimental Social Psychology, 17*, 351–372.

Swoboda, J. S., Elwork, A., Sales, B. D., & Levine, D. (1978). Knowledge of and compliance with privileged communication and child-abuse–reporting laws. *Professional Psychology, 9*, 448–457.

Taylor, D. A., & Altman, I. (1987). Communication in interpersonal relationships: Social penetration processes. In M. E. Roloff & G. R. Miller (Eds.), *Interpersonal processes: New directions in communication research* (pp. 257–277). Newbury Park, CA: Sage Publications.

Taylor, S. E., & Crocker, J. (1981). Schematic bases of social information processing. In E. T. Higgins, C. P. Herman, & M. P. Zanna (Eds.), *Social cognition: The Ontario Symposium* (Vol. 1, pp. 84–135). Hillsdale, NJ: Erlbaum.

Tedeschi, J. T., Schlenker, B. R., & Bonoma, T. V. (1971). Cognitive dissonance: Private ratiocination or public spectacle? *American Psychologist, 26*, 685–695.

Thibaut, J. W., & Kelley, H. H. (1959). *The social psychology of groups*. New York: Wiley.

Thomas, A. N., & Stewart, N. R. (1971). Counselor response to female clients with deviate and conforming career goals. *Journal of Counseling Psychology, 18*, 352–357.

Tilby, P. J., & Kalin, R. (1980). Effects of sex-role deviant life-styles in otherwise normal persons on the perception of maladjustment. *Sex Roles, 6*, 581–592.

Truax, C. B., & Carkhuff, R. R. (1965). Client and therapist transparency in the psychotherapeutic encounter. *Journal of Counseling Psychology, 12*, 3–9.

Truax, C. B., & Mitchell, K. M. (1971). Research on certain therapist interpersonal skills in relation to process and outcome. In A. E. Bergin & S. L. Garfield (Eds.), *Handbook of psychotherapy and behavior change* (1st ed., pp. 299–344). New York: Wiley.

VandeCreek, L., & Angstadt, L. (1985). Client preferences and anticipations about counselor self-disclosure. *Journal of Counseling Psychology, 32*, 206–214.

Vargas, A. M., & Borkowski, J. G. (1983). Physical attractiveness: Interactive effects of counselor and client on counseling process. *Journal of Counseling Psychology, 30*, 146–157.

Waldo, M. (1989). Primary prevention in university residence halls: Paraprofessional led relationship enhancement groups for college roommates. *Journal of Counseling and Development, 67*, 465–471.

Walster, E., Berscheid, E., & Walster, G. W. (1973). New directions in equity research. *Journal of Personality and Social Psychology, 25,* 151–176.

Walster, E., Berscheid, E., & Walster, G. W. (1976). New directions in equity research. In L. Berkowitz & E. Walster (Eds.), *Advances in experimental social psychology: Vol. 9. Equity theory: Toward a general theory of social interaction* (pp. 1–42). New York: Academic Press.

Walster, E., Walster, G. W., & Berscheid, E. (1978). *Equity: Theory and research.* Boston: Allyn & Bacon.

Warner, R. (1978). The diagnosis of antisocial and hysterical personality disorders: An example of sex bias. *Journal of Nervous and Mental Disease, 166,* 839–845.

Warner, R. (1979). Racial and sexual bias in psychiatric diagnoses. *Journal of Nervous and Mental Disease, 167,* 303–310.

Webster's seventh new collegiate dictionary. (1963). Springfield, MA: G. & C. Merriam Co.

Weigel, R. G., Dinges, N., Dyer, R., & Straumfjord, A. A. (1972). Perceived self-disclosure, mental health, and who is liked in group treatment. *Journal of Counseling Psychology, 19,* 47–52.

Weigel, R. G., & Warnath, C. F. (1968). The effects of group therapy on reported self-disclosure. *International Journal of Group Psychotherapy, 18,* 31–41.

Whitaker, C. (1982). A family is four-dimensional. In J. R. Neill & D. P. Kniskern (Eds.), *From psyche to system: The evolving therapy of Carl Whitaker* (pp. 304–316). New York: Guilford Press.

Whitehurst, T. C., & Derlega, V. J. (1985). Influence of touch and preferences for control on visual behavior and subjective responses. In S. L. Ellyson & J. F. Dovidio (Eds.), *Power, dominance, and nonverbal behavior* (pp. 165–181). New York: Springer-Verlag.

Wilson, G. T., & Evans, I. M. (1977). The therapist–client relationship in behavior therapy. In A. S. Gurman & A. N. Razin (Eds.), *Effective psychotherapy: A handbook of research* (pp. 544–565). New York: Pergamon Press.

Wilson, G. T., & O'Leary, K. D. (1980). *Principles of behavior therapy.* Englewood Cliffs, NJ: Prentice-Hall.

Wilson, J. M. (1982). The value of touch in psychotherapy. *American Journal of Orthopsychiatry, 52,* 65–72.

Winstead, B. A. (1986). Sex differences in same-age friendships. In V. J. Derlega & B. A. Winstead (Eds.), *Friendship and social interaction* (pp. 81–99). New York: Springer-Verlag.

Winstead, B. A., Derlega, V. J., Lewis, R. J., & Margulis, S. T. (1988). Understanding the therapeutic relationship as a personal relationship. *Journal of Social and Personal Relationships, 5,* 109–125.

Wise, T. P. (1978). Where the public peril begins: A survey of psychotherapists to determine the effects of *Tarasoff. Stanford Law Review, 31,* 165–190.

Wolpe, J. (1982). *The practice of behavior therapy* (3rd ed.). New York: Pergamon Press.

Won-Doornick, M. (1979). On getting to know you: The association between the stage of relationship and reciprocity of self-disclosure. *Journal of Experimental Social Psychology, 15,* 229–241.

Won-Doornick, M. J. (1985). Self-disclosure and reciprocity in conversation: A cross-national study. *Social Psychology Quarterly, 48,* 97–107.

Wortman, C. B., & Dunkel-Schetter, C. (1987). Conceptual and methodological issues in the study of social support. In A. Baum & J. W. Singer (Eds.), *Handbook of psychology and health: Vol. 5. Stress* (pp. 63–108). Hillsdale, NJ: Erlbaum.

Yalom, I. (1975). *The theory and practice of group psychotherapy* (2nd ed.). New York: Basic Books.

Yalom, I. D. (1980). *Existential psychotherapy.* New York: Basic Books.

Yalom, I. D., & Elkin, G. (1974). *Every day gets a little closer: A twice-told therapy.* New York: Basic Books.

Young, J. E. (1982). Loneliness, depression and cognitive therapy: Theory and application. In L. A. Peplau & D. Perlman (Eds.), *Loneliness: A sourcebook of current theory, research and therapy* (pp. 379–405). New York: Wiley-Interscience.

Young, J. E. (1986). A cognitive–behavioral approach to friendship disorders. In V. J. Derlega & B. A. Winstead (Eds.), *Friendship and social interaction* (pp. 247–276). New York: Springer-Verlag.

Zajonc, R. B. (1968). Attitudinal effects of mere exposure. *Journal of Personality and Social Psychology, 9,* 1–27.

Zeldow, P. B. (1984). Sex roles, psychological assessment, and patient management. In C. S. Widom (Ed.), *Sex roles and psychopathology* (pp. 355–374). New York: Plenum Press.

Zetzel, E. (1956). Current concepts of transference. *International Journal of Psychoanalysis, 37,* 369–376.

Index